MW00399504

The Windmill Chaser

Triumphs and Less in American Politics

The Windmill Chaser

Triumphs and Less in American Politics

Bob Livingston

University of Louisiana at Lafayette Press
2018

© 2018 by University of Louisiana at Lafayette Press
All rights reserved

ISBN 13 (hardcover): 978-1-946160-27-0

http://ulpress.org
University of Louisiana at Lafayette Press
P.O. Box 43558
Lafayette, LA 70504-3558

Printed on acid-free paper in Canada.

Front cover photograph: courtesy AP Photo/Pablo Martinez Monsivais.
All other photographs: courtesy of Bob Livingston.

Library of Congress Cataloging-in-Publication Data:

Names: Livingston, Robert L., 1943-
Title: The windmill chaser : American politics : triumph & less / Robert L. Livingston.
Other titles: American politics, triumph and less | American politics, triumph & less
Description: Lafayette, LA : University of Louisiana at Lafayette Press, [2018] |
Identifiers: LCCN 2018023879 (print) | LCCN 2018029396 (ebook) | ISBN 9781946160379 () | ISBN 9781946160270 (alk. paper)
Subjects: LCSH: Livingston, Robert L., 1943- | Legislators--United States--Biography. | Legislators--Louisiana--Biography. | United States Congress. House--Biography. | Lobbyists--United States--Biography. | Lawyers--Louisiana--Biography. | Legislators--Louisiana--Biography. | Louisiana--Politics and government--20th century. | United States--Politics and government--1989-
Classification: LCC E840.8.L58 (ebook) | LCC E840.8.L58 A3 2018 (print) | DDC 328.73/092 [B] --dc23
LC record available at https://lccn.loc.gov/2018023879

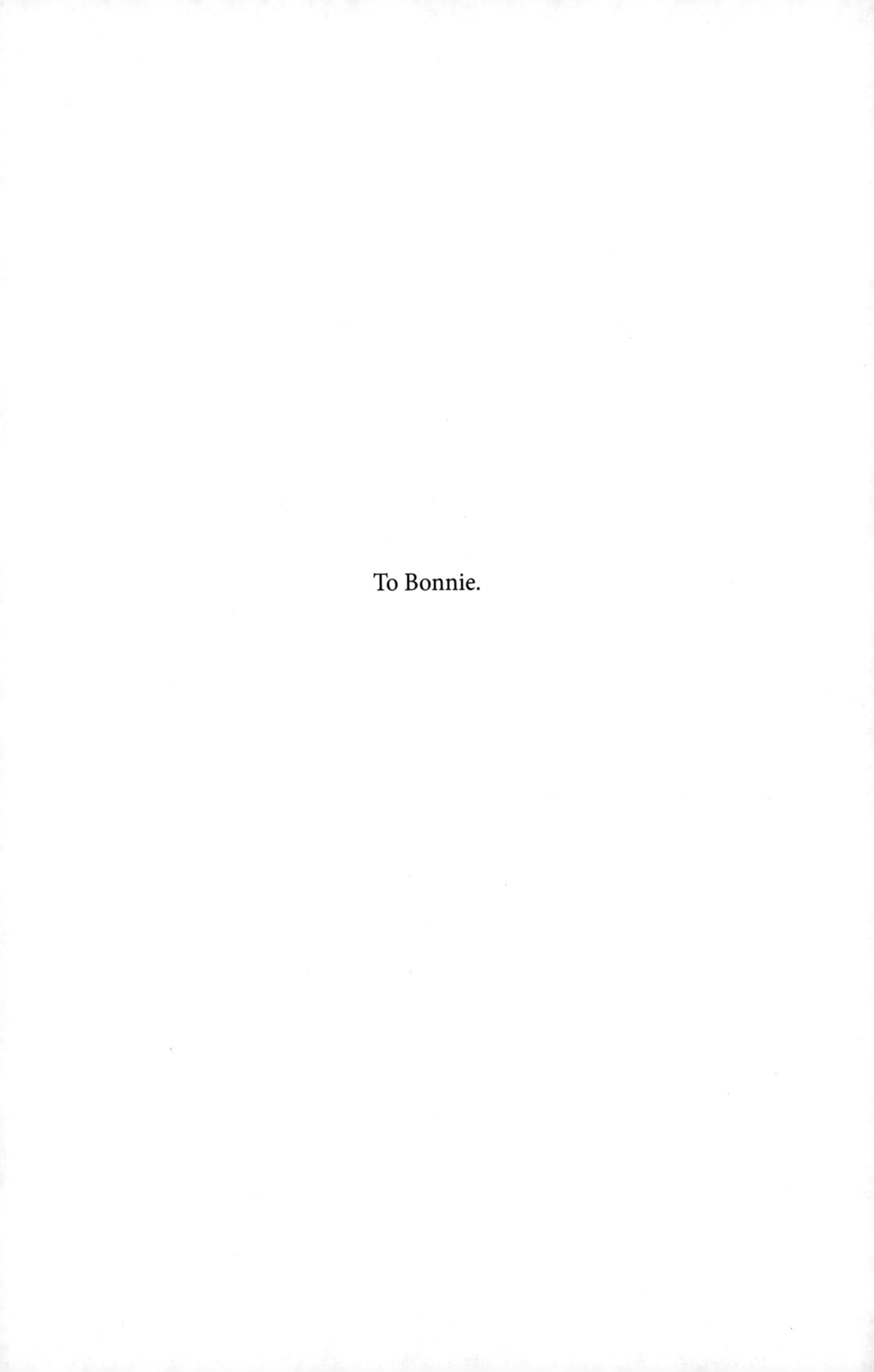

To Bonnie.

Table of Contents

Foreword
by Newt Gingrich

Bob Livingston has written a remarkably candid and courageous memoir.

Virtually anyone could learn from this intriguing and very eclectic book. It is part biography, part New Orleans tales (a city always worth writing about), part political memoir, part public policy analysis, and always personal and candid.

Bob had a remarkable career having helped create the Louisiana GOP, served as a prosecuting attorney in a city and state notorious for public corruption, helped grow the first House Republican majority, and directed Congress to finally balance its budget, a feat that has not been repeated since and is unlikely to happen in the coming decades.

Bob had a deep interest in national security and helped with the Reagan program to win the Cold War and worked consistently to strengthen our national security. In the 1990s he was the most outspoken critic of the Clinton policy of appeasing the North Koreans. In retrospect Livingston was 100 percent right and the appeasers were 100 percent wrong. If he had been listened to we would have avoided a quarter century of growing threat from that dictatorship.

Bob was always supportive of my efforts to elect a House GOP majority (we had not had won since the 1954 elections and for aggressive, smart people like Livingston it became very frustrating always being in the minority).

What made Bob unusual was his candor. When I made a mistake during the long (sixteen year) effort he would tell me directly but in a positive way. He always communicated that he strongly supported my goal of a GOP majority and that his concern for my mistakes was that they made it harder to achieve our goals.

When I investigated the corruption of Speaker Jim Wright, Bob volunteered to review all the work we had done. As a former very successful prosecutor he had a very high professional standard for evidence which as a historian I did not have. After a few days he came back and said I was about a third of the way there but needed a lot more work. It wasn't the answer I wanted but it was the professionally correct answer. We went back to work and dug a lot deeper and began to win the argument.

When we became the majority it was clear we could not allow the ranking Republican to become chairman because he was under indictment (he was ultimately found not guilty and was just one more example of the liberals in the Justice Department's anti-Republican bias). As the new Speaker I was very concerned that the Appropriations Committee has strong leadership. It was the most powerful single committee with the daily duty of supervising and approving all federal discretionary spending.

As soon as we named Livingston chairman he came in to my office and objected to our plans to replace all the professional staff with Republicans. He argued that the constant stream of funding decisions made the Appropriations Committee a uniquely demanding institution. He asserted that we needed continuity and a purge of all the Democratic staffers would cripple the committee and ultimately make us look stupid.

With enormous reluctance we gave in to now Chairman Livingston's demand. I have to admit he was right, and his subsequent leadership of the committee in the difficult struggle to create a balanced budget more than vindicated his position. He also got the professional staff to put aside their partisan and ideological positions and work relentlessly to achieve our goals. It was a great study in leadership.

Looking back I suspect that if I had been 10 percent more like Livingston and 10 percent less my normal aggressive, confrontational self I would have been a more effective Speaker and probably would have served several more terms (I had established a self-imposed limit).

I also agree with his critique of how we mishandled the impeachment of Clinton. If we had been more patient and allowed the country to focus more on the nature of perjury, the importance of protecting the rule of law, and the seriousness of a felony, the process would have worked much better. Our willingness to be aggressive simply played into Clinton's and Carville's ability to lie about the issues and to polarize in a way that submerged the President's illegal behavior into a swamp of partisan vitriol. Livingston's book is worth reading for this thoughtful analysis.

Bob has a much better sense of humor than I realized. His tales of

New Orleans politics and law enforcement made me laugh out loud. His descriptions of four-term Louisiana governor, and subsequently convicted felon, Edwin Edwards are worth the entire book.

Finally, the courage of the book includes a very honest recounting of his life and his remarkable wife Bonnie. They have been married fifty two years, have four children, lost one child to a tragic industrial accident, one of their children is adopted from Taiwan. Their children have all had good lives with solid educations, good jobs, and beautiful families. Bonnie clearly grew the family and held things together while Bob pursued his legal and then his political career.

It is impossible to read this memoir without a deep sense of how much Livingston has grown over the years, how much he has tried to understand his own strengths and weaknesses and how grateful he is to his wife and children for standing with him through all the challenges of public life.

Anyone reading this book will find themselves enriched about politics, about government, and about life.

"For the want of a nail, the shoe was lost; for the want of a shoe the horse was lost; and for the want of a horse the rider was lost, being overtaken and slain by the enemy, all for the want of care about a horseshoe nail."

- Benjamin Franklin

Prologue

We were just a bunch of kids, eight or nine years old, gathered outside the old Chief Theater on Pikes Peak Avenue in old Colorado Springs.

"Yeah, it's impossible for that old man to beat up all those guys all at once!"

"Whadaya mean? That's Hopalong Cassidy . . . he can do anything!!" we protested.

"You think so!?" yelled the red-headed kid. "Heck, I can beat him up by myself."

"The heck you can," I retorted, defending the honor of my hero. "You can't beat up anybody. You're a jerk."

"Yeah, you're a jerk, Parks!" my friends all yelled in chorus.

"I'll show you who's a jerk. I can beat you up," Parks said.

Now it was serious. I'd never been in a fight in my life, but what the heck? "No, you can't!"

"Yes, I can."

So there we were, on the grass of my grandparents' neighbor's front yard, on my eight birthday, and I'm wondering whether Hopalong Cassidy shouldn't be there defending himself. Parks was a year older and much more compact than my long, gangly, skinny self, but we agreed to fight, so here I was.

"All right, this is just wrestling, right? No punching??"

"Yeah, right," said Parks. "No punching."

"OK, let's go."

With that, we began circling like the wrestlers we'd seen on Movie Tone News. We grabbed one another by the arms and shoved. It wasn't long before Parks' sturdier frame prevailed, and I went down with him landing on my chest. We struggled. He righted himself on my stomach—I remember hearing the guys cheering for me to throw him off.

I tried to push him off with all my strength, but he laid into me with all fists flying. A few whacks to the face and a well-placed blow to my skinny chest, and I could hear the wailing of some distant creature in distress. The neighbors and my grandparents came running, but it was too late to stop the humiliation (or the pain) of losing in defense of my movie hero.

My collar bone was broken, and the doctor said there wasn't much they could do except to strap me up for a few weeks. I've thought about that incident many times over my life. In retrospect, I guess it wasn't unusual for me to wade into a fight I couldn't win, but what the heck? Someone had to do it. Why not me? Maybe if my dad had been around more, he'd have convinced me to not always lead with my chin.

Heritage

I was born on April 30, 1943, one hundred and forty years to the day after the signing of the Louisiana Purchase. My dad came from a long line of one of the oldest, and at times wealthiest, families in America, including a stellar list of contributing statesmen in American History. He was on the declining leg.

The first Livingston in America, by twenty years of age, was a well-educated and engaging immigrant son of a prominent minister in the Church of Scotland. Fluent in English, Dutch, and passable French, he arrived in Boston and made his way to Albany, New York, in 1674 or 1675. His proficiency in languages established him as an intermediary between the Dutch fur traders, the incoming English government, and the resident Native Americans. He worked hard and was appointed secretary of the colony's Board of Indian Commissioners, clerk of the Albany General Court, and eventually Albany tax collector.

Public service proved good for business. Livingston rapidly became a successful merchant and entrepreneur. In 1679, he met and wooed the widow of a ranking Dutch merchant who had left her a sizable estate. Once married, her new husband's prowess in business blended well with his political dominion over real estate transactions, so in due time, it happened that much land in the hands of the Indians along the Hudson Valley found its way to him. Sometime after his death, Livingston became known as "The First Lord of the Manor." His progeny, and there are many (estimated to be about 1 million people today), succeeded in building mightily on his success, acquiring a major portion of New York State by the early nineteenth century.

Politics was a necessity for a family of such prominence. Producing large families was the custom of those days. There were numerous aspiring candidates in my lineage, many of whom became successful politicians. They included leaders in business, law, the military, and the executive and legislative branches of government, both before and after the American Revolution. There were several members of Congress, both Continental and current. Philip "the Signer" signed the Declaration of Independence; Robert "the Chancellor," the highest ranking legal officer in New York, swore George Washington into his post as the first President of the United States. The Chancellor was later appointed America's first Secretary of State, following his purchase for President Jefferson of the Louisiana territories from France on April 30, 1803.

His brother, Edward, younger by twenty years, was disgraced when $100,000 disappeared during his service as U.S. Attorney, Chief Customs collector, and Mayor of New York City, whereupon he fled to New Orleans and established himself as one of the foremost attorneys in the history of the nation. Successful attorney; Louisiana state legislator; author of the Louisiana Civil Code in use today, and the Criminal Code—never adopted by the legislature because of its progressivism; member of the U.S. House of Representatives for Louisiana's First Congressional District—the same seat I held for almost twenty two years; member of the U.S. Senate, and Secretary of State under President Andrew Jackson. Despite the early controversy over the missing customs revenue, Edward Livingston enjoyed a lengthy and remarkable career.

After Robert, "The First Lord of the Manor" (1654-1728), the next several generations, Philip (1686-1749), Robert (1708-1790), Walter (1740-1797), Henry Walter (1768-1810), and Henry Walter II (1798-1848), each held up the family name with successive achievements of distinction.

Philip, "The Second Lord of the Manor," served as Deputy Secretary of Indian Affairs under his father and, in 1725, succeeded him in the office. He also served as member of the Albany City Council, County Clerk, and member of the Colonial Legislature.

Robert, "The Third (and last) Lord of the Manor," served as member of the Colonial Assembly, and with his brothers and cousins threw his considerable influence on the side of liberty in the Revolution. With the creation of the new government came the abolition of the feudal, manorial system. Yet land titles in the name of the family prevailed. As the families grew, the land was subdivided and sold off, and today, relatively little of the land remains in the hands of Livingston descendants.

Public service continued as a hallmark of the family. Walter, one of Robert's thirteen children, served in a number of important posts of the day: member of the Provincial Congress in 1775; member of Assembly, 1777-79; Speaker Of Assembly, 1778; Commissioner of the Federal Treasury, 1785; Commissary of Stores for the Province of New York; Deputy of the Northern Department, 1776; and one of the

Commissioners to enforce the Militia Laws. He was not atypical.

Henry Walter, a Yale educated lawyer, was appointed by Gouverneur Morris of New York as his Secretary of Legation at Paris in 1792 to 1794, followed by service in the New York Assembly and then as a member of Congress (1803-07).

Henry Walter II had ten children of which the seventh was a son, Robert Linlithgow (1834-1877), who spent time as a junior officer in the Union Army during the Civil War. His son, Robert L. (1876-1925), my grandfather, allegedly served with Teddy Roosevelt's "Rough Riders" in Cuba and became a respected banker in New York City. Much of the family money had been disbursed elsewhere among the many branches of the family by then, so in time-honored fashion, my grandfather Robert replenished the family coffers by marrying one of the two daughters of a man known as "the richest man in Denver."

Dennis Sheedy

As was often the case among western families with significant resources, Marie Sheedy was sent by her father, my great-grandfather, from Denver "back east" to be educated. There she met and married Robert L. Livingston, my grandfather. The merger of name and money was one of great promise that was unfortunately compromised by the untimely death of my grandfather from influenza at age forty eight. He left behind his widow and five children, the eldest of which was only twelve years of age.

My father had every opportunity in life. He grew up with lots of money; he was tall, handsome, athletic and extremely likable, but he was possessed of another habit to surface from time to time in his family. Like his mother who had married into the Livingston clan, he was possessed of the "Irish disease." And when they were drinking, they weren't very nice. In fact, she was a pathetic but demanding creature who was raised in an environment of incredible wealth. As she grew older, she ruined everything and everyone with whom she came in contact. Spoiled to the core, she was a lost soul, born and raised by an Irish father who accomplished more in his lifetime than most people dream about in any age. Without her father or husband to provide stability, booze ruled her life, and she ruined the lives of her children.

* * * * *

Dennis Sheedy, her father and my great-grandfather, was born the last of thirteen children to a prominent farming family in Ireland in the midst of the Potato Famine in 1846. His family suffered financial failure and was forced to flee to America shortly after he was born. They settled in Rockport, Massachusetts, chosen by the elder Sheedy in order to best educate his children. His family remained there until he was twelve and then relocated to Lyons, Iowa, where Dennis's brother had moved and established a general merchandise store. Dennis worked in the shop as clerk, errand boy, and porter, becoming familiar with the merchandising needs of the western part of the country.

Calamity struck his family when Civil War gripped the country, so at the age of sixteen, he yielded to the allure of the Wild West. He took on odd jobs across the country and made his way west, where he began a successful pattern of merchandising of goods and buying and selling of livestock. Gradually learning the cattle business, he began buying herds in Texas and Arizona, then driving them north to Kansas or west to California where they brought a much better price. He fought off outlaws and Indians and managed to accumulate a quite sizable fortune. When he settled down in Denver, he helped found the Denver National Bank and began The Denver Dry Goods Company, which by the mid-1920s became the largest department store between Chicago and San Francisco. He was so successful that when he passed away in 1927, he was quite literally billed by the *Denver Post* as the "richest man in Denver."

Dennis married twice and had two children by his first wife. Marie was the eldest. Sister Florence married well, and she enjoyed a happy and productive life. Had they lived today, they would have been considered among the jet-set elite. In their own time, F. Scott Fitzgerald would have been proud of them. In fact, he may well have known them.

With her five children, Marie frequently shuttled between New York, England, and France by steamship. My dad attended a Roman Catholic Prep school in England, and he spent so much time with his mother and siblings in Paris that he spoke French like a Parisian. As a teenager in the '30s, he made brief trips to Germany and picked up a smattering of German, which got him assigned to the Intelligence Corps of the Army when World War II broke out. For whatever reason, he never left the States during the war.

Marie had money, and she knew how to spend it. She just didn't know how to hold on to it. Although she was one of the richest people in the country in the '20s, when she died thirty years later, she was heavily in debt. Granted, her bankers did little to protect her from the ravages of the depression, but had she been even the slightest bit frugal, she would have enjoyed a moderately generous lifestyle, as would have her children who might have lived in comfort long after she was gone.

When her husband passed away, her spending found no restraint. In fact, when she died, the IRS swooped in on her two-story penthouse in New York City and seized everything they could get their hands on.

It seems that Marie Sheedy Livingston hadn't believed in paying taxes. Each of her children waited eagerly for their inheritance, but there wasn't much left.

This was shattering for young people who had been raised wanting nothing. My uncle Barklie, the youngest, was the only one to escape a life of unhappiness when he was killed at the age of nineteen in an automobile wreck while in the army.

The rest all suffered greatly throughout their much longer lives. Robert, my father, and his sister, Sylvia, both died relatively young of alcoholism after multiple marriages. My Aunt Jacqueline, an incredibly beautiful woman in her day, took to bed late in life as a total recluse, estranged from her children, and remained so until her death, living for years on the generosity of others. Aunt Denise, the eldest and most normal of the bunch, was likewise estranged from her children and lived her later years in a nursing home in France until her death in 2001. Several of their children broke through the downward spiral begun by their grandmother, Marie, and have led happy, productive lives, but others, less so.

I have been fortunate in many different ways. Most all, I had the good luck to have been born to a great mother, and despite my missteps, I've been blessed to have been married to a wonderful woman, Bonnie Marie Belzons Robichaux, for fifty-two years. We had four terrific children and, at last count, nine perfect grandchildren and one beautiful great-grandchild.

Childhood

My dad left home when I was seven. He left my mom with little else but the Coke bottles kept for deposit refund on the back porch. She had no job, and my two year old sister and I had a nagging habit of eating on regular occasion. That posed a small problem which she managed with no small difficulty, but she managed nonetheless.

Her father was an asthmatic lawyer/insurance salesman who moved to Colorado Springs from Ft. Worth, Texas, for the climate. He and my grandmother were earnest, hardworking Americans of traditional values and fine reputation. They put my mother through college "back east" at Pine Manor for a couple of years followed by a stint at Colorado College, where she met and ultimately married my father.

While it was a fine wedding, complete with morning suits and top hats, I recall stories of a small problem at the reception when my old man got drunk and punched my grandfather. Evidently, they never got along very well after that.

I think my grandparents felt that when my father took off, it wasn't soon enough, and they pitched in to help my mother financially as she took one job after another to raise her two small children. Eventually she found herself in the personnel department at Avondale Shipyard in New Orleans and stayed there for fifteen years until her remarriage in 1965 to Adolph Billet, a really great guy. (They were married on the same day that Bonnie and I were, but that's a story to be shared later on.) Mom and Adolph lived quite happily together in New Orleans until his death at the age of ninety one in 2005. Mom died just before Christmas, 2010, just shy of her ninetieth birthday.

Once separated, my dad left for New York, and later to Spain, to avoid paying alimony and child support. I only saw him four or five times after that; the last time was when I was called to his home in Benidorm, Spain, to collect his bloated body. I closed his home, wrapped up his affairs, bought him a casket, and returned him to Hyde Park Cemetery, in New York, where he rests today. He'd drunk himself to death at the age of fifty one.

I was a normal, tall but skinny, uncoordinated kid, not given to athletics, always reading, and I often listened to the radio. In the early '50s, my favorite program was *No School Today* with Big John and Sparky, the gremlin who always wanted to be a real boy. Every Saturday morning, I'd march around the living room to the sounds of John Phillips Sousa in my pajamas and bathrobe.

That program fostered one of the great bloopers later touted as mistakes in the media when one Saturday at the end of the theme song, "Teddy Bear Picnic," Big John thought he was off the air, but he was heard on coast-to-coast radio as he declared, "I hope that'll hold the little bastards for this week!"

When I was in fifth grade, my mom's folks helped her take me out of the neighborhood Catholic school and send me to St. Martin's, a private Episcopal school out in Metairie, a suburb of New Orleans. This was a traumatic event for me, who as a product of divorce was more than unsure of his place in the world. My new teacher, Mrs. Schamanski, was a dominant and over-bearing person who both scared and infuriated me. She scheduled a bike riding "field trip," but when she learned I still couldn't ride a two wheel bike, she embarrassed me in front of my new class. Memorization was difficult for me, and when I didn't learn the capitals of the states as directed, she did it again. Near the end of the year, I failed to complete my Latin American scrapbook on time and played hooky through the entire last week of school. That earned me a pretty good whacking when my mother found out.

I must have softened with time, for years later, Mrs. Schamanski sold me some encyclopedias for my kids.

As an adolescent, I was shy and self-conscious. As uncoordinated as I was, I didn't learn to ride a bike until I was about ten. But I always had a strange desire to be liked, and I was trusting to a fault. Once while on the moving school bus, someone threw me Alice Ryan's tennis shoes and yelled, "Quick, throw them out the window!" So I did.

My mother sensed my discomfort in my new school, so she threw a birthday party for me and my classmates in Audubon Park. We were to play baseball and have hotdogs and lemonade for refreshments. Lots of boys in the class showed up, and it was a perfect day, until we worked up a thirst and guzzled the lemonade from a jug that my childhood friend, Hoy Booker, and I had washed out. I guess we didn't adequately wash the soap from the dispenser, and by the end of the day every single kid was throwing up. That's a birthday that I've never forgotten.

I was an eternal klutz. There was a brand new fifteen-foot-high slide at school that everyone was proud of. After several safe journeys down the slide, I got overly confident. Once at the top, I caught my foot on the rung of the ladder and toppled over sideways. The collarbone I'd broken a couple of years earlier—broke again. So much for the slide. It was gone when I got back to school. These days, my future would have been assured by the countless trial lawyers who might have signed me up before I hit the ground.

Nixon Adams was three years older than me, twice as heavy and half as tall. He'd catch the school bus at my stop, and if we came home together, he'd drill me for what seemed like hours trying to teach me how to sail clam shells down the street. I never got the hang of it, but I could have paved someone's driveway with all the shells we tossed. I dreaded even seeing him in the school bus, but twenty years later, Nixon was a good friend and was a supporter of my political efforts in St. Tammany Parish, notwithstanding that he was a die-hard Democrat.

In eighth grade, I went out for football. I got a brand new helmet and a jersey, and I paraded around home in my new outfit. It made me look twice as heavy as I really was, and I was very proud of it, at least until the very first scrimmage at school when Eddie Elsey ran right over me and planted his cleats in my face. I went home and never wore it again. They say that's fun!!??

Reading was more fun for me. Every summer, my mom would pile my sister, Carolyn, and me into our old Jeepster with the plastic snap-on windows, and we'd drive to Colorado Springs to see my grandparents. Mimi and Granddad, as we called them, made sure I split my time between swimming and sports at the YMCA and loading up books from the library. Many of my favorite hours were spent stretched out on the couch on their front porch looking out at Pike's Peak, reading about pilots, cowboys, and soldiers. American heroes like Kit Carson, Will Rogers, Daniel Boone, and Paul Revere inspired me as role models.

I was also a big fan of comic books. When I could get away with it whether in New Orleans or Colorado Springs, I constantly raced through stories about Superman, Green Arrow, Batman, and all the Disney characters. I acquired an almost perfect collection of the "Classic" comic books. Three large stacks of comics were in my room when

I later joined the Navy, but my mother didn't get the memo, and she threw out what might have been a couple of hundred thousand dollars in my comic collection.

My grandparents couldn't afford membership in a country club, but they were frequently invited by friends to dinner, and I was often able to go swim with friends at the Garden of the Gods Country Club. I never saw them, but every so often, I heard that Bob Hope or Bing Crosby had been there to play golf. One of my favorite memories was having dinner there with my grandparents one evening in 1955, and someone pointed out Walt Disney sitting a couple of tables away. An addicted Mickey Mouse and Donald Duck fan, I couldn't resist walking up to his table and asking him for his autograph. He couldn't have been nicer, and he autographed a cardboard drink coaster. I don't know whatever happened to it, but I was thrilled. I've loved the Disney Empire ever since, so much so that Bonnie and I took our children and grandchildren on a Disney cruise. It was great fun!

Adolescence

I began making friends after that first year at St. Martin's. In seventh grade, my mother, sister and I moved to an upstairs rental unit near Tulane University, and when two classmates from Uptown, John Woolfolk and Johnny Bolles, showed up on their bikes at my house one Saturday, I never looked back. We rode our bikes all over town together. And we remain good friends to this very day.

In those days, New Orleans was very safe, and we had a ball exploring the city. When the Girod Street Cemetery was closed by the City, we found some souvenirs to decorate our club house behind Woolfolk's house. Today, we'd probably have been arrested for that, but the statute of limitations has long passed.

Not being an athlete in high school in the '50s could have been a real drag; but it wasn't. In fact, I was in a terrific school and while I wasn't overly academic, I learned a lot. I also had a lot of fun. Once I became used to my surroundings and my place in life, I made friends easily.

In most localities in the United States, drinking alcohol is frowned on if one is under twenty-one years of age. In New Orleans in the late '50s, if you could see over the bar, you were old enough to buy a drink. As the tallest kid in my class, I was buying and drinking by the time I was fourteen. I remember my first high school party when I enjoyed the buzz of getting drunk so much that in time, I repeated the performance on many, many occasions.

Fortunately, while the love for booze was in my genes because of my father and his family, the Good Lord also vested me with the brakes to make it very, very painful. I have always gotten terrible hangovers, and though I drank to excess at party time throughout my early life, the hangovers finally caught up with me, and the pain gradually outweighed the "fun." These days, if I have more than a couple of drinks in a month, it's unusual. It's just no fun anymore.

But it certainly was back then. I joined the high school fraternity, OBD, after my first beer party. It was great fun until initiation day, when my friends and I all got the living hell beaten out of us. We knew it would be bad, but after dressing up in ludicrous costumes complete with several extra pairs of underwear, we traversed the city on a silly scavenger hunt, ending up in someone's back yard. There we spent Saturday afternoon reaching for our toes while one frat member after another broke his three or five ply paddle over our butts.

That evening, my behind was black and crusted, and as insane as I thought it was at the time, I repeated the performance to the backsides of other neophytes the next year, perhaps with a little more sympathy than had been given me. High school fraternities are outlawed in New Orleans today, and that is probably a good thing. But indeed the experience formed bonds with friends that have held strong all my life.

Somehow I survived, and life endured in normal routine for a kid in the 1950s. Never the athlete except for a stint of running track, I opted for going to school and studying during the week and having fun on the weekends. That worked during the school year, but since my mother was working to support my sister and me, I had to work during the summers if I wanted any spending money of my own.

High School

My first job was only a few blocks from our apartment near Audubon Park. At fourteen years old, I worked half days for $0.73 an hour taping down lines on the sand tennis courts, chopping weeds with a sickle, picking up paper with a stick, nail, and a sack, and most delightful of all, cleaning up after monkeys on "Monkey Island" as well as elephants after they were chased from their steel housing.

Now, in New Orleans in July, the very humid temperature ranges well into the high 90s, so the latter was indeed a memorable experience. My weapons for the task were a wheelbarrow, pitchfork, and a clothespin. The trick was to stand outside the steel house, place the clothespin on my nose, hold my breath and after several deep breaths, run into the 130 degree enclosure with the wheelbarrow and pitchfork. Before I fainted, I had to fill the barrow up with elephant pies as fast as I could and run out. There was no air in the place, and the heat was unbearable, so it wasn't an environment that anyone but an elephant could wish to hang around in. If elephants could talk, I suspect that they'd say they didn't like that hot house any more than I did. I often said in later years that it was my first experience with my Party Symbol.

In six subsequent summers, I worked at Avondale Shipyard as a mail carrier; a pipe fitter's helper; a ship fitter's helper; a machine shop "expeditor;" and an assembly line worker on the night shift. My mother worked in the shipyard personnel office, first as a secretary, and later as the assistant manager of the office. She actually ran the office, but those days preceded any talk of the "glass ceiling," so she always played second fiddle to her boss, who rarely showed up for work.

Years later, after my time in the Navy, I sold Fuller Brushes for a summer on the streets of Uptown New Orleans. But I'm getting ahead of myself. The point is that I was never unduly burdened as a youngster, but I wasn't idle either. There was never a time when I had more than a week off from school or work of some type. And it was with that training that I essentially became a workaholic. If I ever wanted or needed something, I knew I had to work for it if I felt it attainable. If not, I did without it.

During the school year, weekends involved hanging out with classmates at parties or football games where I watched the action from the stands. But in my senior year, I was hired as water boy (more appropriately perhaps, "mascot") for the football team. At six-foot four-inches tall and 120 lbs., I wore a t-shirt that was small even for me, emblazoned in the back with red letters "DOC." That had become my nickname for Stanley's famous "Dr. Livingstone, I presume!" Unfortunately, my job also earned me a jingle, best forgotten, that went, "He's our pride; he's our joy; he's our little water boy!" I had no pride whatsoever in those days.

On non-football weekends, it wasn't unusual for six of us to pile into Jimmy Conner's '49 Packard, buy some quarts of beer at our favorite black-owned grocery store, then park in front of the empty Winn-Dixie, turn up rock 'n roll on WTIX, and sing at the top of our lungs until the neighbors closed us down.

Some of my very favorite memories were of packing up with many of my friends for weekend trips to the De Soto National Forest in Mississippi. Most of us weren't hunters, and few of us were even experienced campers, but we were undaunted. And we had a ball! We all brought prepackaged food and more equipment than we'd ever need. We built fires, burned our food, sipped booze from our flasks (flasks were big back then), and told stories. Finally we'd climb into our sleeping bags on the ground and get up in the morning and start all over.

Nep Smith was most proud of his new "jungle" hammock that he tied and suspended between two trees. He actually had to be zipped into it by someone outside in order to be fully comfortable. But Nep (Howard is his real name, but no one used it) was famous for his fear of snakes. So when he finally got comfortable in his jungle hammock, all zipped up and ready for the night, he grew a little apprehensive when he felt something move around his feet. It was only the black snake that Jerry Friedrichs had slipped into the hammock just before he got in, and the fact that black snakes are not poisonous was an argument that was of no great import to Nep.

When Nep realized that indeed a snake was locked inside with him, the hammock began to bounce and lurch three feet in every direction as he tried to extricate himself. Eventually, we suppressed our hysterics and hilarity and cut him down and pulled him out. Fortunately, he didn't have a heart attack; but the humor escaped him as we laughed about it throughout his life.

I recall that the trips ended when Carlos DeArriganaga, Lee Estes and Doug "Mad Dog" Howard, all of whom were experienced campers and hunters, got drunk and began shooting bird shot at each other through the trees from about one hundred yards apart. No one was hurt, but the experience dimmed the attractiveness of the trips for the rest of us.

The summer before we graduated, six others of us planned and traveled to the Appalachians in Tennessee. We drove two cars to the trail near Gatlinburg, Tennessee, where we spent a few days hiking up and down mountains. We also strayed off to spots like "Fiery Gizzard" where we dove off a thirty foot cliff into a pool of cold mountain spring water, or "Point Disappointment," a beautiful view from a ledge that loomed over a thousand foot drop off. We were told it had been the site of a number of suicide jumps.

Finally, we explored "Buggy Top Cave," a cold, black, and very deep mountain cave into which we wandered for a couple miles while trying to find the source of the "Nile," or rather the mountain stream that bore deeply into the mountain. Fortunately, John Oudt declined to go into the cave with us, and when we failed to emerge as we struggled to find our way back to the entrance, it appeared that he was going to have to get the Forest Rangers to come find us. It didn't become necessary, but it explains why John made millions of dollars in business later on and the rest of us did not.

Forty one years later, the same six guys got together and reenacted the earlier event with another trip to the Appalachian Trail, where we spent three days hiking with slightly lighter packs, but still much heavier than we needed. For guys in their sixties it was harder by increments, but we had a great time avoiding the bears and almost getting lost. We clearly weren't the same people we'd been forty one years earlier, what with a couple of divorces, the death of one spouse and more than one child, and varying degrees of wealth or lack of it. But once we got on the trail, it was just like the good old days, and we were young again.

We took another trip five years later, but there were no more extensive hiking trips on our calendar. Adding two more old friends to the original six, we stayed at John Oudt's fabulous home in Colorado. From a platform of exquisite comfort, we launched our expeditions of hiking, horse-back riding, and white-water rafting. The latter was more memorable from the bottom of the river—under the water—than from the top . . . since the raft flipped and all of us fell out. But the beds at Oudt's house were dry and a lot more comfortable than sleeping bags on the ground had been five years earlier.

Back in our days in high school we were just a bunch of kids, raised in a safe and relatively nice environment, and looking forward to graduation with the world of 1960 ahead of us. We could not possibly have imagined the changes ahead in our lives, in our country, and indeed, in the world.

College

Between 1960 and 1968, I received two degrees from Tulane University, a BA in Economics and a JD in Law, as well as an honorable discharge following two years of active and four years inactive duty in the United States Navy. Whereas some people would have tackled each task in singular and orderly fashion, I mixed them up and completed the tasks according to my own uncharted agenda.

I enrolled at Tulane's Engineering School as a Freshman, but when Dr. Restor talked over my head and put me to sleep for a semester if and when I attended his physics class, my grade average wasn't enhanced by the "F" on my record. Strangely enough, I enjoyed physics lab and got a "B" for that class, and my other grades were sufficient to help me escape with an overall "C" average, notwithstanding my plebian role at the DKE fraternity house, Tulane's version of *Animal House.* Crashing the physics course was followed by withdrawal from the Naval ROTC unit on grounds that my studies and drilling commitments were interfering with my social life at the frat house.

The ROTC instructor was indignant. I vividly recall him saying that if I couldn't hack ROTC, I was certain to be somewhere other than Tulane in the following school year. Insulted by his absurd prediction, I nevertheless enrolled in the School of Arts and Sciences in the second semester, sans engineering and Naval ROTC. I aimed for an economics major with a math minor and some accounting thrown in. Two weeks later, I'd dropped accounting. The course was worse than a foreign language, and since I assiduously avoided homework, I couldn't figure it out and thus escaped the inevitable poor grade.

Still, I had a great time that year—drinking, carousing, dating various girls, and enjoying myself at the DKE House. But the ROTC officer proved as right as Caesar's soothsayer foretelling the Ides of March. Despite a 2.2 grade point average ("C"), I knew intuitively that I was having too much fun and that I should do something else for a while. I'd always wanted to go to sea, so I decided to join the Seafarers International Union (SIU) and ship out on a merchant marine ship for a cruise. I figured it would only be for a few months, and that I could re-enroll in school upon my return. I applied for and received my seaman's papers designating me as a "wiper" or engine room grunt, and I looked forward to the adventure. It meant I would finally escape New Orleans. I planned to see a little part of the world and go back to college when the trip was over. But just as I was about to ship out, the ILA (longshoreman's union) went out on strike in the Port of New Orleans without any indication that the strike would be a short one.

Navy

My frustration was short lived. A family friend, Bache ("pronounced Beach") Whitlock, found his own college career disrupted for lack of educational devotion, and he told me he was considering joining the Navy.

We went to the recruiter together and within a day or so, we'd both enlisted as "E-1's" in the U.S. Navy Reserve. We were issued our uniforms and attended a couple of drills. At the first opportunity, we were to be sent to boot camp together on the "buddy system." As it turned out, Bache failed the eye test and was confined to a slower admittance schedule than I wanted. So I went ahead by myself and boarded a train for the Great Lakes Boot Camp, just north of Chicago. Bache was later sent to San Diego, and I didn't see him again until years after I left the Navy.

I never had a chance to visit San Diego until twenty-five years later, and when I finally did see how nice it was, I wanted to sue the Navy for misdirection. Boot Camp anywhere was hard, but the thing I really remember about it was that come winter, the Great Lakes base was so terribly cold. Marching around the barracks on night watch in the middle of December was brutal, especially for a kid from New Orleans.

My enlistment required me to spend two years on active duty, inclusive of boot camp. So during a break for Christmas, I bid goodbye after apologizing to my then girlfriend at Newcomb (the women's college of Tulane) for leaving town. In early January, I flew to Portsmouth, New Hampshire, where I boarded the USS *Boxer* (LPH-4), a traditional aircraft carrier originally built about the time of my birth. Converted to an early edition of "amphibious assault" ship meant that she was a troop carrier for Marines and helicopters bound for the fearsome war zones of the Caribbean Sea via her homeport in Norfolk ("Dogs and Sailors, keep off the grass!"), Virginia.

Two years is a long time for anything, but for an eighteen year old kid used to living at home in relative comfort, it was an eternity. In fact, a four hour watch on the quarter deck, up on the bridge, or in the bowels of the ship, could be a test of patience every time it began. In so many instances, I was required to just stand still without any activity apart from watching the second hand on a clock tick away ever so slowly. There were lots of those watches over time, and I never enjoyed any of them.

In January, 1961, I boarded the *Boxer* to take my assignment in the ship's personnel office. This was not my choice, but one made for me by the omnipotent Bureau of Naval Personnel with which it was futile to argue. I suppose some bureaucrat saw my one year of college and astounding capacity to type nineteen words per minute on a typewriter and divined that I was best suited for a permanent desk job. That wasn't quite the case.

I stayed there plunking on the typewriter for roughly three months. I was constantly erasing mistakes, cursing the triplicate carbon copies as I corrected each one, and spilling the mimeograph ink all over my uniform. I absolutely hated the assignment, and I wasn't the only one. My shipmate, Tom Bruffy, had actually graduated from college. Bruffy was a nice guy, but every time the Bosons' Mate announced "Cast off all lines; the ship is underway!" he ran to the ship's head (bathroom) and buried his head in a toilet for the next three days until he got over his inevitable sea sickness.

Unless you are in a typhoon on an aircraft carrier, you really have no idea that you are not standing in the equivalent of the third floor of the New York Stock Exchange—even though you could be steaming along at twenty knots in the ocean. With the exception of full hurricanes, there was virtually no movement other than the vibrations of the engines, which were a full five decks below us. But you couldn't convince Bruffy of that. Like clockwork, every time we left port, he got very sick. After a few months on board, the Navy sent Bruffy a letter advising him that he had been accepted to OCS, and he left to get his commission. I loved the thought of Bruffy becoming an officer.

The other guys in the personnel division were good folks as well. It was just the incessant agony of typing—in triplicate—dabbing "white-out" on mistakes; mimeographing; filling in DD 214's; and filing, filing, and more filing, that got under my skin from the beginning. The Chief of the Personnel Division, a chief petty officer and the king of the roost, didn't make the job any more enjoyable. He really wasn't a bad guy, but this was a man who loved forms, all forms, in triplicate, quadruplicate, and infinitecate. He just couldn't appreciate anyone in his lair who didn't love them as much as he did.

It took me about three months from the time that I boarded the ship to hit the point that if I had to type a single additional form, my eyes were going to roll in my head like the wheels on a Las Vegas slot machine. I hated what I was doing, and my work reflected it. One day, the Chief called me over to his desk to tell me that I was doing a lousy job. That was the trigger. I guess I could have been court-martialed for whatever I told him, but when I'd settled down, I let him know I had no desire to remain in his Division.

I said that I'd really wanted to get into Navigation and be a Quartermaster, but that the "Great Brain" in Navy Central had sent me to Personnel. So we came to an agreement. The Chief told me that he would definitely transfer me. If I worked hard for two or three more weeks, my destination might be Navigation but in all likelihood, I would end up in the Ship's Laundry where the mean temperature at any given time was 130 degrees. That was an easy choice, so I really applied myself and improved my typing speed up to twenty words a minute.

A couple of weeks later, I was transferred to Navigation for the balance of my two years. Somehow, I'd neglected to tell the Chief of Personnel that the reason I didn't get Navigation in the first place was because I had failed the color blindness test in boot camp. Those little red and green numbers on the charts just never stood out for me like they do for other folks. But how important could that have been, anyway?

The balance of my time on active duty was more fun than in the beginning, but it was still very much enough for me to decide that I wasn't inclined toward a naval career. I worked my way through Quarterdeck and Bridge watches and on a stint of watches in "after-steering" from which the ship is steered from the bottom in the event the Bridge is knocked out in hostile action.

Each Division is responsible for the upkeep of its own quarters, so daytimes were consumed with cleaning, painting, chipping old paint; and repainting with lots of lead-based red paint known as "Red Lead." (They say lead paint is potentially harmful to the brain—but there's really nothing wrong with me . . . *&$ percent*@*# . . . !!) The Navigation Division controlled several ship compartments from the bowels of the ship to the very top, and they all had to be cleaned and painted regularly. One of my favorite missions was winding the ship's clocks, a task that had to be done by one of our number every single day. That meant traveling to every other Division and visiting with friends all over the ship.

Once underway, steering the ship and keeping the ship's logs were most enjoyable. Navigation was interesting, but once when those little red, green, and white lights merged into one another, I caused the ship to drift off course late one night. For whatever reason, my future as a naval navigator was somewhat abbreviated. But I survived my two years in the Navy, and I enjoyed my assignment in the Navigation Department. Notwithstanding some great moments, I was convinced that I wasn't cut out for a naval career, and I couldn't wait to get out.

The United States had launched the Bay of Pigs invasion of Cuba in the spring of 1961, shortly after John Kennedy was inaugurated President of the United States. Then Russian Premier Khrushchev began construction of the Berlin Wall just before I entered boot camp. The "Cold War" was growing more and more intense. But for the average sailor stationed aboard ship in the Caribbean, life was fairly peaceful.

We steamed on a number of cruises to the Caribbean, and I always enjoyed cruising at sea and visiting various islands down south, much preferring that to being locked at home-port in Norfolk. Va. The Norfolk routine allowed us to leave the ship on liberty every other day, but with no old friends in the area, we did little more than visit the local honky-tonks with shipmates, consume all the "3.2 beer" we could handle, and roll back to the ship by curfew at midnight.

But in October, 1962, the routine began to vary. When I returned to the ship one Tuesday night, I noticed that several ships had departed from their moorings. Heading home from the bars on Thursday night, I noticed that several additional ships were missing. By Saturday, the *Boxer* was gone ... and we were headed for something that would later be known as "The Cuban Missile Crisis."

We didn't learn until we were well underway that we were to be part of the force deployed to face off against Fidel Castro following his introduction of Soviet missiles in Cuba. Khrushchev and the Cubans eventually backed down when confronted by President Kennedy, but until then, there were some tense moments in the halls of power. I don't think I ever truly realized how tense the situation was until I saw Castro interviewed on television some many years later. He told an inquiring reporter that if he had had his own finger on the button, he would have launched missiles at our carriers. Since I was a sailor aboard the *Boxer* (LPH-4) within sixty miles of the shores of Cuba, I took the news somewhat personally. I waited fifty years for him to croak, but the guy lived to his 90s.

The sacrifices throughout history of men and women in our Armed Services have been beyond honorable. Just since my days in the Navy, Americans have sent their young people to death and destruction in South East Asia, the Mid-East, and other dark and strife-ridden corners of the world. My experiences in the Navy were not emblematic of those horrors. In fact, I've so often admired the stories of the many who have served our nation with honor that it's with some embarrassment that I recall my toughest time in the Navy. In November, 1962, we'd been at sea circling Cuba for over sixty days without returning to port. We couldn't replenish our stores, and the scarcity became so bad that I found weevils in my Rice Krispies.

In John McCain's *Faith of My Fathers*, I noticed that he was a fighter pilot aboard the *USS Enterprise* in Norfolk at the same time I was there. He was an officer, of course, so we didn't hang out in the same bars. But it was an interesting coincidence that we were within rock throwing distance of one another, only to serve together in the Congress many years later.

The rest of my time in the Navy was unremarkable, save the two fights I had a year apart from one another while waiting for the long boat to take us back to the ship at the Port of St. Thomas in the Virgin Islands. While I always got along fine with most of my shipmates be they sailor or Marine, on two occasions, each after long days of fun and frolic, I found myself in dispute with some Marines temporarily assigned to the *Boxer*. I survived the battles, but in each case when morning came, I had to move my nose from the side of my head to the center of my face. One guy later threatened to kill me in compensation for the front teeth he was missing, but the "dogging wrench" (an eight-inch lead pipe used for battening down the water-tight hatches) in my back pocket must have dissuaded him through the end of the cruise.

In retrospect, I was quite fortunate that those two years in the

Navy were as uneventful as they were. I couldn't wait to go home when my enlistment was over, but the experience left me with full admiration and great respect for the sacrifices made by the people who serve in our Armed Services. Vietnam found its way to the forefront of consciousness throughout our nation for the next decade, and the suffering from that war continues to this day. Yet had I been asked to find that country on a map when I returned to civilian life in 1963, I doubt that I would have been able to do so.

Not many of our people volunteer to serve in the Armed Services any more, and far too many of our citizens fail to appreciate the sacrifices of the ones that do. Nor do they appreciate the strain on the families who manage in the absence of loved ones. My own limited experience inspires both Bonnie and me not to miss an opportunity to thank young people in uniform for their service. We were extremely proud of our son, Richard, who enlisted in the Army and served with honor and distinction for three years.

College (again)

And so I emerged from the Navy in time for the fall semester of college in 1963. Although I'd attained the rank of Quartermaster Third Class (QM3) or E-4, neither that nor the many stories of alcoholic excess in the Caribbean earned me more than the title of "sophomore" when I returned to class at Tulane University. Most of my DKE brothers had begun to plot their paths in life and were now "seniors." But not all were that lucky. Some had suffered mishaps along the way and had faltered. For example, one old friend had an especially bad semester while I was gone. When the dust settled on the five courses in which he'd registered, he received four "F's" and one "D" for the term. Everyone said it was because he'd spent too much time on one subject. He wasn't there when I returned.

A couple of other things had happened before I returned as well. After assuring all the gamblers and whorehouses that he would be friendly to their cause, Jim Garrison was elected District Attorney of New Orleans in 1961. Shortly after taking office, Garrison earned himself a profile in *Time* magazine by personally leading the police on a round of very public busts of his old friends' businesses. Among them was the famous whorehouse run by the infamous Madam Norma Wallace on Conti and North Rampart streets a block from the police station. Norma had served (or is it "serviced"?) many a Tulane and Loyola college student over the years, and she was reputed to offer discounts for regular customers. Her place was well known to the DKE house as "H. Monroe's," since one of our more affluent brothers couldn't very well write checks to Norma Wallace on the account his father set up for him. Good jock that he was, he always wrote them out to "H. Monroe's Sporting Goods," and Norma cashed them easily.

When Garrison and the police knocked down Norma's door, they found and arrested one of the DKE brothers inside, but *Time* magazine was nice enough to spell his name wrong.

The other item of note happened well before I returned from the Navy in 1963. In May 1962, President Jack Kennedy came to New Orleans to speak at a Port ceremony. A couple of miles away, the DKEs threw a party on the front porch of their house at 1469 Henry Clay Avenue. Wonder of wonders, the President's motorcade brought his open convertible right past the DKE house and across the giant letters spelling out "Drunk Zone" on the pavement across the width of the street.

The DKE's were ready for him as he passed. They'd hired a famous New Orleans rock 'n roll band to play "Hit the Road, Jack!" as the motorcade approached. Then out of nowhere, someone in the crowd kicked a beach ball that flew over heads of the Secret Service and bounced on the hood of the President's vehicle. Breaths were held and guns drawn, and there were some tense moments while the fun of the day was suspended. But all was well, and the motorcade proceeded unharmed.

Eighteen months later, Jack Kennedy was assassinated in Dallas while riding in what was quite likely that very same car.

I was back at Tulane by then and was napping at home after class. My mother called me from work to see if I'd heard the news. She said, "Turn on the TV! The President has just been shot in Dallas." I ran to the television and watched the tragedy unfold and then I ran the block and a half from our apartment to the DKE house. The guys had just heard and had the TV blaring on the front porch.

A couple of hours later, one of my DKE brothers, Kaul Buhler, boarded a New Orleans Public Service bus on Freret Street. Several black people were on the bus with Kaul, and the white bus driver was listening to the radio reports of Kennedy's death. The driver turned to the riders and said to no one in particular, "Boy, I'm glad that son of a bitch is dead." Buhler, a compact five-foot eight-inch law student, stood up, walked to the front of the bus, and quietly asked the driver to step outside. The burly driver had no sooner stepped of the bus, when Buhler decked him. When the police showed up, the people on the bus defended him, "That white boy didn't do nothing! That bus driver picked on him for no reason!" The cops let him go.

Upon return to Tulane, I enrolled in my post-engineering curriculum: heavy on math and chemistry, a little English, but no history and only so much social science as I absolutely had to have. Economics 101 was on the menu, and since I had no idea what I wanted to do with my life, I kept my sophomore year curriculum fairly general in nature. But with the passage of time, I decided on an economics major with a math minor. Unfortunately, after successfully navigating through sixteen hours of math, just short of the seventeen hours needed to qualify for a minor, I became suddenly aware that I couldn't understand anything more that math had to offer. Calculus centered on infinity, and that was a concept I never could grasp. Suddenly English became the substitute for math, and since I always enjoyed reading, it became an enjoyable alternative. I still greatly regret not having taken more history in college.

Since then, I've loved reading history and historical fiction. While I never took any structured history courses, I suppose I've compensated for that by now. I deeply appreciate the challenges and accomplishments of those who precede us. But as a kid who was himself greatly distracted by the advent of television, I believe a great cause of the lack of education and understanding of young people today is that they simply haven't been sufficiently exposed to history and the foundations of our democratic system. If we don't know how we arrived where we are, we really can't appreciate the gifts we've been handed in this remarkable American system of ours. The peoples of other nations in the world would readily trade places with us if they could, yet far too many of our own fail to appreciate how truly lucky we are.

I don't intend that as a platitude. Reading about Washington, Adams, Franklin, Hamilton, Madison, and Jefferson has given me deep appreciation for their gift to future generations, not just Americans, but to the untold millions of people who live in relative freedom throughout the world. I've come to believe that so long as our leaders adhere to our Constitution, our system of government provides more benefit to more people here and abroad than any monarchy, dictatorship, communist society, or authoritarian government of any kind anywhere else.

Fear of what we might have been motivated me to take a personal interest in politics. Franz Kafka's *The Trial* alarmed me to the horrors of overbearing faceless bureaucracy. Ayn Rand's *Atlas Shrugged* lit the fire in me to fight the threat of top-heavy government and convinced me that one man can make a difference if only he is motivated to step up and challenge the status quo. As we see in today's world, these lessons are eternal, but they must be learned and re-learned by successive generations.

In my early days back in college after the Navy, I was serious about my studies, at least for a few months. I averaged a B+ for my courses that semester but as the old ways settled in, I became more comfortable at the DKE House again, and booze and girls reasserted their presence in my life. We studied a bit, but we also enjoyed ourselves. It simply became a question of whether the party routine continued at the DKE House through the weekend . . . or into the next week.

Beer on Friday afternoons was a constant at Bruno's on Maple Street or Grafagnino's (we called it Graff's) on Calhoun, where you could get an icy glass mug of beer for a quarter. It was fun to read the graffiti on the bathroom walls of Graff's . . . and just about any other New Orleans bar. Aside from the phone numbers of dates for sale or companionship (be they male or female) or far too many crude depictions of some sick jerk's dreams, there were the amusing comments about life, women, your mother, or other contemporary humor.

For whatever reason, one of the more memorable was when after a couple of beers, I felt the call of nature and had to sit on one of the dirtier toilets in the city. I wasn't happy to be there and was concentrating on the issues of the day, when I noticed something written in small letters across the bottom of the stall door. I squinted my eyes, but I couldn't read it. I leaned forward, but I still couldn't read it. So I leaned really far forward, hoisting my butt off the toilet seat. Finally, I read it, "You are now shitting at a forty five degree angle." I was.

The rest of my sophomore and junior years were spent in that continuum. My grades were decent, but nothing worthy of the Mensa Society, and I had a great time dating and drinking my way through the weekends at frat parties, etc.

By the end of my junior year, my friends who hadn't for whatever reason discontinued their studies had either graduated or moved on in life, or they were enrolled in law school, med school, or some other graduate endeavor. A couple of friends even rolled out as officers and went to Vietnam. But all my friends were making major decisions in their lives, and I was still hanging around as an undergraduate. I felt left out. Then one day, I saw my old friend, Johnny Bolles, emerge from a freshman tort exam in law school, and he handed me the test he had just taken. I knew nothing about law school, but while we were riding to Domilise's to get a world-famous New Orleans po-boy sandwich, I looked it over and began thinking, "That looks easy enough; I can do that."

As it happened, I had completed virtually all of my required courses for a Bachelor of Arts degree, but I hadn't taken my elective courses. So the number of hours required for graduation became more important than the course load. When I mentioned that to my friends, they told me that I would probably qualify for admittance to law school on the "3 & 3" program, which permitted me to take law classes as my remaining undergraduate elective courses and thus allowed me to complete a law degree in six rather than seven years. I took a couple of economics classes over the summer to round out my major and was subsequently admitted to the Tulane law school.

Summer, 1965

I didn't intend it to be so, but as it turned out the summer of 1965 was a most memorable summer for me. After economics class, I became a Fuller Brush salesman, trooping around uptown New Orleans in ninety-plus degree weather hoping to sell enough brush and cosmetic specials to make some money for the school year. I was doing ok, but it was no way to retire rich.

With only a few weeks on the job, I was asked to train my friend and DKE brother, George Riess, so that he could join me on the sales force. One very hot July day, he and I were making the rounds when we spied a fairly heavy older woman, rollers in her hair and dressed in her house coat, trimming the vegetation in front of her shotgun house. We walked up to the front gate, and I asked her if she would like a free sample of our very best perfumed hand cream. She said she would, so I squirted some in her hands. As she churned her hands, they turned a milky white while I began to explain our specials in hair brushes, bath brushes, clothes brushes, dog brushes, and tooth brushes. She continued to wipe the stuff on her forearms and her upper arms, and then her face. I showed her my display of floor mops, kitchen ware, dish soap, bath soap, shoe polish, and shoe brushes.

As she stood there in the sweltering heat, her hands, arms, and face covered with this white cream, she tried to wipe it on her clothes. I was in full throttle with my specials pitch when she barked out, "Hey, how do you get this **** crap off!!!!" We missed the sale, but I sure was impressed with that hand cream sample. George lasted another couple of weeks before he turned in his sample case and looked for other employment.

When I wasn't selling Fuller Brushes, I managed to show up for my two economics classes in the mornings with little mishap. Evidently, I didn't get as much out the classes as my classmate, Burden Lawrence. A few years ago, Burden sold Kirby Barge Company for many millions of dollars.

Earlier in May, I'd negotiated with my friend, Jimmy Conner, to resurface the bottom of his wooden outboard Lyman motor boat if he would let our DKE brother, Lou Martin, and me use the boat when we were finished. Jimmy had a dishwashing gig in some New England resort, and he was going to be gone all summer. Well, that deal didn't work out too well for any of us. It took Lou and me every evening all summer after pushing Fuller Brushes to finish the boat. The summer was over by the time we finally had a chance to take it for a ride in Lake Pontchartrain. We enjoyed that single ride before Conner returned to reclaim the boat, but it sure wasn't worth our effort and work. Jimmy's luck wasn't any better. His job entailed washing dishes the whole time he was gone, and he didn't get to see anything of the New England countryside while he was there.

But the summer certainly wasn't a total loss. Once Lou and I had had our fill of sanding, staining, grouting, filling, more sanding, and painting that damned boat, we'd knock off and go for a beer at Bruno's Bar on Maple Street. Leo Bruno had been a bootlegger in the '30s. He'd cashed in and bought himself what was to become the best college bar in the city of New Orleans. His bar was the recreational meeting place for all my friends from the time I was about seventeen on. Weekends and beer and pinball were synonymous at Bruno's. It was as close a home away from home (other than the DKE house) as there was in the latter days of high school, my first year in college, and once I returned from the Navy,

Old Leo stood in the door virtually all the time he was open until his health demanded that he slow down. When he couldn't be there, the place was manned by George, a black ex-boxer who headed the bar squad, broke up fights, and provided personal and/or marital counseling to any who needed or asked for it. Both Leo and George took a personal interest in their customers. They made the place available for weddings and receptions. Leo gave wedding gifts and baptismal presents to his customers, and I even saw him take money out of his pocket to lend to patrons who were down and out or to provide cab fare for those too drunk to drive home.

It is hardly surprising that it was on one of those hot July evenings of 1965, after futilely refurbishing Jimmy Conner's boat in Lou's garage, that we adjourned to Bruno's for a beer, and I met the lady who would become the mother of my four children and my bride for these last fifty-two years.

I'd sold my share of Fuller Brushes that day and spent a couple of hours toiling over Jimmy's boat with Lou. We knocked off and capped the day off with a beer at Bruno's. At six-foot-four, skinny as a flag pole, hot and dirty, I stood at the bar in my filthy t-shirt and Bermuda shorts, foot on the rail and talking trash with Lou and my old friend Johnny Bolles. I noticed this attractive blonde speaking with some guys I didn't know at the end of the bar. I remember looking her over and remarking to Johnny that she was good looking. He didn't know her, so I wandered over that way, and out of the blue, she said, "Don't you sell Fuller Brushes?" "As a matter of fact, I do," I replied.

Bonnie Marie Belzons Robichaux was the daughter of Dr. Richard E. Robichaux Sr. and Estelle Scheuermann Robichaux of Raceland, Louisiana. Her grandfather had been a successful Cajun retailer and State Senator from Lafourche Parish, forty miles west of New Orleans at the edge of the Acadiana region settled by the predominantly French population of south Louisiana. Senator Alcide Robichaux married Allie Moore, of Scots-Irish descent from north Louisiana. Of their four children, Bonnie's father and uncle both became country doctors. Her Uncle Philip was elected and served as Lafourche Parish Coroner for many years. Subsequently, Bonnie's brother Dickey and two of her cousins, Mike and Phil, all became physicians, as did four of our brothers-in-law, a nephew, and our son-in-law, Kevin Kirchner. Everywhere I might go, family members talked about hematomas, gall bladders and such.

Bonnie's mother was of German descent from New Roads, Louisiana, and Bonnie herself, one of six siblings, is an attractive blonde and blue eyed blend of western European Americana.

She had been engaged to some guy in Florida, but he wasn't around to protect his turf, and by November, we were married. Coincidentally, it was on the same day that my mother was married to Adolph Billet. Adolph was a wonderful guy with four grown daughters, all within a year or two of my age. He was amazingly tolerant of our intrusion into his big wedding day that had been planned for quite a while. Ours was not. He and Mom had a big wedding reception, and for those few who knew about our own marriage earlier that day, it served as ours as well. Our first son, Robert L., III, a/k/a "Shep," was born the following June.

Marriage & Law School

I began law school at Tulane the same year I was married. I was not a superlative law student, but I hung in there as student, husband, and father; I passed most of my courses, graduated in 1968, and passed the Bar Exam after a summer of cramming in all the knowledge that I had barely absorbed in the previous three years.

Our first year of marriage was spent in a tiny two room apartment in the back of a shotgun house on Soniat Street not far from Tulane. We had an old car that Bonnie used to drive to school to teach elementary children, and I got around on a Honda 50cc motorbike. I rode it all though my freshman year of law school and across the Huey P. Long bridge to Avondale Shipyard where I worked as a laborer the following summer. But one day I almost killed myself by carelessly running into the car in front of me on River Road, and that was the end of my motorcycle days. Anyway, once Shep was born, it wasn't the optimum vehicle for a family of three.

As noted, I wasn't much of a student. Despite some reverses, I always managed to bounce back academically. Socially, I was doing fine. Bonnie and I enjoyed all our friends and we partied hearty, given the need to take our baby son with us wherever we went. I don't recall when I acquired a taste for politics, but I was elected President of my junior and senior law school classes, and I brokered John Branham's election as President of the Law School Student Body.

That was the extent of my political activism in those years. Though I had registered as a Democrat in 1964, I cast my first vote for President of the United States for the Republican candidate, Senator Barry Goldwater, since "in my heart I knew he was right." I acquired a strong distaste for Lyndon Johnson and the apparent corruption of his administration, especially his micro-management of the Vietnam War. As a veteran, I'd felt that the war was a just one intended to contain Communism, but I thought Johnson was not letting our troops do the job they needed to do to win. I was pictured in the Tulane newspaper, the *Hullabaloo*, standing in the rain, decked out in a black raincoat and burning—not my draft card as was in vogue—but rather some antiwar literature. I changed my registration to Republican in 1967. Better late than never.

I had no earthly idea what I wanted to do when I graduated from law school. Since I'd been working as a title-chaser at Lawyer's Title Insurance Company for a very nice guy, retired IBM executive Jim Mills. I thought about going to work for him in the public relations end of his business. My grades had barely kept me above water in law school, so I had not given much thought to practicing law. But I spotted a notice on the employment bulletin board for a young associate lawyer at Beard, Blue, Schmitt, and Treen (BBS&T). I'd heard that Dave Treen had unsuccessfully run as a Republican for Congress a few times against the well ensconced incumbent Democrat, Hale Boggs. So I decided to give it a try and seek an appointment.

Young Lawyer

To this day, I don't know why he hired me, but he did. So as a twenty-five-year-old lawyer with a wife and son and another on the way, I signed up for $500.00 a month to do general civil litigation under David C. Treen, Tulane grad, member of the Law Review and Order of the Coif, Republican and conservative activist in a town that had been dominated by Democrats ever since Reconstruction ended.

In two years' time, I came to love Dave as a friend and mentor, but I also found that I despised the civil practice of law. I think I may have tried three small cases in all that time, each trial taking no more than four hours from beginning to end. I handled some divorce cases, enough to know I sure didn't want to do that for the rest of my life. And I mastered the hourly billing system to the point that I became absolutely convinced that there has never, ever been a more corrupt system….one that either defrauds the client through padded bills, or else leaves the honest lawyer bereft of just and adequate compensation for the time he spent on behalf of the client.

I liked the people I worked with at BBS&T, but I really can't recall anything I liked about what I was doing to earn my living. In fact, there were many times when I would simply close the door to my small office, put my head down on my desk, and go to sleep to avoid thinking about what I was doing. I really hated it—and I most certainly would have been fired, had Dave Treen not saved my life with an idea he had in late 1969.

Richard Nixon was elected President in November 1968. By that time, I had taken an interest in Republican politics in New Orleans. I'd joined the Young Republicans, and with Treen's help, I gained a seat on the Orleans Republican Executive Committee. That didn't mean much, but it kept me in the loop as I stuffed envelopes for aspiring candidates and it gave me parole power to get clients or friends arrested on misdemeanors released from prison. Treen ran again for Congress, and I met many of the people supporting him. Gradually, I became an insignificant fixture among the small Republican circles.

Dave knew that I was not flourishing as his legal assistant, and I think he was trying to come up with reasons to let me go without simply putting me on the street. Anyway, Nixon replaced the Democratic U.S. Attorney, Louie LaCour, with the flamboyant and crusading President of the Orleans Levee Commission, Gerald "Gerry" Gallinghouse. Dave offered to put in a good word for me to work at the U.S. Attorney's office if I was so inclined. I knew my days at BBS&T were numbered, and I desperately wanted to do something else anyway, so I jumped at the suggestion. Dave made the call and I went over for an interview in late 1969. They gave me five pounds of forms to complete, and we began the process. It took about four months for the FBI to clear me, and in April 1970, I was sworn in as an Assistant U.S. Attorney in the Criminal Division for the Eastern District of Louisiana.

Assistant U.S. Attorney

With the help of fellow Assistant U.S. Attorney Dan Markey, I tried my first criminal case against veteran defense attorney G. Wray Gill. It was a multiple car theft case in Judge Herbert Christenberry's courtroom, and it took two days to try. I won the case, and that was when I knew that I had found something that I would love to do for as long as they'd have me.

Dan, Pat Hand, and Richard Olsen were hold-overs from the LaCour office, and they broke the rest of us new guys in. Joe McMahon, C.J. Aucoin, Mike Ellis, and Pat McGinity joined me as part of the new guard. Some had experience at the local District Attorney's offices, but most did not. I was the only one with purely Republican credentials, so they all gave me a hard time until I gradually brought most of them over to my side. Julian Murray, who had been a successful prosecutor under DA Jim Garrison, became the Chief of the Criminal Division when Gene Palmisano left, and under Julian, we became a small but crack team of committed prosecutors.

It was a wonderful time in my life. I liked all the guys I worked with. We established a great record of aggressive but fair prosecutions under "Captain America," the name we gave our blustery and incorruptible boss, Gerry Gallinghouse. And we tried everything. We didn't make political decisions, and we didn't back down. We took on the best defense attorneys in the region, and while we didn't win them all, we were certainly a force for law and order in a time when the country and the State of Louisiana were crying for it. And we played hard as well.

Whether it was the volleyball games in Dan Markey's office —later to be mine when Dan left—or the drunken nights of victory celebrations (or commiserating the losses) in the French Quarter where our office was located, or raucous parties in the "Attic Bar" down the block or in C.J.'s apartment in the Pontalba Apartments near Jackson Square, we had great fun together.

One of my favorite memories is of Dan Markey and me standing at the otherwise empty Attic Bar at the corner of St. Louis and Chartres Streets on a cool spring Friday afternoon. The doors and windows were open, and the gentle breeze wafted through the bar. One of the most infamous and aging French Quarter characters, four-foot ten-inch tall Ruthie, the Duck Lady, wandered up to the bar and stood next to Dan. Dressed in her flowing, unwashed hippie robes, she ordered a shot of whiskey. Ruthie had been known in the Quarter for years…and everywhere she went, usually between bars, she was usually accompanied by a mother duck and her little ducklings close behind.

This day, Ruthie had a little black puppy on a leash. Dan, whose dry wit was infamous around the Federal Court complex, glanced at Ruthie, looked down at the puppy, and then back at Ruthie. "What's the matter, Ruthie, Dog eat your fuckin' duck?" "Shaddup!' she shot back, and gulped her drink and left dragging her puppy behind her.

Then there was Pat Hand, short of stature but tough as nails. At least he was tough in court. One night when we'd been seeing the sights in the Quarter, we decided to have a night cap in a bar across from our office. We hadn't realized that it was a fairly new hangout for lesbians.

Pat discovered the fact to his dismay when he accidentally pushed the motorcycle jockey beside him, and the woman, dressed in leather riding pants, a tight T shirt with Lucky Strikes folded in her sleeve, black leather vest and a black cruiser's hat complete with chain on her head, spun around, grabbed him by his collar, threw him up against the wall and punched him in the face.

In those days, the FBI loved to investigate car thefts and bank robberies, and I began with the car cases and worked up the chain. I convicted a Jefferson Parish Assistant DA for running a car theft ring, and I tried several other cases of that sort. One of the various car theft defendants was out on bail, and when he didn't show up for trial, the judge put an arrest warrant out for him. The U.S. Marshal found him and brought him to me. I was to take him to the judge before trial.

Judge Lansing Mitchell was a heavy, jovial sort of fellow who had been having back and neck problems brought on by his weight. He'd rigged up a system in his office that enabled him to put a brace on his neck hooked to a line that went up to the ceiling over his desk, through some pulleys on the ceiling, and down behind him to a series of weights that hung down while pulling his head up and relieving the strain on his neck.

When the Marshal retrieved and arrested the recalcitrant defendant, they brought him to me; he was obviously worried about what the judge might do to him. As we walked to the judge's office, I took advantage of his mood by telling him how mad the judge was. I told him that it was all out of my control, and that I just didn't know what was going to happen to him. I opened the door and pushed him through. As he entered the room, I saw his eyes grow wide as he focused on the man at the desk with his head suspended by weights. I whispered in his ear, "That's what they did to the last guy who didn't show up!"

Time passed, and I tried lots of eclectic cases of varying types. I tried and convicted a lawyer for tax evasion and, shortly afterwards, a man who'd kidnapped a young woman in Alabama and brought her to Louisiana where he tied her to a tree and assaulted her with a broom stick. Gerry Gallinghouse brought an indictment against some business executives for taking call girls across state lines in violation of the Mann Act. When he looked around for someone to handle the case, I got the short straw since my reputation was that I was willing to try anything. I went after it with all I had, but I think I lost it in the picking of the jury of eleven men and a barmaid. I proved the case, but those folks simply didn't want to convict the pillars of society, so after a lengthy trial, they returned a verdict of "not guilty."

In fact, that case was indicative of Gerry's approach to his job. He would challenge anyone, the more prestigious the better. Gerry himself was a big man, and when he was in the Grand Jury, he could be incredibly intimidating. No one was immune from his scrutiny, and his aggressive prosecutorial approach did much to inspire his staff and shake fear in the hearts of the business and political community in the Greater New Orleans Area in the 1970s. Most of us were proud to have served on his team, and while I don't know if he ever heard our nickname for him, we only knew him as "Captain America" when he wasn't around.

Mike Ellis and Gerry Gallinghouse tried a case against Louisiana Attorney General, Jack "P.F." Gremillion, about whom someone once said, "If you wanted to hide anything from him, simply put it in a law book!" I assisted on the periphery of that case, and I remember walking to the Court House in the old Wildlife and Fisheries Building on St. Louis and Royal streets with FBI Agent Chris Dauwalder, who was one of the few FBI agents assigned to work the strippers on Bourbon St.

If you wanted information on local hoods, the best place to get it was from the strippers and hookers. Dauwalder excelled at the job.

It was a beautiful day in the French Quarter, and as we approached the magnificent old court house, Chris casually turned to me and said, "Bob, you know the people of Louisiana will not tolerate corruption!!I thought that was a strange thing to say in view of where we were headed. And he quickly said, "They demand it!!!"

One person on Gerry's staff who didn't share his "full speed ahead" attitude toward prosecution of evil doers was my friend, C.J. Aucoin. C.J. graduated from M.I.T., and after law school at Loyola, he joined the FBI for a few years. He came home and was hired by Gallinghouse about the same time that I was. We became good friends. C.J. was small and slight, very bright, and quite cynical about just about everything. He and his wife, Mary Ann, had been married for several years; they had no children and lived comfortably in a classic apartment in the two-hundred-year-old Pontalba Apartment House on Jackson Square. They had a sailboat at the New Orleans Marina on Lake Pontchartrain, and they were living large. C.J. rarely lost a case, and he methodically went about his business without rancor and without making waves. But he really didn't like the loud and blustery Gerry Gallinghouse, and he stayed as far from him as he could. Gerry interpreted C.J.'s withdrawal as a disinterest in his job. It wasn't true, but the two lived in entirely separate worlds.

Mary Ann suddenly became pregnant long after they had concluded that they would not have children. They gave up the Pontalba apartment and the sailboat, moved across the Mississippi River to the suburbs, and began a life completely apart from anything they had experienced before. One day, C.J. announced his desire to quit the job, leave the practice of law, and open up a camera store on the West Bank of the river. Everyone was shocked, even Gerry Gallinghouse. A couple of days before C.J. left, Gallinghouse wandered into C.J.'s office and tried his hand at psycho-analysis.

"C.J.," he said. (Actually, Gerry Gallinghouse was the only person I ever met who could take two syllables and turn them into four.) "Ci-ee Jay-iee," he said, "Ci-ee Jay-iee, you know what your problem is?? Ci-ee Jay-iee, your problem is that you don't give a shit!" I almost dropped to my knees when C.J. fired back, "Mr. G, I don't give a shit!" And those were the last words they ever said to one another.

In time, I became the deputy chief of the criminal division behind Joe McMahon and was placed in charge of white collar crimes. They were often difficult trials, but they were the most interesting ones in the building. After I had convicted the lawyer for tax evasion, I charged a prominent grocer for dealing in illegal food stamps worth thousands of dollars. That one never got to trial for the day the indictment came down, the poor soul went home and shot himself. I felt awful about it, but the case was a sound one, so I never could second guess myself.

On a lighter note, I brought charges against a beach bum named Radcliffe Wills for stealing sailboats in New Orleans and sailing them around the horn of Florida to Miami, where he jiggered the records and sold them to unsuspecting buyers. Radcliffe was a good looking and good natured guy with wavy blond hair and an outgoing personality. His attorney moved for a change of venue from New Orleans to Miami, and the judge granted his motion. We shipped the whole file down to the U.S. Attorney's office in Miami, but for whatever reason, they didn't want to try the case. So we were faced with the decision to drop the case or send me down to Miami to prosecute the case. It wasn't a difficult decision for me, and Gerry Gallinghouse never dropped a case without good reason.

So, once the preliminary motions were disposed of, I packed my bags and traveled to Miami for a week or so. Chuck Farrar, a law school chum in the local U.S. Attorney's office, invited me to stay at his place for the trial, so finding a room was no problem.

The trial was fun from the beginning. Many of the witnesses were local, and those that weren't came from New Orleans or the FBI Lab in Washington, D.C. The judge was experimenting with a six person jury, and Mr. Wills did not object to it, so that's what we used. The court room was smaller than most, and everyone in court seemed relaxed and laid back. But no one was more laid back than the defendant. Even though he was in custody of the U.S. Marshall, every morning he would greet the judge, the jury, the clerks, and me with a big smile and a "How're ya doin?!" Then his wife and four girlfriends would rush up and ask if he needed coffee or a sweet roll, and they would hover around him until the trial started. As the trial proceeded, I began calling witnesses. When there was a break, the ladies would return and bring Radcliffe refreshments to keep him going. Once refreshed, they would all . . . wife, girlfriends, and Radcliffe, himself, turn to me and tell me what a good job I was doing. And that was the mood for the whole week that it took for me to try the case.

When it was all over, the jury came back in less than an hour with a verdict of "guilty" on all counts. Radcliffe smiled, thanked the jury, congratulated me, and waited patiently in his orange prison jump suit as the judge sentenced him to six months in the slammer. He waived to his groupies, and the Marshal took him away. The judge thanked the jury, congratulated me, and adjourned the trial. I called Chuck Farrar to thank him for his hospitality and drove to the airport for the next plane back to New Orleans.

Everyone in that courtroom liked Radcliffe Wills, including both the judge and me! I didn't go back to Miami, but a few weeks later, I heard that Radcliffe's attorney had filed a motion to reduce the sentence. The judge refused the motion, but he did give Radcliffe credit for time served and released him on probation for the duration of his sentence. I liked the guy so much that I didn't mind. I don't know if Radcliffe stayed out of trouble after that. Many years later, Chuck Farrar became the U.S. Attorney for the Miami District of Florida.

In those three years, I tried well over one hundred jury trials. My favorite centered on a fraud case against two men charged with "advanced fee swindles." For some time, the Bureau (FBI) and I followed the activity of Robert Lee Frick and Quemet "Kim" Peterson who were taking advantage of legitimate businessmen having difficulty getting loans from banks and other lending institutions in an era of very tight money. These guys would print up phony documents offering commitments to a target, assuring him that for an advanced fee, they would shop the application and give him a guarantee to be used at a bank to make a sought-after loan. Once the victim had paid a fee of several thousands of dollars and then tried unsuccessfully to shop his commitment to receive his loan, Frick and Peterson were long gone—with his advance fee.

When I felt that I had a good enough case, I had the FBI pick them up. In the course of the arrest, a briefcase in their immediate possession was seized by the case agents. As I prepared for trial, I reviewed the documents in the briefcase and was delighted to find one special item.

The trial lasted five or six days. In a routine offer of evidence, I added a mountain of documents from the briefcase that supported the testimony of various witnesses to the effect that these guys had intentionally defrauded victims out of the fees they had paid. I easily proved that in several instances, when it was time to actually effect the loans, the defendants were nowhere around and the guarantees were essentially worthless.

But the hardest thing in a fraud case is to prove that there was intent in the minds of the defendants to defraud a victim in what otherwise would be a normal business deal. Any business deal can go bad, so without intent to defraud, there can be no culpability.

Frick's and Peterson's intent became crystal clear in this case. The hundreds of documents and miscellaneous papers I'd introduced from Frick's briefcase included a single handwritten draft. At first glance, it looked like a draft of a typical business form with no consequence whatsoever, and I had no difficulty getting it into evidence. But in closing arguments, I unveiled a three-foot by four-foot blown-up copy of it to make sure the jury could note what I'd seen.

The hand-penned drafted legal document noted that Robert Lee Frick and Quemet Peterson were Chairman and Chief Executive Officer of "Mortgage Corporation of America" with all sorts of "Wherefores" and "Whereases" and lots of legalese . . . all to be signed by the two of them and the client at the bottom of the lengthy document. On the left bottom were spaces for both men to sign in their official capacities, and on the right, a space for the prospective client/borrower to sign . . . except that on this particular handwritten form was a word substituted for "Borrower." I'd circled it with a bright red marker. The word was "Sucker!"

The jury wasn't out very long, and I convicted them both.

Months later, I tried an interstate prostitution case against Kent "Frenchy" Brouillette, whose career as a pimp was memorialized in Mathew Randazzo's hilarious book, *Mr. New Orleans*. Traditionally, a madam would use a "trick book" to log in the names of her clients together with the amounts paid and little notations in the margin about fetishes, etc. The FBI had seized their books, and as was the custom of all prosecutors in such cases, I perused them to see if any friends or acquaintances were logged in. As I scanned the pages of their many customers or "Johns," I delightedly stumbled across the name of Robert Lee Frick! In the margin, a comment clearly noted, "Don't take checks!!!"

There were so many funny and unusual incidents that I can't recount them all here. But one of the more memorable happened when Julian Murray tried the pastor of the Mid City Baptist Church for running off with the church treasury. An elderly man who had devoted his life to the church was called as a witness to the grand jury. Julian had the old man sworn in and began asking him some preliminary questions. Suddenly, the elderly gentleman exclaimed, "If it's the last thing I do, I'll get that son of a bitch!" With that, the poor man suffered a major coronary and keeled over and died.

Of course, the grand jury was horrified. It was late on a Friday afternoon, and Julian immediately called the coroner to come and remove the body. Sam Moran, the old crusty coroner's investigator showed up, impatiently looked at his watch and then at the body. He confirmed the death and then rifled through the old man's pockets and placed a call on the telephone in the room.

"Hello," he said. "Hello, Mrs. Jones? Yes, Mrs. Jones, this is Sam Moran from the Coroner's office. Yes, it's about your husband . . . . Yes, well, I AM from the Coroner's Office!!!" And that's how Mrs. Jones found out that her husband had passed away.

We really were a band of brothers in the U.S. Attorney's Office. I stayed only three years, and in that time, lawyers came and left. But the core of our group were so committed and effective that as I look back on it now some forty-plus years later, it really was one of the most fun and interesting times of my life. Trying cases; mostly winning, sometimes losing; celebrating wins and commiserating losses in the French Quarter; playing volleyball or throwing craps in the office during working hours; hearing that one of our own was caught "in flagrante delicto" with one of the secretaries in the library; speaking with my boss in his office one Saturday morning when we were startled by a live TV broadcast of a shootout between the police and a druggie at the Howard Johnson's Hotel; those were memorable and exciting times.

But they weren't all happy. In February, 1972, I received a call from Florida ("Flor-ee-da"), the Spanish caretaker for my alcoholic father who fifteen years earlier had moved to Benidorm, Spain, to escape paying alimony to my mother. He'd literally drunk himself to death and died of cirrhosis. He was fifty-one years old.

I turned my cases over to my colleagues for a couple of weeks and flew to Spain to gather my father's remains, close down his property, and bring him back to the U.S. for burial with his family in New York. Bonnie was pregnant with our third son, and she met me in New York for the funeral.

Later that year, I joined her and her family to bid farewell to her youngest brother, Rene, who at the age of eighteen was killed in a car wreck while on his way with friends back to LSU. Bonnie's family never fully recovered from Rene's death, especially since four years earlier, they had lost her younger sister, Estelle, in a previous auto accident. Two of six children were lost in separate accidents, and so too was the marriage of Bonnie's wonderful parents. They divorced a year or so later.

Civil Law (again)

My days at the U.S. Attorney's Office came to an end when something in me decided that if I didn't leave, I'd be prosecuting for the rest of my life . . . and some of my friends did just that. I took a pay cut to return to civil law, this time working for two tough but lovable Dutch lawyers, Arthur and Richard Reuter. They were terrific attorneys, and the people at the firm were all wonderful, especially my new friend, "RT," the son of Arthur Reuter.

But in a single year, I again realized how much I truly hated practicing civil law and anything to do with it. I hated it for a multiple reasons, but primarily, I became once again convinced that the "billable hours" system employed by attorneys was a fraud. Either it defrauded the client, in that many lawyers required to keep track of every productive minute inevitably pad their time logs if only for simplification. On the other hand if they were meticulous, it became a fraud on the lawyer. As a young lawyer, I felt I could never adequately bill for the time I put in.

The final blow hit me when I was asked by some local civil lawyers to tell them how much I would charge to represent their client, Falstaff Brewing Company, which had just been indicted for some odd trade practice in Federal court. It seemed to me that this was a good opportunity to try an important case, so with little thought ahead of time, I quoted them my going rate at the time, $35.00 an hour.

They immediately hired me and turned over the files. I looked them over and concluded that the case had no merit, so I filed a motion to dismiss the indictment. A hearing was scheduled, I argued the motion, and I won. When I computed the value of my time in the case, it came to a grand total of $178.00. I billed them and suggested that since I had just freed a major U.S. Corporation from a federal indictment, my work was worthy of a hefty bonus. But the company CEO didn't feel compelled to pay me beyond the terms of my contract, so I received a check for $178.00—without even a "thank you" note.

And so it was that I began to look around for an alternative career. Fortunately, another door soon opened.

As noted above, James "Big Jim" Garrison won the job of Orleans

Parish District Attorney, and shortly after taking office, he made a splash as a crusading "reformer" by closing down the whorehouses in New Orleans. But he wasn't the person he held himself out to be. He didn't shut down all the vice in the city. Gambling persisted during his tenure and as time passed, he gradually showed his colors as one of the more reprehensible people ever to occupy public office.

His infamy in American memory arose in 1967 from his indictment and trial of Clay Shaw, a tall, distinguished, openly gay New Orleans businessman, for the assassination of President Kennedy. When Garrison first began the investigation and charged Shaw, the whole world and especially the people of New Orleans thought he walked on water for doing what no "Warren Commission" or subsequent investigator of Kennedy's death had been able to accomplish. In short, the world thought that District Attorney Jim Garrison had solved the most notorious crime of the century—the assassination of President Jack Kennedy.

As time passed, the world, along with every honest, intelligent person in New Orleans, came to understand that Jim Garrison was a huge fraud and that his case was one of total and complete fabrication. As the case progressed, he sued the Federal government for access to its files and for a long time the government resisted, giving currency to his claims of a cover up. But before the trial was over, the government called his bluff and provided access to the records. Mysteriously, he concluded the trial shortly afterwards without any supportive evidence of his claims. The jury quickly returned a verdict of "Not Guilty," but Clay Shaw's reputation was destroyed in the process. His fortune was depleted, and he died a few years later a broken man.

Garrison remained in office for several more years, but in 1973, Gerry Gallinghouse, assisted by the FBI, filed an indictment against him for corruption and bribery at the hands of the pinball machine industry. I didn't have any direct role in the trial itself, but I did review the transcripts of wire taps that were obtained by the FBI in the months preceding the case. The transcripts were classified, so I can't comment on specifics. But I can truthfully state my own opinion, and that is that Jim Garrison was a hideously corrupt and mentally unstable man.

But he wasn't stupid, and when the trial began, he dismissed his own counsel and represented himself. An old legal saw avers that "An attorney who represents himself has a fool for a client." That was certainly not the case with Garrison. He successfully appealed to the jury on the grounds that the government sought revenge against him because of his attempts to uncover the conspiracy of the "Military Industrial Complex" to kill President Kennedy. He won an acquittal and it was a hard loss for Gerry Gallinghouse, since he had put his heart and soul into the prosecution of the case.

Garrison was triumphant and his theory of Kennedy's death was later enshrined in his book, *On The Trail of The Assassins* (1988). Anyone who had followed the facts knew that the whole story was fabrication, but he made a lot of money on the book, especially when it was picked up and made the foundation for Oliver Stone's hallucinogenic movie, *JFK* (1991). Garrison, himself, played the role of the judge in the movie.

Years after the movie came out, Garrison was redeemed in the public eye and was elected in 1978 to the Louisiana Court of Appeal where he served until just before his death in 1992. The movie *JFK* lingers on and serves as a reminder that Lincoln wasn't completely right. You CAN fool most of the people most of the time! But Jim Garrison couldn't fool his Maker, and I have some confidence when I think about him and where he is today. I always look down, not up.

Assistant District Attorney

I knew Harry Connick Sr. from my work in the U.S. Attorney's office when he represented a black pimp who had been running a bunch of black hookers and was charged for violations of the Mann Act. I had a solid case on the guy, but Harry stood valiantly in his defense. His legal argument was unique. He said the Federal Government couldn't have had jurisdiction over the case, notwithstanding the interstate aspects of the defendant's transportation of the girls across state lines for the purposes of engaging in prostitution. Harry maintained that the statute couldn't apply because it was otherwise known as the "White Slavery Act" and quite obviously, neither his client nor the girls were white. I didn't put a lot of faith in that argument, and the judge didn't either. The man was easily convicted.

But Harry is a very nice guy, and in a gutsy move in late 1973, he challenged the infamous Garrison for the post of District Attorney. Harry was a Democrat as was almost everyone else in the city other than me, so party politics had nothing to do with the race. In fact by this time, the only elected Republicans in the state were my friends, Charlie Lancaster in the Louisiana House of Representatives and recently elected Congressman Dave Treen, my former employer. After three unsuccessful runs for Congress and another for governor, Dave was elected in 1972 to the U.S. Congress in the Third Congressional District, west of New Orleans. It was his fifth bid for elective office. He became the first Republican Congressman (and in 1980, the first Republican Governor) in Louisiana since Reconstruction.

Though Harry was a quintessential old-line "yellow dog" Democrat, I backed him, and Bonnie and I even threw a fundraiser for him in the back yard of my house. I was convinced that Jim Garrison was almost evil-incarnate, and Harry was the only hope to remove him from office. Harry ran a great campaign, and when the dust settled, he won in a fairly close election. He was sworn in on my thirty-first birthday, April 30, 1974, and began what became a thirty year tenure in office.

Because of our past association when I had defeated Connick in trial and because of my support for his candidacy, Harry offered me the chance to become one of his top prosecutors. I was delighted to escape my civil law practice once again, so I jumped at the chance. The salary was meager so Harry let me retain a small private practice on the side. If I could have supported my family, I think I'd have taken the job for free since this was my chance to get back in the court room to put crooks in jail. I had come to realize that criminal prosecution was my real joy.

This time, the forum was at "Tulane & Broad," the street corner where the New Orleans Criminal Courts Building, also known as "the snake-pit," stands. Every low life scum-bag in the world has appeared before a judge in that building—and then there were the defendants!

Harry initially assigned me to head what was already known to be "The Armed Robbery Division," and for that, I was given my own office in a room with a sink and white asbestos wall board that resembled peg board found in many old radio stations. When I moved in, I noticed that I also had a narrow closet inside which was about three-and-a-half feet of stacked folders, pictures, and accumulated evidentiary material. I examined some of the stuff and suddenly realized that it was all of the trial material from the Clay Shaw trial. I made a mental note to come back on the weekend and go through it extensively. But when I returned that weekend, it was gone—every last speck. It wasn't re-discovered until many years later, when Harry learned that it had been taken by former DA investigator Gary Raymond. Harry launched a proceeding against Raymond to get it back, but I never did get to review the material.

Dan Markey, Joe McMahon, and Mike Ellis, all friends from the U.S. Attorney's office, were among the top members of Harry's initial prosecution team. I was especially delighted to be working with Dan Markey again. Ever since he helped me win the first criminal case I had ever seen, I felt a close relationship with him. An old-line Irish Democrat from the union-dominated sectors of New Orleans, our backgrounds were very different. But the swarthy and overweight Dan had a quick wit, a *joy de vivre*, and was always fun to be around, drunk or sober. From the volley ball games in his office at the U.S. Attorney's office, his brief stint in private practice, to his arrival at the DA's office, he easily attracted lifelong friends, many of whom rallied to him and his family sometime later.

Dan baptized my new office in the Criminal Courts Building by stepping up to the sink one mid-afternoon and pissing in it. No women were around, but the four or five guys in the office gave him hell, and Dan just laughed it off. Crude as he may have been, he was a really fine trial lawyer, and he had once convicted a room full of doctors and lawyers in an incredibly complex case of insurance fraud. While the effete men with multiple advanced degrees sneered at the implication that they would have anything to do with the dope addicts and hookers who testified about their collaboration to defraud insurance companies in phony automobile accidents, Dan won a verdict of guilty on all counts with a fictional quote from the late John James Audubon, "Birds of a feather flock together!"

Dan became notorious in the DA's office for practical jokes. He put tropical fish in the drinking water jug. On a blistering hot morning in July, he opened the over-heated car of an administrative colleague with whom he didn't get along and threw a live chicken inside, only to have it discovered at the end of the day. I heard the result was not pretty.

But Dan didn't take care of himself and a few years after he'd left the DA's office and set up his own private law practice, he suffered a major stroke and became fully incapacitated. He suffered greatly and died absolutely destitute a year later, leaving an impoverished wife, Betty, and two children. Dan's friends helped Betty to the extent possible but she had a very difficult time of it, and she passed away within five years after her husband. Both were in their forties when they died.

Harry's long-time friend, Bill Wessel, became his Chief of Staff at the DA's office, while Garrison hold-overs Ralph Whalen, Ralph Capitelli, Mike Gross, and Larry Centola were retained to round out the leadership team. Capitelli was my chief lieutenant in the Armed Robbery section, but after a month, Harry and Wessel reorganized the place and made Whalen and me the two "Chief Special Prosecutors." That meant different things for each of us. Whalen, a superb prosecutor and later an excellent defense attorney, stayed around for several years and set a record for the most capital case victories.

Unlike my friend Ralph Whalen, I was given the distinction of trying the "dogs"—cases that had been reversed on appeal or for whatever reason were deemed to be the really big "heater" cases, i.e.: politically sensitive or just plain tough. Those included a reversed conviction of a "cop killer" which I ended winning but with a reduced verdict, as well as various and sundry murder, rape, and kidnapping cases. I was especially excited to learn that I was to try the case against arch-racist and Klansman, Byron De La Beckwith.

De La Beckwith was well known for having been tried twice but turned loose after two hung juries in Mississippi failed to convict him for the 1963 murder of Medgar Evers, the civil rights leader and the first Mississippi field officer for the NAACP. The evidence was convincing that De La Beckwith had committed the murder, but circumstances in Mississippi in the mid-1960s were not conducive to such trials, and all-white juries were not likely persuaded of guilt. In 1973, De La Beckwith was tracked and caught by the Louisiana State Police and the NOPD with a trunkload of explosives in his car. Working through informants, they established that De La Beckwith was driving to New Orleans with the intent to blow up the home of A. I. Botnick, a prominent Jewish leader who had challenged the Ku Klux Klan over the years. De La Beckwith had enough explosives in his car to blow up an entire city block.

Once in jail in New Orleans, the Magistrate assigned him a court appointed attorney. My friend and former colleague from the U.S. Attorney's Office, Pat McGinity, who was by this time in private practice, was chosen by the Magistrate to represent De La Beckwith. The Klan certainly doesn't like black people or Jews, but they aren't too keen on Catholics either. So when Pat went to the prison and introduced himself to the thin, wiry, grizzled man in his sixties, De La Beckwith looked him up and down and said,

"McGinity . . . McGinity . . . Are you Catlick?"

"Yes, Sir, I am, and I'm here to represent you."

"Catlick, huh? . . . Well, I guess that's ok. I got a few friends who are Catlick!"

And so, my friend was appointed to represent this racist, and I was to be the prosecutor. I prepared the case for trial and was ready to go to the mat. But two days before we were to begin the trial, I caught the flu and was bedridden for days. The trial was postponed, and had I not once again changed jobs in late 1974, I would have prosecuted him. But as will be seen shortly that was not to be, so I reluctantly turned my carefully prepared trial brief over to Bill Wessel, who tried and convicted De La Beckwith in the summer of 1975.

The judge sentenced him to the maximum of four years in prison. He served his time in Angola State Prison and was released in 1980. But in 1994, Federal prosecutors in Mississippi brought renewed civil rights charges against him for the death of Medgar Evers. Because the state charges were never pressed after the hung juries, and since federal charges are exempted from a claim of "double jeopardy," De La Beckwith was exposed. This time, a Mississippi jury convicted him and closed an ugly chapter in Mississippi history. De La Beckwith died in prison in 2001.

I recovered from the flu and continued at the District Attorney's office in my assignment to odd and unusual cases as "Special Prosecutor." The most significant among them was a case against Clyde Cain and William Burman for killing of Donald Ruiz, an attorney I had known years earlier.

Ruiz had a reputation of being a stereotypical "ambulance chaser." Short and pudgy of stature, he was not a man to inspire the best qualities of humanity. He and his wife, Mona, lived on Memphis Street in Lakeview, a quiet and pleasant middle-class community close to Lake Pontchartrain in New Orleans. (Roughly thirty years later, the entire community was almost wiped out by Hurricane Katrina, but at that time, it was a lovely, modest neighborhood.)

Cain and Burman were a couple of thugs with criminal records who were working "odd jobs" for Ruiz as "investigators." Ruiz owned a country home in Lumberton, Mississippi, where James Wheatly worked for him as caretaker. On the evening of November 20th, 1973, Ruiz and his friend, William "Red" Moore, had dinner with Clyde Cain and Ruiz's secretary (and one of Cain's girlfriends) Evelyn Sanders.

After dinner, Ruiz and Moore drove to Lumberton in Evelyn's car intending to pick up an old Oldsmobile to trade it in for a new car for Ruiz's estranged wife, Mona. Mona was staying with her parents in Delisle, Mississippi, and Ruiz hoped that he could entice his wife back to the marriage. The plan was to trade cars in Lumberton, drive to Delisle, again swap cars, and bring Mona's Oldsmobile back to New Orleans to trade in on a newer car.

Wheatly testified that he waited for Ruiz and Moore in Lumberton and joined them when they arrived from New Orleans. Leaving their car at the farm, the three of them, Ruiz, Moore, and Wheatly took Ruiz's farm truck from Lumberton to Delisle, Mississippi, where Mona was staying. Wheatly said he remained outside while Ruiz and Moore entered the Delisle house to speak with Mona and that she was unaware that Wheatly was with them. He said that when the two men came back outside, Wheatly climbed into the back seat of the Oldsmobile and that Ruiz drove it from Delisle back to New Orleans. Red Moore followed in the truck.

They returned to New Orleans early in the morning of the twenty-first. Wheatly testified that around 4:30 a.m., Ruiz and Moore parked the two vehicles in front of the Memphis St. home while he remained stretched out in the back of the Olds. Within seconds after Ruiz and Moore entered Ruiz's residence, Wheatly testified he heard shots and some muffled screams, and he lurched up and looked out the car window. Moments later, he said he saw two men emerge from the rear of the residence. One he knew to be Clyde Cain and the other he later identified as William Burman. He said he stayed out of sight as they passed the Oldsmobile without noticing him. Another car driven by a third figure pulled up from down the block; it stopped while they both got in, then drove away. Wheatly said he waited a while, and when nothing happened, he jumped out of the car and quickly walked away from the neighborhood to the Greyhound bus station where he caught the first bus back to Lumberton.

Muriel Campbell, Ruiz's maid, arrived at the Memphis St. house about noon that day. She couldn't enter the front door with her key because the chain lock was latched inside, so she went around to the back door. Once in, she discovered the bullet-ridden bodies of Donald Ruiz and Red Moore on the kitchen floor.

And so began the saga of what was positively the most wild and fantastic trial I ever personally experienced. Unfortunately, I was forced to try it twice and the second time was not a charm.

I couldn't have had a better judge. Frank Shea was known as the toughest, most hard driving, and most prosecutorial judge at Tulane and Broad. Had I completed the first trial, I'm certain that the defendants would have been convicted. But it was not to be.

I was assisted by Ernie Chen, a Chinese American lawyer who

would later become a very successful trial lawyer in Los Angeles. And years later, Ernie's brother, Ed, interviewed me several times in his role as reporter for the *Washington Post.*

Cain was represented by John "Buster" Unsworth, a contemporary of mine going back many years, while Burman had hired Thomas Johnson, son-in-law to a very famous trial attorney in New Orleans, Freddy Gesivius. When I'd first met him, Tom Johnson was a red-headed, young, bright, and energetic lawyer. But by the time of the first trial, he'd taken to drinking ice tea glasses full of bourbon more than once a day. When we were well into the case, one of the first indications that this was a trial from the *Twilight Zone* occurred when, in the middle of routine testimony of a prosecution witness, Johnson rose from his chair and yelled, turned bright green, and keeled over on the floor with what appeared to be a liver attack. The trial adjourned for a while until Tom recovered, and we began again. Tom completed that trial, but he died of cirrhosis a couple of years later. He was in his early thirties.

Much of the time spent in the trial was pretty straight forward stuff in a criminal trial. Muriel Campbell told about entering the house and discovering Ruiz and Moore. The police and coroner's office testified to the location and condition of the bodies. Collateral testimony revealed that Mona Ruiz had befriended Clyde Cain, and that she and Cain had begun liquidating her husband's effects soon after he died. Mona's mother testified that her daughter had taken up with Cain in an intimate relationship. Other witnesses testified that Cain and Mona were seen together and gave the appearance of intimacy both before and after Ruiz's death. The suggestion of conspiracy between Mona and Cain to murder Ruiz and live together off his estate became a significant backdrop to the case. But there was no hard evidence to confirm the theory of conspiracy.

We established that Cain, Moore, Saunders, and Ruiz had dinner the evening before the murders. We showed that Ruiz and Mona had been estranged, and she had been living with her parents in Delisle. But Ruiz was attempting to win his wife back by trading in the Oldsmobile for a new car for Mona.

What actually happened thereafter could only have come from eye witness testimony, and that's why Jim Wheatly was so critical to the case. By the time I'd gotten through his testimony, I felt fairly confident that we had a winner. Wheatly told his story well and there was little that Unsworth and Johnson could do to tear apart his recollection. Anyway, they were unable to do it with any significant impact. We bolstered Wheatly's story with incidentals. The maid in Lumberton, Mississippi, testified that Wheatly had been in Lumberton the previous night, that he'd left with Don Ruiz, and that he wasn't there until much later the next day. But the crux of the case was Wheatly's story and identification and description of Cain and Burman at the scene.

Had I stopped there, we might have had a different outcome. But to enhance the implication of conspiracy and bolster the story of the relationship between Cain and Ruiz's wife, Mona, I called to the stand John Ruiz, an attorney and Donald's youngest brother. Donald's father had offered a reward for the apprehension of his son's killers, and it was well known that his father and his two brothers would have done anything to wreck retribution on the people responsible. That they were all personally convinced of the guilt of Cain and Burman was undeniable. I probably would have done well to leave John off the stand.

But knowing he was a lawyer, I thought it was a safe gambit so I had him sworn in. He testified about seeing Mona and Cain in Ruiz's office in intimate circumstances several times before Ruiz's death. Later, after Ruiz's murder, he said he went to Donald's office and observed Burman wearing some of Donald's clothes and jewelry while he loaded office effects onto a flat-bed trailer. He said he called the police, but Burman offered up his driver's license and told the police that Mona had given him several things, so they turned him loose. Later that day, John said that Cain called him on the telephone and threatened him. But the *coups de grace* occurred when Tom Johnson took John Ruiz under cross examination:

> Johnson: "Are you familiar with the $20,000.00 reward that your father put or caused to be advertised in the newspaper for anyone who could lead to the identity and conviction of anyone connected with the death of your brother?"
>
> Ruiz: "I think my father knew that both . . . ."
> Johnson: "I am asking you if you are familiar with that particular . . . ."

> Ruiz: "I am responding to your question, and I think my father knew that Clyde and Bill Burman were convicted felons trying to get . . . ."
>
> Johnson: "Your Honor, I have to move for a mistrial."

John Ruiz, an attorney himself, knew full well that reference to prior convictions without judicial clearance was not permitted in any criminal trial. The trial was over! No verdict; no resolution; no conviction; no acquittal. The mistrial was granted and the judge ruled that we should try the whole case over again the following week.

We did, and it all went according to plan, except for one small addition that had been overlooked by my police detectives and for that matter, almost everyone else—me included. At the conclusion of Jim Wheatly's testimony, Buster Unsworth earned his money as a defense attorney. He had somehow found out that at one point in his life, Jim Wheatly had been committed for mental disorders, specifically for schizophrenia! Unsworth had the medical record, and by the time he was through his cross-examination, even I could not be sure that Wheatly had not made up the whole story. The jury acquitted both Cain and Burman in short order.

I don't know if John Ruiz intentionally blew the first trial or if he was just so dumb that he didn't know any better. But almost a year after the September 1974 trials, Bill Burman drove his plumbing supply truck up Veteran's Highway in Jefferson Parish just outside New Orleans. His window was open, but he didn't notice the car that pulled even with his truck. An assailant leaned out the passenger window of the approaching vehicle and fired several rounds from a heavy caliber pistol through the truck window. Struck in the head, Burman lurched forward, pulled his wheel to the left, and plunged into the adjoining canal.

Nine years later, two men were arrested for the Burman killing, but to the best of my knowledge, a motive for the slaying was never identified.

Cain remains alive. He lived with Mona in a communal relationship with Evelyn Saunders and other women and various children until at age fifty, in 1991, he was arrested in Texas on charges of child abuse and possession of illegal weapons. Thanks to the dedicated investigative work of Louisiana State Police Sergeant and, later on, U.S. Marshall Genny May, he was convicted on a separate murder charge for which he received a maximum non-capital sentence of life imprisonment. At minimum, he had to spend the following fifteen years behind bars. He allegedly ruled the roost in confinement and was eligible for parole in early 2009, but as of the date of this writing, he still has not been released. I won't mind if he is never turned loose.

I was with Harry Connick less than a full year. After the Cain Case, I had no idea what might be in store for me, but one of my "Special Assignments" led me to conclude that I was not going to stay at Tulane and Broad for the rest of my legal career. Harry asked me to review a police "intelligence" finding Joseph Marcello should be denied a liquor license for his proposed Broussard's Restaurant in the French Quarter.

Joe's brother was the reputed Mafia Don who lived and owned a good bit of property in Jefferson Parish, just outside New Orleans. Carlos "Little Man" Marcello was the center-piece of one of the several conspiracy theories regarding the killing of President Kennedy. Unlike Jim Garrison's hair-brained theory, this one bore credibility years later when Congressman Lou Stokes (D-OH), chairman of the Congressional follow-on to the Warren Commission, officially concluded that it was quite possible that Kennedy could have been killed in retribution for his brother Bobby Kennedy's actions against the Mafia.

The story held that Joe Kennedy, Jack's father, used the Mob and its influence with the unions to steal votes in both West Virginia and Chicago in the 1960 election against Nixon. These votes made a difference in the close election, and the Mob expected gentle treatment from the Kennedy administration. But Bobby Kennedy aggressively prosecuted labor bosses and the Mob with tooth and tong. Sam Giancana, the Chicago Mafia boss, who had a girlfriend named Judith Exner, wasn't pleased with Kennedy for a couple of reasons. He wanted Bobby off the Mob's case. Furthermore, coincidentally or not, one of the many ladies that Jack Kennedy entertained in the White House was none other than the very same Judith Exner.

Everyone has a theory about the Kennedy assassination, and many contest the findings of the Warren Commission. Congressman Stokes concluded that there was enough evidence to suggest (but not prove) the possibility that Giancana was sufficiently angry with the Kennedys that he ordered or requested help from Marcello to arrange the hit on Kennedy. An additional theory holds that when Kennedy pulled his support from President Diem of Vietnam, thereby encouraging Diem's assassination only a few weeks before his own, he disrupted the heroin trade from Vietnam to Marseilles, France, and that that was another reason the Mob wanted Kennedy dead. Marcello was implicated because of his alleged reach into Dallas and possible association with both Lee Harvey Oswald and Jack Ruby. But while Kennedy was killed in Dallas weeks after the assassination of President Diem, nothing was ever proven to implicate Marcello.

True or not, the fact remained that Marcello was a very strong power in the greater New Orleans underworld, and while his listed occupation was "olive oil salesman," the FBI felt he was such a vital component of the Mob that they once tried but failed to deport him. Later, they allegedly coerced him into striking an FBI agent and sent him to prison for six months.

I use the word "coerced" because of a story I heard when I was at the U.S. Attorney's office. I have no way of knowing the truth of the story, but since it centered on a far different FBI than exists today, I suspect there may be some truth in it.

The story began in the town of Apalachin, N.Y. in 1957, where there had been a meeting of Mafia Dons from all around the country. The Bureau got wind of it and raided the meeting. Many if not all the Dons were arrested and photographed, among them, Carlos Marcello.

Chairman Lou Stokes' House Committee on Investigations relates:

> 323 In late 1966, Marcello's status in organized crime was underscored when he was arrested in New York along with Carlo Gambino, then the Maria's reported "boss of all bosses" at a summit meeting of La Cosa Nostra leaders. (43) On September 22, 1966, New York police arrested those two Santos Trafficante, Joe Colombo, Thomas Eboli, Mike Miranda and several others at the La Stella restaurant on Long Island; this mob gathering was quickly dubbed by the newspapers 'the Little Apalachin' conference. (44) While

authorities came to believe that the La Stella 'luncheon"' was actually a pro forma gathering following a more serious meeting (probably of the night before), the assemblage has never been fully explained. (45) In his testimony before the committee, Marcello stated there had been no substance to the gathering: 'We just walked in. When we walked in we got arrested. We didn't have time to eat or talk.'(46) None of those arrested were convicted of a crime. The seating arrangement was as follows:

Seating Arrangement at La Stella

324 Eight days after, the La Stella arrests, upon his return to New Orleans International Airport, Marcello committed the only Federal offense for which he has been tried and convicted in recent times. On September 30, 1966, as he made his way through the crowd of newsmen and spectators who had gathered to watch his return, Marcello had a verbal exchange with a man in the crowd who he believed was impeding his way. (47) Shouting "I'm the boss here!", Marcello took a wild swing with his fist at the man. (48) The man turned out to be FBI Special Agent Patrick Collins.(49) Arrested by FBI agents on the following day and charged with assault, Marcello was eventually tried in Laredo, Tex. The trial resulted in a hung jury (the New Orleans Crime Commission subsequently conclude that "There were substantial reasons to suspect jury tampering had occurred."). (50)

325 Under the vigorous direction of the New Orleans strike force, Marcello was retried and subsequently convicted in Houston, Texas, on August 9, 1968. (51) Originally sentenced to two years in Federal prison, Marcello served less than six months, he was released on March 12, 1971. As the New Orleans Crime Commission noted at the time the large number of prestigious individuals who sought to intercede on his behalf, urging clemency, further underscored the depth of his influence in Louisiana. (52)

326 During the late 1960s and early 1970s, Marcello

> and his organized crime activities were the subject of renewed public attention. He was referred to ,by the chief of police in Youngstown, Ohio, as "the archetype of the devious pattern of the Mafiosi." (53) On September 1967, *Life* magazine also identified Marcello as one of the "handful" of men who controlled organized crime throughout the Nation.(54) In a special investigative report, the magazine reported that Marcello was personally directing a national La Cosa Nostra scheme to secure the release of Teamster leader James R. Hoffa from Federal prison through attempts to bribe the former chief prosecution witness against him to recant his testimony.(55) Life said that various key Mafia leaders in the east had given the alleged free-Hoffa assignment to Marcello, along with personal pledges of between $1 to $2 million to effect the plan. (56) (The effort was to fail.) In its following issue, *Life* went on to portray Marcello as "King Thug of Louisiana," reporting that he was one of the State's wealthiest men and "the lord of one of the richest and most corrupt criminal fiefdoms in the land." (57)
>
> (source: http://www.madcowprod.com/2013/11/22/barry-seal-the-dallas-get-away-plane-the-jfk-assassination/)

FBI Special Agent Patrick Collins was assigned to the Bourbon Street beat in New Orleans, meaning that like Agent Chris Dauwalder mentioned earlier, Collins's job was to hang around the street, talk to the strippers, pimps and whores, and develop intelligence on the bad guys. Collins, a big, good looking guy, was a notorious lady's man and was known to be enthusiastic about his work. He also allegedly spoke fluent Sicilian, the native language of many of the old line mobsters.

As I heard it, when Marcello was arrested, the entire press establishment across the country carried the story. New Orleans was no exception, so when Marcello flew home, he was greeted by a bevy of reporters at the gate in the airport. In the throng was Collins, disguised as a reporter.

When Marcello met the crowd, Collins wiggled in next to him and allegedly whispered in his ear in Sicilian, "For the last two years, I've been banging your brother's wife, and in the last few weeks, I've gotten yours as well!" Pow! Marcello lashed out and pasted Collins on the chin. The Bureau arrested him for striking an FBI agent, and Marcello wouldn't defend himself by telling the truth, so he was convicted.

It was ironic that the fat and out of shape Marcello was sent to the Federal Hospital in St. Louis, Missouri, on a sentence of six months confinement under the care of government physicians, and he trimmed down and reconditioned himself. The sentence likely added years to his life!

Both the Office of the U.S. Attorney and the Federal Probation Office were located in the same building on St. Louis Street. Years after his conviction when he was still on probation, I found myself in the same elevator with him. He looked in pretty good shape to me.

So it was with this background that I reviewed the police file assertions that while the Mafia had a strong presence in Jefferson Parish, it still had little or no significant presence in the City itself. As a result, the New Orleans Police Department Intelligence division, then comprised of some honest and effective policemen, recommended against granting a liquor license for Broussard's, a restaurant owned by Carlos Marcello's brother, Joe. They claimed that if Joe were given the license, the Mafia would gain a legally sanctioned foothold in the city of New Orleans, where until then it had held only a shadowy presence.

I reviewed the file and essentially agreed with the Department's rationale, so I recommended that Harry go along with it. Harry Connick was and is a friend even though back then he was a "Yellow Dog Democrat" ("I'd vote for a Yellow Dog before I'd vote for a Republican.") Many years later, he became a Republican after his successor took over the DA's Office and fired every last white person in the office.

But in late 1974, Harry invited me to present my case on Joe Marcello, Carlos's brother, in front of his entire staff on a Saturday morning. I was reasonably persuasive, but when I was through, Connick postulated, "Just because a man's name ends in a vowel doesn't mean he's a member of the Mafia!" So I realized that once again, it was time for me to seek other employment.

Louisiana Attorney General's Office

As luck would have it, Julian Murray, my once senior colleague and friend from the U.S. Attorney's Office, was leaving his post as Chief Prosecutor of the Organized Crime unit under Louisiana Attorney General William Guste Jr. He was kind to call and ask if I was interested in taking his place. When I acknowledged that I was, he persuaded the AG to hire me. Billy Guste was a wonderful guy and former State Senator who had won his post as a Democrat a couple of years earlier. He wasn't very interested in criminal law, and he left this particular office alone for the most part to run itself. A civil lawyer by preference and training, he and his wife, Butsy, were kind, gentle and deeply religious people who had been raised in the traditionally affluent and liberal Catholic environment of old New Orleans. His family owned and operated "Antoine's Restaurant," one of the most famous of old-line restaurants in the city. But Billy devoted himself to the law, and he ran an honorable and straightforward office.

Our office was formed along the lines of the Federal Organized Crime offices of the early Nixon administration. Police Investigators and administrative personnel worked alongside three or four staff attorneys and kept an eye on criminal targets of interest around the state. But as I was to learn after I signed up in January 1975, there was more investigative than trial work, and as one who felt more comfortable in the court room than behind the desk, it wasn't a perfect arrangement. But it was interesting—and it wasn't civil law.

Bill Faust was the Executive Director of the office. A lawyer who shared my distaste for civil practice, Bill preferred the role of administrator, and he kept the trains running on time. The police investigators were all interesting people; State Policemen Chet Traylor and David Hunter, former Orleans Parish Policeman and Jefferson Parish Deputy Walter Reed, and Gretna Policeman, E.J. Geiling, a short, stocky street cop who knew everyone in the greater New Orleans area. There was also Dave Gensler, an ordained Catholic priest from an old line Catholic family, who, once ordained, decided that he'd rather carry a gun and go after the bad guys than work a parish.

Chet Traylor loved the State Police, and he looks after the department to this day. But while on the job back then, he attended law school and later entered private practice, subsequently to run for and become elected to the Louisiana Supreme Court, from which he retired after a couple of terms. Dave Hunter stayed with the State Police and rose to become one of the top officials in that organization.

Walter Reed also attended law school at night while at the AG's Office, and in due time, he earned a law degree which he parlayed into his election as District Attorney for St. Tammany and Washington parishes. Walter introduced me to St. Tammany Parish when I began running for Congress. His family had been there for generations, and he had relatives everywhere. I had been there infrequently in my life, but when Walter took me around the parish, the way was paved for me to gain acceptance from people who wouldn't have considered voting for a non-resident Republican in earlier times. He was invaluable to me, and we became good friends.

I was not surprised when Walter was later elected DA, nor that he retained power for as long as he did. He became one of the longest serving District Attorneys in the state. Unfortunately, his tenure caught up with him and ended in 2014 when after some thirty years in office, Walter was indicted by the Feds for permitting his personal expenses to exceed his budget. He and his son were charged and convicted for various forms of embezzlement. His conviction may ultimately be overturned on appeal. But back in 1975, he was just one of our police investigators.

In those days, St. Tammany Parish was a solid old-line conservative Democratic bastion. But it was also the only parish that stayed entirely within the First Congressional District for my entire tenure, notwithstanding five reapportionment efforts in twenty years. By the time I left Congress in 1999, the parish was so Republican that it was exceedingly difficult for anyone to be elected under any banner other than Republican. In fact, toward the end of my tenure, I could usually count on upwards of 90 percent of the vote in St. Tammany. But it certainly didn't begin that way.

The two most memorable incidents during my time in the Attorney General's office included a trial of a local deputy sheriff for killing an unarmed black teenager in a honky-tonk bar in Rayville, in the northeastern part of the state. The second involved a trip with Attorney

General Guste to Lake Charles, to investigate some labor unrest that resulted in the death of a laborer.

The former was a tragic incident involving Ernest Kennedy, an old white man who should have been removed from his uniform years earlier. He was moonlighting as a guard in a predominantly black bar owned by a local white goon. The victim was a black youth who probably shouldn't have been in the bar in the first place. Once inside, the owner ordered the young fellow to run an errand for him. When he refused, the owner began cursing him and the kid gave him some back-talk. The owner then told Kennedy to take the kid in the back room and teach him a lesson. Kennedy reached out to grab him, but the boy dodged away and pushed the older man. Kennedy stumbled and fell on his back. The crowd in the bar apparently laughed at him. Obviously embarrassed, Kennedy got to his feet, drew his gun, and shot the boy dead.

The local District Attorney wanted nothing to do with the case, so the court called in the Louisiana Attorney General. That meant that I, as the Chief Prosecutor for the Organized Crime Unit, had another beauty on my hands. Having never been to Rayville, a small quiet town in what is truly the Deep South, I soon learned that the Ku Klux Klan had a strong presence in the area and that the bar owner was a prominent member. I can't say I received an overwhelmingly warm welcome in the town. But we quietly went about the process of procuring multiple eye witnesses to testify that Kennedy had shot the unarmed boy without substantial provocation. Unfortunately, once the trial began, I was stuck with an all-white jury while the Grand Dragon of the local KKK took a front row seat in the spectators' section throughout the proceeding. Under normal circumstances, it was an open and shut case. But these were not normal circumstances. The jury quickly returned a verdict, and despite my best efforts, Officer Kennedy was acquitted.

The other incident was of a different sort. In January of 1976 Attorney General Guste and I traveled to Lake Charles after a worker was killed in a labor dispute while he attempted to unionize a chemical company. We were able to assist in quelling the violence, and some of the offenders were arrested and the issues were resolved. But I vividly recall Billy Guste looking at a newspaper headline in the airport when we arrived. "Congressman Hebert to Retire!" it blared. Guste looked at me, well knowing I was a Republican and said," Why don't you run for that?"

"I don't even live in the District!" I responded, and I didn't give it another thought for another few months—until May of that same year.

Congressional Vacancy

F. Edward Hebert served in Congress for thirty six years and in time ascended to the lofty post of chairman of the Armed Services Committee. A crusty, elderly conservative Democrat, he was of an era when the Southern Democrats were a mighty force in the Democratic Party and in Congress. As the party moved to the left, the power of the few conservative "Old Bulls" were chairmen of key committees in the House of Representatives and served as a check on the more liberal members throughout the early 1960s. But with the passage of time and administrations, their power waned, and the Civil Rights Act of 1964 and accompanying "Great Society" legislation was passed by northern Democrats and sympathetic Republicans despite objections by Hebert and his southern allies.

The Vietnam War changed America and the fall-out took its toll on the "Old Bulls." Appropriations Chairman George Mahon, House Administration Committee Chairman Wayne Hays, Ways and Means Committee Chairman Wilbur Mills, and Armed Services Committee Chairman F. Edward Hebert either died, were chased from office by scandal, or were ultimately stripped of their power by the incoming liberal class of members elected in 1974 known as the "Watergate Babies." It was they that led the charge for impeachment of President Richard M. Nixon, and it was they that were the product of the changing mood of the country—anti-war, leftist in philosophy, angry, and activist. They wanted nothing more than to change the face of American politics, and in large part, they succeeded.

Eddie Hebert, as he was known to his friends, was a prime target. He represented a conservative district in southeast Louisiana, and had exerted very little effort to gain reelection every two years. A former newspaper reporter who had "made his bones" with award winning articles on the corruption of Louisiana politics following the assassination of Senator Huey P. Long, Hebert had worked for the *New Orleans Times-Picayune*, and he blew the whistle on alleged misappropriation of highway funds during the administration of Governor Richard W. Leche. Leche and his predecessor Governor "O. K." Allen were part of the Long political machine, and the charges of corruption during his administration were so pervasive that contemporaries dubbed the scandals "The Second Louisiana Purchase." Leche, who is alleged to have said shortly after his election, "When I took the oath of office I didn't take any vow of poverty," was convicted for corruption in office and sentenced to prison where he served five years of his ten year sentence. He was subsequently pardoned by President Truman.

In any event, Hebert was acclaimed for his stories and was elected to Congress in 1940. As he progressed in tenure and seniority, his ego expanded disproportionately. By the time I first arrived on the scene in 1976, his role as chairman of the House Armed Services Committee entitled him to a military aide assisting him in his every activity and his office in the new Rayburn Building was fronted by a water fountain in a foyer and was twice the size of any other Congressional office. In case anyone doubted his estimation of self-worth, they need only look to the title of his autobiography—*The Last of the Titans.*

But Hebert's view of himself was not shared by the "Watergate Babies." A strong and committed southern conservative, he was out of sync with the incoming class of new Democrats. He had frequent disagreements with them, most notably the freshman Congresswoman and member of the Armed Services Committee, Patricia Schroeder (D - CO). They clearly didn't get along, but as chairman of the committee, Hebert always had the last word.

One day they were engaged in a heated discussion about the future of American Armed Forces, and Hebert gaveled her down, thereby denying her the opportunity to speak further on the topic at hand.

Schroeder, an ardent feminist, blurted out, "Mr. Chairman, you only did that because I have a vagina!"

Hebert shot back, "If you used your vagina half as much as you use your mouth, you wouldn't be in so much trouble around here!"

He later moved to expunge the record.

But the chairman couldn't suppress the movement against him. He and other "Old Bulls" were challenged by the newer members of the Democratic Caucus and were stripped of their chairmanships. Once he'd lost his base of power, he announced his retirement from Congress. In January 1977, Chairman F. Edward Hebert vacated the office in the House of Representatives that he had held for thirty six years.

By that time, Bonnie and I had bought and renovated a lovely old Victorian house on Lowerline Street in New Orleans. We and our three boys, Shep, Richard and David, were enjoying life in what looked to be the neighborhood of our dreams. I made enough to pay the bills, but little else.I had become convinced that I didn't want to do what I was doing at the AG's Office for the rest of my life and I was still certain I didn't want to practice civil law, so I was in a quandary. I can remember sitting in my yard watching my kids play ball, and thinking that something different needed to happen in life. It soon did.

I was fortunate that while working for Harry Connick in the DA's Office and later for the Attorney General Billy Guste, both allowed me to have a small law practice on the side. It earned me a bit of outside income that wasn't much to brag about. And even though they were both Democrats, they allowed me to continue working behind the scenes on Republican politics. In retrospect, I especially appreciate this very real benefit of my employment. There were so few Republicans in New Orleans in those days; I think they each regarded me as a quixotic dreamer rather than a political threat of any kind. In fact, I supported both of them, so there was no reason to stifle me.

Dave Treen finally was elected in the Third Congressional District in 1972 after three unsuccessful runs for Congress and one futile shot at governor of Louisiana. He became the first Republican Congressman to represent the State of Louisiana since Reconstruction a hundred years earlier. Two years later, after a heavily contested election in the Sixth Congressional District was thrown out for vote irregularities in Baton Rouge, that race was re-run, and Henson Moore became the second Republican in the Louisiana delegation. Republicans developed confidence that they could win anywhere in the state if the candidates and circumstances were right, and they began seeding a statewide organization. The envelope stuffers, neighborhood canvassers, telephone bankers, and young Republicans went to school under the leadership of the national Republican Party, and they began to emerge as a viable political entity in New Orleans and around the state.

The trend began with State Chairmen Charlton Lyons of Shreveport and later, Jimmy Boyce, a successful bigger than life heavy-equipment vendor in Baton Rouge. They, together with Dave Treen, John Cade, and Billy Nungesser, the nuclei of the Treen organization, and subsequent State Chairmen George Despot and Charlie DeGravelles, brought the party from a laughable afterthought to a competitive threat throughout the state.

Henson Moore's victory beat the odds and convinced people that the burgeoning Republican movement was not just a fluke and that something was seriously changing in the State. With the indulgence of Harry Connick and Billy Guste, I matured politically within the movement. Bill McNeal, a waterways and barge consultant from Algiers on the West Bank of the Mississippi River, became my mentor and guide in political organization and it was under Bill, who became chairman of the Orleans Parish Republican Party, that I came of age in the local and statewide political apparatus.

By February, 1976, Michael Starr, CEO of a few radio stations in the greater New Orleans area, was running to succeed Chairman Hebert. He had run against Hebert two years earlier, and I had assisted him by stuffing envelopes, getting out mailings, and other similar duties. He had little or no chance of defeating the venerable chairman at the time, and when the race was over, one could hardly claim that he'd been a serious candidate. But now that the seat was open with Hebert's announcement of his own retirement, Mike was in the race in a big way. I was once again stuffing envelopes for him, and I had every expectation of supporting him throughout the race. However, sometime in late April, Billy Nungesser, Dave Treen's friend and campaign co-chairman, called me out of the blue!

He said that Mike Starr's personal life was deteriorating and that because of health and family problems, Starr would not be able to make the race, so would I be interested? I told him I didn't even live in the District, and he said I could move. I said I didn't have any money, and he said we could raise it. I told him I'd have to quit my job to avoid a conflict before running, and he said that was OK. So I told him I'd have to speak with Bonnie and my kids and get back to him.

Campaign # 1

After speaking with Bonnie, I told Billy I'd do it. With no more than $5,000 in the bank, I quit my job. With the help of some of the guys in the Attorney General's Office and some young Republicans, I packed up essentials from our beautiful house and moved my family across the river to a small and far less than lovely rental apartment on Kabel Drive in Algiers.

And there I was, a young lawyer with a wife and three kids, giving up a decent job, abandoning the home of our dreams, uprooting my family and moving across town, becoming a candidate for the first race I'd ever entered with no money, no campaign organization, and no plans for making it all possible. And the filing deadline was two weeks away.

Geographically, Algiers is across the Mississippi River from the Central Business District of New Orleans. But back then, it was fairly central to the whole Congressional District, which encompassed half of Orleans and all of St. Tammany, St. Bernard and Plaquemines parishes, or basically the southeastern toe of the Louisiana boot. The city of New Orleans was divided fairly simply, with Lindy Boggs of the Second District representing the French Quarter, the Central Business District, Uptown, and the silk stocking area. The First District encompassed the West Bank, Lakeview, Central City, and New Orleans East, all in Orleans Parish. Despite the fact that the urban areas in the First District contained more housing projects for poor people than did the Second District, the First was far more conservative than the Second simply because the outlying parishes were so much more conservative than the city itself. Even so, 32 percent of the district was African-American.

The die was cast. I quickly found myself, a city-bound white guy with little money in a full blown Congressional race in a very urban, suburban, and rural area in much of which I had spent little if any time in my life. I had never run for anything and didn't know enough to know that I was on a fool's errand. And as soon as I qualified, I found myself on a plane bound for the school for House Republican candidates in Washington, D.C. I'd only visited the nation's Capital on two occasions, so just the trip itself was a new experience. I found myself surrounded by other more experienced political types who were also candidates for office, and I was confronted with issues I had never heard of—things like "cargo preference" and "windfall profits taxes." Well, it's not a stretch to say that I was overwhelmed and dazed for the entire week of campaign school.

But I was a true believer in basic Republican principles, and as I articulated my conviction that the rights of the individual were at the core of American values, I gained some attention at campaign school. I believed the admonition that "big government," whether right or left, was a threat to the well-being of American democracy. I believed "that government is best which governs least." I believed in a strong national defense and that a lightly regulated free enterprise system was vastly superior to any totalitarian entity. I believed in low taxes, freedom of religion, an unfettered press, and quite simply, the right to be left alone as long as one did not intrude on the rights of one's neighbor. As a former criminal prosecutor, I believed in strong but non-intrusive law enforcement and in the principal that we all stand accountable for our actions. Intent was paramount; motive was not. I have never thought that "hate crimes" should be at issue for it does not matter why you acted or whom you harmed, but only that you intended to inflict injury upon another.

And then I came home. I had no job and little money in the bank. Yet, with an incredibly supportive wife and three young boys, we began our campaign lives in our cramped West Bank apartment. Fortunately, I had a lot of friends, and when I gave my first speech at Lenfant's Restaurant in Lakeview, many of them even showed up. My speaking prowess was lousy, but I was a believer in less government, lower taxes, and greater individual freedom, so away I went. My longtime friend from the DKE house and a practicing West Bank lawyer, Ted Nass, signed on as campaign manager, and longtime Republican friend, Marilyn Thayer, headed up a campaign office near my apartment in Algiers.

I immediately began hosting coffees and teas in the mornings at various Republican Women's Clubs around the District, and the ladies that turned out became the backbone of my volunteer force. Since we had no money for the campaign, we enlisted their children to help produce hundreds of hand-painted blue and white silk-screened signs, "Bob Livingston—Congress," and my friends began posting them in hard-to-get places all over the district. Similarly, we silk-screened t-shirts with the same logo and little kids wore them everywhere. They became collectors' items for years afterwards.

The New Orleans *States-Item*, an afternoon newspaper now long gone, did an early story on the candidates in the race. The parties were to hold primaries for multiple candidates and there were eight Democrats signed up—and me, the Republican, who had no primary opponent, hence no primary. But apart from my friends, Charlie Lancaster, the first Republican to be elected to the state legislature, and Dave Treen, who by then was running for his third term in Congress from Jefferson and other parishes west of New Orleans, there were no elected Republicans in the area. Hence the *States-Item* omitted any story on me, since it was obvious I had no chance of winning. They just wrote about the eight Democrats in the race.

Meanwhile, for reasons apart from my magnificence as a candidate, the NRCC (National Republican Congressional Committee) began sending political advisors down to New Orleans to advise on my campaign. Some of them were even good at what they did. But in all honesty, I think their enthusiasm had far more to do with the hotels and parties in the French Quarter than the prospects of my campaign.

As I traveled around the District, I began to attract adherents and supporters. My policeman friend from the AG's office, Walter Reed, introduced me to his many generations of family in St. Tammany Parish, and they, along with Margaret Sloan, Penny McWilliams, and the Republican ladies of St. Tammany, became an incredible force that changed politics from the sleepy "good ole country boy" domination by Democrats in the parish of the past, to a network today that makes it extremely difficult to get elected if you have a "D" behind your name. But it wasn't always that way, and it took a lot of people and a lot of hard work to change their minds. "My granddaddy was a Democrat, my daddy was a Democrat, and I will always be a Democrat!" I used to hear that mantra frequently, but rarely do I hear it any more.

During one visit in northern St. Tammany, my new friend Fred Bass was showing me around his area to meet some farmers, when someone told me that the famous local union leader, Hezzie Parker, was nearby at his farm. Hezzie had been the political kingpin of the parish in his day, so I jumped at the chance to meet him. We rode deep into the backwoods in this other fellow's Cadillac until we came to a pretty little lake. Hezzie, a strong, compact man whom I'd never met, was standing by himself just gazing out at the water. I got out of the car and strolled over the pasture toward him. When I was within earshot, I stuck out my hand and said, "Hezzie Parker, I'm Bob Livingston!" I guess he'd heard of me for he broke into a grin. He reached out to grab my hand, and as he shook it vigorously, he said, "I'd vote for a gorilla before I'd vote for a Republican." I laughed and told him I didn't need his vote, but if he ever needed my help, just call. I can't say that I ever really had significant union opposition in St. Tammany after that. But I'm positive that I never got Hezzie's vote.

Plaquemines and St. Bernard are the two southernmost parishes in Southeast Louisiana. They comprise all of the eastern and some of the western sides of the Mississippi River, and they are considered by many as hosts to the best fishing in the United States. Plaquemines is also a major throughway from the Gulf of Mexico to the port of New Orleans and all points north. It has enjoyed abundant access to minerals of all sorts, especially sulfur, oil, and gas. Oil wells dotted the shoreline of both parishes, and as resources ran out, the coast line was riddled with canals and access ways for pipelines bringing the resources to market. Over the years, the canals have been blamed with some validity to a significant loss of wetlands.

Until his death in 1969, politics in both parishes was dominated by the imposing force of Judge Leander Perez, an ally of Huey Long's when he was the virtual emperor (as Governor and subsequently, Senator) of the state until his assassination in 1935. Huey had successfully challenged the oil and railroad industries that controlled the state before he arrived on the scene. He transformed Louisiana politics for generations, empowering the poor, building roads, bridges, public buildings, and hospitals, and siphoning much of the state coffers off for himself and his cronies, Leander Perez being one. He was a brilliant demagogue with a Populist (read "Socialist") message, "Every man a king and a chicken in every pot!" In at least one of his nationally acclaimed radio broadcast speeches, Huey advocated the nationalization of assets in excess of one million dollars from every American family.

But, like many of today's socialists, he certainly didn't intend his proposal to limit his own grasp of power and wealth nor of those of his immediate cronies. Together, they became quite wealthy.

Huey divided the mineral wealth of the state among seven geographically diverse Louisiana families. Leander Perez got Plaquemines and St. Bernard, and until a suit was filed and adjudicated in the 1980s, his family continued to reap the rewards from mineral rights to public lands so acquired in the '30s. To this day, there continues to be a lot of poverty in those parishes, but despite the mineral wealth of the terrain, the poor failed to benefit significantly from it. Yet until much later, they voted over and over for the Perez machine.

Leander, or "The Judge" as he preferred to be called, was a noted holdout for segregation and is remembered for his reaction to the "Freedom Riders" of the 1960s. Had they actually arrived in Plaquemines Parish, he threatened to have them arrested and locked inside old Fort Jackson deep in the parish. A remnant of the previous century, it had been renovated but bore little offer of comfort in the snake and alligator infested wetlands surrounding the fort. Their decision to avoid the parish was probably wise. The "Judge" was not known for his vigor as a civil libertarian.

Leander died and was buried in Plaquemines Parish in 1969. When I began running for Congress in 1976, his two sons, Leander Jr. and Chalin, were in charge of his domain. Lee Jr. was the elected District Attorney in St. Bernard, and he and his protégé, Sheriff Jack Rowley, controlled everything political in the parish. Likewise, Chalin was the uncontested king of Plaquemines Parish. Chalin and Lee didn't get along, but as long as they stayed away from one another, all was well. Both were brilliant lawyers like their father, but Lee was jovial and urbane, while Chalin was rough, curt, and a "take no prisoners" sort of guy.

It was my race for Congress that ultimately prompted their irreparable quarrel and the dissolution of their empire. Chalin and Lee joined forces in 1976 to support retired Marine and then New Orleans City Councilman, Jimmy Moreau, one of the leading Democrats in the mix, to replace Chairman Hebert. Moreau had been a longtime friend of Hebert, and he was his hand-picked choice as a successor. In the early days of the campaign, he looked to be the slam-dunk, odds-on favorite, but fate had other things in store for him.

I had been reading political philosophy in books by Congressman and former NFL quarterback Jack Kemp, House Minority Leader John Rhodes, and other prominent Republicans, and I'd developed my speeches by focusing on the conservative rhetoric of lesser and frugal government, a philosophy shared by Jimmy Moreau. But Jimmy, an extraordinarily nice and decent person, wasn't the most articulate of candidates, and when we engaged in our first debate, I began to think my chances were better than perceived by conventional wisdom. The District was conservative and I held my own against the predominantly liberal field. But when Moreau declared that his top priority as Congressman was to push for a "Shadow Congress" to replace all our elected officials in the event of a nuclear attack, well, it dawned on me that I might actually have a chance to win.

As it turned out, Jimmy Moreau was not the problem. Beyond all expectations, another far more populist candidate by the name of Rick Tonry rose from the pack and rapidly became a front-runner among the Democrats. An entire book could be written about Tonry. A Catholic Seminarian and teacher at Jesuit High School in New Orleans, he had been elected recently to his first term to the Louisiana State House of Representatives. Tonry hailed from St. Bernard Parish, and he quickly became the "home-town boy."That enabled him to mobilize much of the vote in St. Bernard and even in Plaquemines Parishes, despite opposition from the conservative Perez brothers. Tonry's message was sufficiently liberal to attract the blue collar, union, and African American vote, and his co-option of the *Rocky* movie theme blared on the loud speakers on his campaign RV added the color he needed to become a real contender.

But the district was still extraordinarily conservative, and under normal circumstances, Jimmy Moreau should have been an easy victor in the Democrat primary. These were not normal circumstances. We all campaigned throughout the summer of 1976, and I continued to pick up steam. I never attacked Moreau, and I pitched his supporters with the theme that if he were to lose, a possibility that none of them had contemplated, at least they would have me as a fall-back candidate in the general election.

But the Democratic primary came first, and in September 1976, people of the First Congressional District went to the polls. All of the pollsters had virtually declared Jimmy Moreau to be the winner—but he wasn't. Rick Tonry won in a fairly close race, at least superficially.

Moreau and his supporters were shocked! They could not—did not—accept defeat. They quickly began examining the voting records, and their investigation turned up evidence of massive vote fraud in many precincts in St. Bernard. The investigators found election workers who were Tonry people and who in the midst of unchecked fun and frolic abandoned any pretense of discipline or protection of voter integrity. People came to the polls in great numbers and repeatedly "rang the bell," meaning they each voted for Tonry multiple times in the voting machines after signing the rolls as "Superman," "Popeye and Pals," "Howdy Doody," "Buster Brown," and so forth.

Moreau, backed by the Perez brothers and Luke Petrovich, a brilliant lawyer and then the President of Plaquemines Parish, filed suit immediately and, to their great credit, took the case all the way to the U.S. Supreme Court. But that took time, and meanwhile, the election process progressed. Suddenly Moreau supporters realized that they had no place to go. If they wanted a conservative to go to Congress, they needed to support the only conservative in the race—Bob Livingston.

As a newcomer to the scene, I was an untested commodity, and some of the hard-core conservatives in the district thought that maybe they needed another alternative choice. I was accumulating both local and national attention as the virtual front-runner against Rick Tonry, when suddenly the race changed once again.

With only weeks to go before the general election, former state judge and one term Sixth District Democratic Baton Rouge Congressman, John Rarick, appeared on the scene. With no support from anyone but the most extreme right-wing in the area (the Ku Klux Klan was still active in St. Tammany Parish at the time), Rarick filed as an independent candidate at the last possible moment. I had never heard of Rarick, but I soon learned that he was an avowed racist who would not even shake hands with black people. He quickly developed a small organization and a following that I initially ignored.

Some weeks before the November election, we held a major fundraiser for my campaign with headliner California Governor Ronald Reagan, who had just run an unsuccessful campaign for the Republican nomination against President Gerald Ford. Reagan was to speak at a formal luncheon at the Fairmont Roosevelt Hotel in New Orleans. In order to accommodate the press, the plan was for him to arrive by small plane at the Lakefront Airport, hold a press conference in the hangar, and take a car to the luncheon, after which he would quickly ride to cut a ribbon at a new Livingston Headquarters in the Lakeview area, and then head back to catch his plane home.

When Bonnie and I arrived at the airport to greet him, a battery of local and national press was waiting patiently to cover the very popular governor. Naturally, his plane was late. We waited for over thirty minutes and finally the plane arrived. I still bear a vivid recollection of then-Governor Reagan as he deplaned and walked quickly up to me. His very first words as he shook my hand and met me for the first time were, "Where's the bathroom?"

Returning from that task, he abided the plan by graciously spending a good fifteen minutes answering press questions despite our being almost an hour behind schedule. As he concluded the press conference, we prepared to enter the limousine to take us all to the hotel when Jeanne Nathan, a TV reporter and former advance person for George McGovern, arrived late. She approached me and asked for a special interview. I told her she was too late but that we'd try to make it up to her later in the trip.

Once downtown, the lunch was beautifully handled. Governor Reagan spoke and all was well, except when Jeanne Nathan came up to me toward the end of the event and told me that if I didn't get her that interview, it would go down as "one loser comes on behalf of another." Since I was gaining strength in the polls every day and was beginning to smell the prospect of victory against Tonry, I mumbled that I'd do what I could.

Back in the limousine, we proceeded to the new headquarters. Reagan chatted casually with Bonnie, her mother, Boo Robichaux, and me. When we arrived, Reagan jumped out, cut a ribbon with me for the cameras, and then began to reenter the car for the airport. I was to remain with Bonnie and her mom, and after saying our "goodbyes," we watched as he began to climb into the back seat of the car. Suddenly, there was Jeanne Nathan on his heels, her microphone stuck in his face as she asked him a question with the big TV camera man capturing his answer on video from over their shoulders. Reagan, ever so gracious, began to answer, but his advance man jumped between Nathan and the governor and pushed her aside as he guided his ward into the car.

Nathan, recalling her McGovern days, was not to be stopped so easily. With her right hand, she pulled the advance guy's coat over his shoulders and pinned his arms. In her left hand was the microphone attached by wire to the camera. She jammed it back in Reagan's face and again he began to answer. I watched it all in slow motion as the advance guy, clearly miffed by her insistence, freed his hands just enough to separate the wire from the microphone as he shoved her aside and closed the door on the governor. The TV coverage was just about what I could have expected, and it was a great story for twenty four hours!

The election was a week away when David Levy, Rarick's campaign manager in St. Tammany, called me up and said, "Bob, let's flip a coin. If you win, we'll get out, and if we win, you get out." By then I'd been running for five months and my polls told me I was on the verge of winning, but I knew that Rarick could take a good bit of the conservative vote. He was a wacko, and in my opinion so was his campaign manager—and I told him so. I refused his offer. The next week, the people cast their ballots. Rarick received 9 percent of the vote, Tonry 47 percent, and I got only 44 percent. President Gerald Ford and I were both defeated in the election of 1976, and Rick Tonry was elected to Congress, while the toothy Georgian peanut farmer, Jimmy Carter, was elected President of the United States.

For many years thereafter, I opened my speeches by explaining to people I didn't know that when I first ran for Congress in 1976, I lost. But the guy who beat me was made ABC's stereotypical freshman Congressman of the Year! That meant that ABC followed him everywhere from the time he was sworn-in in January 1977 until July of that same year when he went to prison. I had another shot.

I always got a laugh but it was true. Jimmy Moreau pursued his case all the way up the court system. He proved unequivocally that the primary was stolen from him, and his evidence led to the prosecution and conviction of quite a few St. Bernard poll officials. There was even evidence suggesting that Tonry, himself, may have cast some illegal ballots. In any event, they built a case against Tonry for vote fraud, and in May 1977, after having his case fully evaluated by the Democrat-controlled House Administration Committee, even they could not overlook the evidence against him. They convinced him that if he didn't step down and run again for his own seat, he might be expelled. Thus, in May, while I was struggling to put a fledgling law practice back together, I was delighted to hear on the radio that the man who had beaten me for Congress was vacating his seat and announcing that he would run again in a special election.

Campaign #2

That's exactly what Rick Tonry did, but not everyone who had supported him the first time around was enthusiastic about his chances. Specifically, a bright and articulate twenty-five-year-old first term state representative, Ron Faucheux ("Fo-shey"), who had supported Tonry in the first go-round, announced that he would run against Tonry in the Democratic primary. Meanwhile, Jimmy Moreau, whose lawsuit had finally created the premise and circumstance causing Tonry to step down, switched parties and announced that he was running against me as a Republican for Congress.

I had followed the process closely for months, and I knew that even if Tonry hadn't stepped down, at least he'd been critically wounded by the investigation. I was prepared have another run in two years when his term ended. So to the degree possible, I'd kept together the political machine that had taken me from nowhere to 44 percent in the previous election. I'd moved my law practice and my home to Algiers. Bonnie and I bought a beautiful old brick building in "Old Algiers" and renovated it as our new home. Known as the "Reineke Shoe Store" where all the neighbors who'd grown up in the area had bought their "Red Goose" and "Buster Brown" shoes as kids, the building overlooked the levee along the Mississippi River. It was empty and abandoned when we bought it, but the *façade* of lovely old (Spanish) French Quarter style grill work with wrap-around the porches convinced us that this was where we should be. We sold our house on Lowerline Street in uptown New Orleans, and we spent the next few months renovating our new home.

I had come too far to quit now, and I was planning to run at the end of Tonry's full term. I had established myself as a reasonably decent campaigner, a solid conservative, and a longtime Republican. So now that Tonry had stepped down, I felt entitled to the Republican nomination, notwithstanding Jimmy Moreau's conversion. Thus, after only six months following my defeat at the hands of Tonry and Rarick, I was back in the race.

This race was wholly different from the earlier one. I now had an organization, and I was ready. We were back in force within a matter of days. Elsewhere in the country, Republicans had won three special elections for Congress earlier that year, so the national folks were feeling their oats and were eager to get in behind me. Dave Treen and Henson Moore, who sensed that they had a chance to bring another Republican into the delegation, mobilized their entire campaign organizations to pitch in to the maximum, and Republican State Chairman Jimmy Boyce activated the state organization behind me as well.

In fact, I had every Republican in the state behind me, save the many personal friends of Jimmy Moreau, who did a great job of switching his Democratic friends over to the Republican side so that they could vote for him. But long time Republicans supporting me from the beginning were furious that after all their work, their candidate might see his candidacy for Congress taken away from him by a newcomer to the party. Moreover, lots of conservative Democrats who had thrown in with me in the earlier race switched parties so that they could vote for me in the primary. Many of them were highly motivated on my behalf. But then, Jimmy Moreau's friends were motivated to stick with him—as new Republicans! After all, his own victory had been stolen from him in the Democratic Primary. So in a few short weeks, the Southeast Louisiana Republican Party grew faster than it had in a century.

It was a relatively brief Republican primary, and when the dust settled, I decisively defeated Chairman Eddie Hebert's hand-picked candidate, Councilman Jimmy Moreau. On the Democratic side, Rick Tonry continued to attract bad luck. Young State Representative Ron Faucheux ran a vigorous race in the primary and defeated the man he'd supported in the first go round. Shortly afterwards, Tonry was indicted in Federal Court on an abundance of charges for election irregularities. In addition to the overwhelming charges of ballot box stuffing, someone had taped a conversation during the general election against me, in which he'd agreed to take money under the table to avoid federal campaign finance law. The evidence was irrefutable.

A charge of vote fraud in the primary would have constituted a felony and caused the loss of his law license. So Tonry negotiated down his plea to a misdemeanor for accepting illegal campaign donations in the general election. The judge still sentenced him to serve the maximum under the law: one year in prison.

The term was later reduced, and he only served about six months of the sentence. His luck improved since he emerged from prison a millionaire. In his absence, his law partner, Wayne Mumphrey, had settled a case for several clients who some years earlier had been injured in an oil fire on the site of Murphy Oil Company in St. Bernard Parish.

But as bright and gregarious as he was, Tonry was a true reprobate, and he continued to generate headlines in one scandal after another for years afterwards. He even went to jail a second time years later for allegedly bribing a chief to put Bingo on an Indian reservation. But that case was thrown out on appeal for failure of the prosecutors to prove federal jurisdiction; hence there had been no federal crime. I do believe that an entire book could be written about his adventures, but that will have to wait for another time.

So here I was, having started, stopped, and started again in a Congressional race that was to last over eighteen months from beginning to end. In that time, I raised almost $1.5 million, an astronomical sum for Congressional races of the day. I'd won the primary, and I thought I would be the front runner for the next general election, but I was wrong.

Ron Faucheux had barely finished college when he ran for and won a seat in the state legislature. A natural politician, he was a fine writer and a good speaker. He'd determined at a very young age to run for Congress and progress politically from there on. After little more than a year in the State House, he beat Tonry in the Congressional primary and was on his way.

Meanwhile, the primary posed a dilemma for the Perez organization in St. Bernard and Plaquemines. They had backed Moreau without reservation. But now he was gone. What were they to do?

Faucheux was the "chosen one" among die-hard Democrats, and he easily convinced Chalin Perez to back him for Congress. On the other hand, Chalin's brother, Lee Perez, was more conservative than he was Democrat, and he backed me. This was their first open disagreement, but there were others to come. They later fought over the use of a parish helicopter, and that argument caused them to sever ties completely.

The split between the Perez brothers gave me a foothold in St. Bernard Parish, while Faucheux fairly well locked up Plaquemines Parish.

Now that Tonry was no longer an element in St. Bernard, I pushed my small band of Republican supporters there to work against all their own "good government" instincts and join with the organizations of DA Lee Perez and Sheriff Jack Rowley on my behalf. Clerk of Court Sidney Torres was a third and lesser power in the parish, and since he was a long time personal friend of Ron Faucheux, I wasn't able to sew up the entire parish.

But I did get the lion's share, and because St. Bernard had twice the population of Plaquemines, it wasn't a bad deal for me even though Chalin Perez literally controlled 90 percent of the vote in Plaquemines Parish. I had received that 90 percent in the general election against Tonry and Rarick, but since it was the smallest part of the District, it didn't make a big difference in the outcome. This time however, with Chalin backing Faucheux, I was to be on the downside of the equation, and Faucheux ultimately received that 90 percent to my meager 10 percent.

Faucheux was clever. He'd followed my speeches against Tonry throughout the campaign, and he aligned himself on the same side with me on virtually all of the issues. That knocked me for a loop. I was used to being the only conservative in the race. But it was commonly accepted in the old Democratic South that if there were a Republican and a Democrat running against one another in the same race, and if they were saying the same things, the Democrat would always win.

To make things worse, independent Democrat Sandy Krasnoff jumped into the race as a third party candidate. Sandy was a notorious character who had served on the New Orleans Police Force, and I could envision another Rarick situation that would bring me "close, but no cigar."

But with historic trends in his favor, Ron Faucheux made a key and critical mistake. He was a fine speaker, and he was actually more assured of himself on the stump than I, especially since he was stealing all my speech material. But as soon as he defeated Tonry in the primary, he announced that he would meet and debate me "any time, any place!" And then he went off to Baton Rouge to serve his time in the state legislative session. It proved to be his undoing.

When I ran against Tonry the first time around, I'd adopted the standard Republican mantra against unions in my speeches and positions. It hadn't proved to be a very effective strategy, since it automatically mobilized the entire AFL-CIO against me, and it cost me a lot of unnecessary votes. Louisiana had become a "Right to Work" state in the previous legislative session. Labor domination of Louisiana politics was diminishing, but the unions were still quite strong in the First District by the time of this Congressional race. In the course of Faucheux's return to the state legislative session, he was forced to vote on a couple of critical issues affecting Big Labor. Since the First District was overwhelmingly conservative notwithstanding the heavy blue collar influence, he voted with business all the way to undercut my well established business support. That alienated the labor bosses, and it caused them to rethink their support in the race. Krasnoff had been a police union member, but as a relatively fringe candidate, he attracted some but certainly not all of their support.

A prominent leader of the AFL-CIO in greater New Orleans at the time was the boss of the Seafarers International Union (SIU), Lindsey Williams. Lindsey was a bigger than life, tough but lovable rogue from the Irish Channel. Before I joined the Navy at age eighteen, I'd signed up for the SIU as a "wiper" on a merchant marine vessel, only to be prevented from shipping out when the longshoreman's union (ILA) went out on strike. In addition, many of the guys in the Fraternal Order of Police (FOP) were friends of mine from my prosecutorial days. And finally, I had mastered the art of drinking beer with world champions. So with such credentials, I asked an SIU friend, Gerry Brown, to set up a meeting with Lindsey Williams at the Half Moon Lounge, his office away from the office a couple of blocks down the street from SIU headquarters. Gerry had headed the SIU office in Mobile, Alabama, and had only recently relocated to New Orleans. We'd hit it off as soon as we met, and he was happy to help me meet Lindsey.

Lindsey, Gerry, I, and two or three SIU lieutenants spent one Friday afternoon drinking beer and swapping stories. We had a terrific time, and I came away from the experience with some new friends. I hadn't bought support, for the AFL construction trades were still very much opposed to me. In fact, had they known that my very first advertising man in the earlier campaign was Jim Leslie, an ad-man who had led the successful fight for "Right-to-Work" in the 1976 legislative session, they would have opposed me with all their might. Leslie designed my logo and bumper sticker in May of that year and then traveled to Baton Rouge to celebrate his legislative victory. He was gunned down by unknown assailants a week later. The murderer subsequently was found to have had nothing to do with his victory over the unions, but at the time, suspicious observers couldn't overlook the coincidence.

Leslie was so talented that I do believe that had he lived, I might have won the first time out of the box. But with the passage of a single year, I had just befriended the president of the most powerful union in the AFL-CIO inner council in New Orleans. The SIU's biggest issue was protecting maritime jobs by maintaining a strong merchant marine through "cargo preference." While in my early campaign days I had no idea what that was, I soon learned all about it and found it an easy issue to support so that U.S. vessels would be preferred for outgoing cargo of U.S. commodities. With active help from the SIU and an actual endorsement from the police unions, I kept the AFL Council neutral. That plus Ron Faucheux's adverse votes in the state House enabled me to overcome a major hurdle that I had not been able to overcome in the earlier race.

There was another piece of good fortune from Faucheux's sabbatical to the Louisiana State Capitol. The First District enjoyed a 32 percent black constituency. As previously noted, there were more predominantly black housing projects in the First District than in Lindy Boggs's Second District. I had done poorly in the black areas against Rick Tonry. So my handlers at the RNC sent in a prominent minority outreach consultant, Bob Wright, to work the district. With his help, we developed a small core of African American supporters like Hosea Ned in Plaquemines Parish, cousins Arthur and Melvin Bush in Algiers, and Dr. Herb Eddington and John Patnett in the Gentilly region of New Orleans. I visited the black radio stations and befriended the DeJoie brothers, Connie and Henry, who ran the black newspaper, the *Louisiana Weekly*. I went to black churches and campaigned in black neighborhoods.

In the first race, we had been out-gunned by Tonry and Democratic machine and had received no more than 2 percent or 3 percent of the black vote in much of the district. This time we actively pursued black voters and turned the tide. We built on our small but enthusiastic black network. Then in response to Faucheux's challenge that he'd debate me "anytime, anywhere," we set up meetings in the black neighborhoods and community centers. We'd give him short notice, then publicize that there would be a Livingston/Faucheux debate—along with free food and T-shirts with my logo. I would appear on a dais along with two chairs and tell the small but effective crowds that Mr. Faucheux was detained in the state legislature. Then Arthur Bush would jump up in the audience and declare, "He's taking our vote for granted!!!" The story was told more than once on black radio or in the newspaper and it had an impact.

I was known to be a full time, non-stop campaigner. I had to be virtually everywhere in the District, and without the ability to transport myself to more than one place at the same time as in *Star Trek*, I did a pretty good job. I worked the black neighborhoods, the white neighborhoods, the black and white media; the white collar and the blue collar haunts. On occasion, I would go bar-hopping with friends to key centers of the community like Bud Rip's Bar on Piety St. and Whitey's on Downman Road. I formed lifelong friendships with people who joined the campaign along the way, like Edward "Bud Rip" Ripoll, himself. Key people included Ann and Frank Hein and Julie and Bob Durocher of St. Bernard Parish; Fred Bass, Francis Barker, Rusty Burns, Margaret Sloan, and Penny McWilliams in St. Tammany Parish; Marilyn and Stu Thayer, Madge and Carey Becker in New Orleans; and Mary Ellen Miller, who came all the way from Oklahoma to manage my phone banks. There were hundreds if not thousands of people, men and women, who gave of themselves in time, energy, creativity, and yes, money, to help me win.

Allen Martin, the very young Executive Director of the South Carolina Republican Party, had come to Louisiana at the request of my friend, Republican State Chairman George Despot, to head our young party in Baton Rouge. Allen and I got to know one another in my first campaign, and when Ted Nass couldn't take any more time from his law practice, I invited Allen to come to New Orleans and run the second campaign as the manager. In the meantime, Ted hired his wife's cousin, Paul Cambon, right out of LSU to drive me around the District. To this day over forty years later, Allen, Paul, and I are still together as founding partners of The Livingston Group.

The straw that broke the camel's back for Faucheux in the election was a TV ad that John Cade and I concocted late in the campaign. John and Billy Nungesser Sr. were Congressman Dave Treen's closest advisors. Unlike the brash and vocal Billy, John was a quiet and thoughtful Christian Scientist who never took a single pill, medication, drink, or even coffee or tea despite horrendous migraine headaches. Regardless of his health problems, John soldiered through life without a complaint. And he was an excellent political strategist.

Toward the end of what was becoming a tight and close campaign, I mentioned to John that I'd worked as a ship-fitter's helper and in other odd jobs at Avondale Shipyard. The more we talked about it, the more it dawned on us that we had the makings of an ad. We wanted to show the difference between Ron Faucheux and me. I had a beautiful wife and three wonderful little boys. Ron was young and unmarried and had gone into politics right out of college. Although successful in politics, he'd not established much of a work record beyond that. I had been working every summer since I was fourteen, and my days at Avondale were worthy of notice in the campaign.

So in the last two weeks of the campaign, our pre-purchased television ads were narrowed to a single thirty second shot of me in blue jean pants and shirt kneeling on flat steel at Equitable Shipyard in the District. I wore a welder's helmet on my head and held a welder's torch in my hand. As the camera zoomed in, I struck an arc sufficiently to convince any welder that I knew what I was doing. The flash from the torch filled the screen for an instant, and then I turned it off, lifted my helmet visor and looked into the camera. The camera focused on my face, the helmet still on top of my head, as I said:

> *I don't do this for a living now, but I used to. I know what it means to work hard, put food on the table for my children, and make ends meet. Now I want to go to Congress to pass good laws so that your job is easier. Won't you vote for me, Bob Livingston, for Congress? I want to go to work for you!*

It was especially pleasing to hear the reaction of Ron Faucheux, an ardent student of politics who had begun a successful political advertising business with his friend, Jim Farwell, and who ultimately received a Ph.D. in political science. He and Jim created TV ads for a living and had done several for Rick Tonry. Ron later told me that when he saw my welder's ad, he knew he was beaten.

He'd been a tough campaigner. As soon as the Louisiana Legislature adjourned, he came home and made up for lost time. He chased and received some newspaper endorsements, and he did well in all the debates but for some Democratic mantra about "counter-cyclical budgeting" that I never did understand. But since no one else did either, I laughingly wrapped it around him as being one more great Democratic "Big Government" gimmick.

So with my inroads into the Labor movement, the Black community, the blue collar neighborhoods, and traditional conservative Republican demographics, we went to the polls in a special election on August, 27, 1977, to fill the vacancy in Congress left by Rick Tonry. This time, I took 51 percent of the vote against both Faucheux and Krasnoff, who received less than 6 percent.

Congress

On September 7, 1977, I was sworn in by Speaker Tip O'Neill with my three boys at my side on the floor of the U.S. House of Representatives. Bonnie looked down from the Gallery as I became the first Republican to hold the First District Congressional Seat in Louisiana in over one hundred years, and only the third Republican in the entire state behind my friends, Dave Treen and Henson Moore.

The Constitution allows a Governor of a State to appoint someone to fill the unexpired term of a departing Senator, but a House vacancy in a Congressional District can only be filled by the vote of the people in a special election. My election was the third successive special election that year, and Republicans had won them all. Jack Cunningham of Washington State and Arlan Stangeland in Minnesota won their seats before I was elected, and Bill Green took New York City, which made it a "grand slam" for Republicans later in 1977. The four of us began a trend that would foreshadow the capture of the majority of the House by Republicans some seventeen years later. But for those seventeen years, I served my constituents as a happy warrior in the minority party.

Being in the minority wasn't all that bad since I had nothing to compare it to. I was honored and delighted to have been elected to Congress, and all the more so as I gradually climbed the ladder of seniority and committee assignments. But, it was two months following my election before I was assigned to any committee at all! In the meantime, I had to acquire and structure my office with new and experienced staff people. Henson Moore loaned me a member of his staff, Sue Cornick, to supervise the structuring of my new people. With Sue's help and with a few other folks that Henson and Dave Treen loaned me, we quickly rounded out our staff and began learning the ropes.

Once complete, half our team were from Louisiana and half were from Republican pools of experienced people around Capitol Hill. Ted Nass, my DKE brother and first campaign manager, left his law practice to come up and serve as my first chief of staff (then called "AA" for "Administrative Assistant.") My campaign manager, Allen

Martin headed my local district office and opened up satellite offices in St. Tammany and St. Bernard Parishes. That worked for about six months until I swapped them around. Allen became my AA, and Ted moved back home to take over the local office for the next year or so.

Bonnie and I had purchased the home in Old Algiers across the Mississippi from downtown New Orleans, and her time was consumed with supervising the renovation of the old brick building while making sure my boys were carried back and forth across the Mississippi River to St. Andrew's Episcopal Elementary School where they had been enrolled before I ran for Congress.

The early years in Congress were thrilling, notwithstanding my standing as a junior member of the minority party. I was ecstatic and honored to have been elected to Congress, and I set about my job as vigorously as the twenty-four-hour day would allow. I was immediately thrown into the fray on the floor of the House, and I quietly watched members politely refer to arch-enemies as "My Good Friend" and "My Distinguished Colleague" as they attempted to annihilate their opponent's arguments with dripping insincerity.

I watched as people like Bob Bauman (R-MD) and John Rousselot (R-CA) took on Jim Wright (D-TX) Phil Burton (D-CA). I learned that Burton's wife was Sala, the daughter of Gus Hall, once leader of the American Communist Party (CPUSA.) I watched the young and dynamic conservative, Phil Crane (R-IL), equal the skills of any on the left; and I saw gruff but gregarious Chicago pol, Danny Rostenkowski (D-IL) rise to post of chairman of the prestigious Ways and Means Committee. John Brademas (D-IN) was as good a whip as the Democrats would ever have. And Democratic Georgia Representative Larry McDonald, later killed in the crash of Koren Airlines flight 007, was more conservative than almost every Republican I ever knew.

When I arrived in Washington, I set about getting to know my neighbors. The first Congressman I visited (apart from Dave Treen and Henson Moore) was Thad Cochran (R-MS). He was kind to see me in his Congressional office, and I recall our discussion like it was yesterday. Thad, like his colleague, Trent Lott, had been an Ole Miss cheerleader and both were elected to the U.S. Senate in later years. As Senator, Thad eventually became chairman of the Appropriations Committee while Trent rose to become Majority Leader after Senator Bob Dole. Their relations with each other were often strained by intramural rivalries, but I considered both to be good friends. Tom Kindness (R-OH) was the first Congressman to visit my office and he lived up to his name. He was a friend until his death some ten years later.

I was often fascinated by the stories of others in Congress. Although we were colleagues in my freshman year, I don't recall meeting Leo Ryan, a Democratic member from California who flew to Jonestown, Guyana, in 1978 to search for a constituent's daughter. She had been a member of the Peoples Temple run by cult leader, Jim Jones. Ryan challenged Jones and attempted to bring some cult members back with him on his plane to the United States. But Jones sent a team out to the plane and they opened fire, killing Ryan, three journalists and a defecting cult member and wounding nine others. By the time police were informed and called to the scene shortly afterwards, they discovered over nine hundred bodies including over three hundred children—all Jones cult members, most of whom had drunk Kool-Aid laced with cyanide. Some who refused were shot.

My friend and constituent, Lou Gurvich, lost a daughter with the cult. Due to his family ties in the law enforcement community, Lou was one of the first Americans on a plane down to Guyana. But when he arrived two or three days after the discovery, the hot tropical sun had done its damage, and men, women and children were virtually indistinguishable. Lou never really recovered from the shock that I suspect took years off his life.

Since I had been sworn in following the third special election of the year, there were no committee slots open for me, and I was without any committee assignment for at least my first couple of months. But I pushed Minority Leader John Rhodes and the Republican leadership and was finally assigned to the Public Works Committee. In those days, the Public Works Committee was wisely comprised of no more than fifty members. As the most junior member of the minority, I sat down at the foot of the dais during hearings, but I became accustomed to sitting through long hours as witnesses would come and justify the expenditure of public funds on their projects of choice. Members were permitted to ask questions in bipartisan fashion under the five minute-rule, meaning that even if they were in mid-sentence at the end of five minutes, a good chairman would interrupt them on the spot and move on to the next member for questions, comments and/or incessant grandstanding. I was assigned to three subcommittees within the committee, and that's where the hearings and most of the substantive work took place.

I especially enjoyed the "Water Resources" Sub-committee, since it governed issues of extreme importance to my district. It allowed me to talk about the need for improved levee protection and lock replacement, issues vital to the folks back home. Never would I realize how absolutely vital those issues were until 2005, long after my departure from Congress, with the arrival of Hurricane Katrina. We always knew the fabled "one hundred year" storm could ravage southern Louisiana and we had suffered greatly from the impact of Hurricane Betsy in 1965. It was a given that we had to spend more money on flood protection, but it was always a constant battle to get sufficient resources to meet the need, particularly since members from other parts of the country attacked our programs and siphoned away tax dollars for their own parochial projects. But it was that battle that enabled me to work my way through the rolls of seniority of the Public Works Committee and gain stature with the Republican and Democratic members alike. I paid rapt attention to committee business and was more than willing to travel with fellow members on investigative field trips or "CODELS."

I got to know and like most of the members of the Committee regardless of party. Serving under Democratic chairmen Harold "Biz" Johnson of California and Ray Roberts of Texas, ranking Republican member Bill Harsha of Ohio, together with my Democratic Louisiana colleague, John Breaux, I did what I could to advance a "bipartisan" approach to legislation. I really had no choice, since the heavy Democratic majority meant it was the only way I could claim accomplishment back home. Widely rejected in today's highly partisan atmosphere, those days taught me the value of compromise, a concept envisioned in the Constitution, but fairly unknown as Congress progressed during the Bush (43) and Obama administrations of the early 2000s. Without compromise, nothing is accomplished, and that's pretty much what Republicans accomplished in those years under Speaker Hastert. Hence, the American people grew tired and threw them out in favor of the Democrats in 2006—who under Speaker Nancy Pelosi, became even more authoritarian and less open to compromise!

In those early days, the strategy employed by Public Works Chairman Biz Johnson and his Republican counterpart, Bill Harsha, in league with the senior Republican on the Appropriations Committee, Silvio Conte (R-MA), was to let members serve on the sub-committees of their choice if at all possible, but they tried not to assign members to hold ranking (leadership) positions on sub-committees if they had parochial interests in the matters of jurisdiction for fear that they would "pork" up the programs. It was a good policy that was quickly forgotten after I left. That's not to say that my dear friend Silvio was above "porking" up the state of Massachusetts. He would take to the floor of the House and rail against salaries of the Capitol Police or subsidies for the sugar growers. But he along with his buddies, Speaker Tip O'Neill and their roommate, Eddie Boland (D-MA), poured taxpayer's dollars into the their home state, most notably with the tunnel boondoggle known as the "Big Dig." It was riddled with problems and cost overruns, but it nonetheless transformed the city of Boston into a great and accessible city.

Party affiliation had little to do with flood control, and for many years, Republicans and Democrats from the South and Midwestern Mississippi Valley drainage states joined together to successfully fight off opposition to adequate funding for flood and drainage projects managed by the Corps of Engineers. But they were never funded to capacity, and it's easy to look back in the aftermath of Katrina and realize that we should have done more than we did.

The Corps of Engineers, wanting to please as many members as possible, did what they were told by leadership and struggled to manage the hundreds of billions of dollars in authorized programs on their books with only the few billions that were appropriated in a single year. That meant that the most critical programs rarely received the attention they deserved because what little money was available was spread all over the country rather than selectively targeted. Some of the flood and navigation projects of South Louisiana had been on the books for fifty to one hundred years, and they suffered greatly from lack of attention.

My very first CODEL (Congressional Delegation trip) was to Duluth, Montana, under the leadership of Jim Oberstar (D-MN) and Norm Mineta (D-CA) later to become the Secretary of Transportation under Presidents Clinton and Bush (43). The purpose was to study the needs of the Duluth water system. Once there, I learned that in early October, Duluth was both dark and cold, and I lost any desire to go there again. But I found that CODELS were important for members to understand how federal programs work and how they do not. If properly managed and staffed, they could provide effective means of investigation, provided that at least 80 percent of the time on the trip was spent on actual work. Foreign travel is also important in that it enables members to probe the depths of understanding between allies and other countries around the world and to assist our State Department in providing a political perspective to improve our legitimate international relationships. Of course, CODELS could be and have been frequently abused. Those are the real "junkets," and the only way to discourage them is with active and fair oversight by both Congressional leadership and the press.

Instead of insisting that CODELS are both responsible and effective, in more recent years Congress has layered on incredibly obtuse ethics rules that outlaw much of the activity that was acceptable behavior in the past. Trips to Israel or Taiwan and other countries paid for by legally acceptable outside entities were not uncommon ways to get a member and his/ her spouse to spend a few days in a host country to understand the culture and society and to meet the leaders and discuss bilateral relations between our countries. That's not as easy any more, and some members are intimidated and avoid traveling on legitimate trips. I believe that's unfortunate, since U.S. interests are better protected with understanding, and that only flows from access and exposure.

Majority Leader Dick Armey (R-TX) was quoted in the 1990s as saying: "I've been to Europe once, and I don't need to go back." That sentiment may be fine for some people, but it would be entirely inappropriate if all of Congress took that attitude. In this global society of ours, our leaders need to get to know one another, for it is through personal dialogue that peace is enhanced, not through walls of separation.

In fact, a trip that Bonnie and I took with Dan Lungren (R-CA) and his wife Bobbi in 1980 changed our lives forever for the better. Bonnie and I had three boys and she had always wanted a little girl. Our youngest boy, David, was eight years old by then, and I wasn't keen on our having another baby. We'd explored adoption a few times, but it had come to naught. But when the four of us spent a few days together in Taiwan, we noticed those adorable children in their little blue and white uniforms walking back and forth to school together. At one point, I asked Bonnie if she would be interested in adopting a Chinese child. She didn't hesitate. So, I inquired of our escort, Taiwanese Naval Attaché (and later Ambassador) Jason Yuan, to put us in touch with a local adoption agency.

The agency we contacted said that we were too old, that we already had children, and that they didn't have any older children, so we put the idea on the shelf and out of our minds for a short while. We returned to DC, and about three weeks later, Jason came to my office and put a picture of this lovely little six-year-old on my desk. Su Shan Fu (later to be named Sushan Alida Livingston) was the child of a small beautiful Taiwanese mother and a (likely large) German father. He had taken off, and the mother was left with the child. It was custom of a mother under such circumstances to contact an orphanage or find a foster home for the child. Susie was fortunate to have been placed with the family of a police lieutenant whom I was told later rose all the way to Chief of Police of Taipei. He had several daughters, and Susie had become just one more in the mix. She was well cared for, and her mother visited her frequently.

When we expressed interest, her biological mother had to make the tough decision to let her go, but she agreed, and after two adoption proceedings, one in Taipei and one in Louisiana, Susie was brought to the United States by a lady from the orphanage. The lady coached her on the trip, and her first English words to Bonnie and me when she got off the plane were, "I love you, Mommy and Daddy." Her new youngest brother, David, two years older than she, had mixed feelings about the family expansion, and he greeted her with a windup buzzer in his hand. Susie shrieked, and quickly learned her second English phrase, "Stop it, David!!" She employed it frequently.

Today, Susie is happily married to her husband, Kevin Kirchner, a practicing ophthalmologist, and they have three beautiful, curly red headed children and a huge rambunctious dog. I believe Susie has finally forgiven her brother David for all his many transgressions over the years. He, his wife Nance, and their two children live a short distance from Susie and Kevin.

So much good can flow from CODELS; they promote understanding between diverse cultures and serve to bring the world a little closer. And they enabled one of the best things to happen to us that we could ever have imagined.

John Breaux (D-LA) and I may not have been closest of friends, but despite political differences, we liked each other and always got along well. The same could be said for my neighboring colleague from New Orleans, Lindy Boggs (D-LA), a member of the Appropriations Committee, and me. In their own ways, each of them was a superb legislator, and I learned a lot from them. We were all partisan to a point, but back then, we avoided interfering in each other's races for re-election, and the whole Louisiana delegation enjoyed a reputation of leaving partisan politics at the state line. When it came time to push Louisiana's interests ahead, we joined together and with rare exceptions, we advanced Louisiana in common cause.

Our ability to work together became most apparent during the "Washington Mardi Gras," which generally preceded the actual Mardi Gras in South Louisiana by a couple of weeks. Every year since its inception sixty years ago, 3,500 of our best friends from Louisiana came to DC and joined in a Louisiana bash. With tons of great food including salty oysters, Gulf shrimp, po-boys, jambalaya, gumbo, and mega-gallons of beer, wine, and whiskey, it was widely known as the best party of the year in Washington. The Saturday morning ritual called for each one of the ten members of the delegation to parade before the "business community"—generally just a large group of Louisiana and DC lobbyists and partiers, whereupon each one of us tried to beat his or her colleagues with pithy and cute quips about what a wonderful place Louisiana was for doing business.

That was often a heavy lift in the "Edwards years" when Edwin Edwards was governor, since everyone knew his administration was significantly corrupt. At this writing, Edwards is approaching his 90s, relaxing with his wife of roughly half his age. After an earlier indictment and trial in which he was acquitted, the government finally caught up with him, convicted him for manipulating gambling licenses, and sentenced him to ten years in prison. To his great credit, Edwards took his punishment stoically and served his time without blaming others for his predicament.

The Mardi Gras extravaganza always grows in intensity over several days before the Saturday night ball, when a couple of hundred members of the "Mystick Krewe of Louisianians" in the Louisiana and Washington, D.C. business, political and lobbying community take over the ballroom of the Washington Hilton on Connecticut Avenue to throw one hell of a colorful party. A King is chosen from a list of wealthy contributors by the chairman, who is always one of the alternating members of the Louisiana Congressional delegation regardless of party. Likewise, the chairman chooses a Queen. She might be the chairman's daughter as was my daughter, Susie, in 1992. If not, she could be the daughter of a close friend, prominent constituent, or volunteer in the chairman's campaign. The Queen is accompanied by the festival queens from select events around the state, as well as maids and princesses appointed by the King and the Congressional delegation.

Back then, the Saturday night event would begin with a recital from the Marine Drum and Bugle Corps to get people revved up, to be followed by floats carrying the King and Queen, the festival queens, and finally the maids and princesses, all dressed in their Mardi Gras finest gowns. The crowd always went wild when the "Frog Queen," "Swine Queen," and "Crab Queen" strolled by on the arms of her proud father, brother, or boyfriend.

The Krewe, dressed in costume, would support the indoor parade complete with floats, bands, and banner carriers for each of the members of the delegation. The parade and Krewe would march around the ballroom amid multiple Dixieland bands while throwing trinkets and strings of colorful beads to the revelers in numbers generally exceeding the limits imposed by the fire marshal. When the parade was over, Krewe members were able to call out ladies in waiting throughout the audience for forty-five-second dances in time to the music of a worn-out orchestra. Once selected, Krewe members might bestow sometimes expensive, sometimes trivial, and mostly tacky gifts on their choices. At the end of the Ball, survivors would distribute themselves, invited or not, to "breakfasts" hosted by "royalty," business groups, or members of the Delegation. Grits, eggs, sausage, and more booze were in abundance.

It was always a colorful, and for first timers, thrilling event. Unfortunately, it lasted from Wednesday through Sunday, and by the time it was over, Bonnie and I were usually catatonic with exhaustion. I grew to dread the thing and often quipped that "everyone should do it once." I did about twenty five of them.

Campaign, 1978

With my reelection at hand in the fall of 1978, I did my best to ingratiate myself with all of my constituents and most especially my Louisiana Republicans. I worked as hard as I could throughout my district for I knew that if I won the next one, I could pretty well count on less opposition over the succeeding years. I managed to keep Republicans out of a primary against me, and I was delighted when Ron Faucheux decided not to run again. But former policeman Sandy Krasnoff was not to be discouraged, so I had a race. Sandy was not a brilliant candidate, but he had been a tough cop and he had friends on the police force who worked vigorously for him. And as a trial attorney after his time on the police force, he knew his way around the courtroom.

Shortly after I filed my papers for reelection, he challenged them on the grounds that I had not properly filled them out. In fact, he found a slight error and he darn near won the argument. In a narrow decision, Judge George Connolly of New Orleans Civil District Court ruled against him, but I sweated out the ruling until the end. I learned a great lesson, and I religiously checked my papers in every election thereafter.

Once the ruling was handed down, Krasnoff tried to shake me down to buy him out of the race, but I refused and we went to the mat. I beat him handily, but I still look back at the court action with relief that I didn't get nailed at the gate. I had many opponents in elections after that one, but despite some five separate re-apportionment rulings significantly reshaping my district in the next fifteen years, I never had a problematic opponent threaten my reelection to Congress. I just made sure that I worked sufficiently hard that they could never catch up. And it's still a source of pride that although the District was almost exclusively Democratic when I first ran, when I left, it was the most fully Republican District in the state.

Once the 1978 election was over, I relaxed my campaign schedule, and instead of going home every single weekend to campaign, I tried to cut back to only three weekends a month. By this time, I'd moved my family to the greater Washington, D.C., area. We'd bought Dave Treen's house. Dave and his wife, Dodi, wanted to live close to the Capitol to cut down on his commute, and he had just begun to think about selling it. I asked him how much he wanted for it. He told me, and I agreed on the spot. It was probably the quickest decision that Congressman Treen ever made. He was well known for taking home every single inconsequential legislative bill filed in Congress to review and ponder before deciding how to vote.

I knew my friend and political mentor well enough to know that the house would be in relatively good condition, and I was not surprised to find nothing wrong with it, save a dent in the side exterior paneling where a tree had fallen against the house. Dave was extremely apologetic about it, and he offered to have it fixed. I think we whittled a couple of hundred dollars off the purchase price, but I never felt the need to get it fixed. That was emblematic of the Treen approach. He was impeccably honest and incredibly deliberate.

The neighborhood was perfect for my family. The house was near a cul-de-sac on a quiet street in Annandale, Virginia, in a peaceful middle class neighborhood that served us well as our children grew up. Bonnie and I placed them in the local Catholic elementary school, and the nuns ran them hard in those early days. There was a small park nearby, so there was lots of room for the kids to roam, have fun, and remain safe. Our golden Labrador, Rascal, accompanied them everywhere, and she had the run of the neighborhood. One Saturday our neighbor, Mr. Goldstein, walked from house to house with a notice telling all the neighbors that the law compelled them to keep their dogs leashed or fenced up. Rascal accompanied him to every house and sat attentively at each stop as he discussed the issue with our neighbors.

When Susie, joined the family, she fit right in without any difficulty, at least when her brother, David, wasn't tormenting her. One day a couple of years after she arrived, a neighborhood kid sat with the two of them on the curbside, and David mentioned that Susie was adopted. "No, she's not!" the boy exclaimed. "Yes, she is," said David, "and what's more, she's Chinese!' "She can't be," the boy retorted. "She looks just like you!"

I always said that Susie never gave me a lick of trouble but that all my boys turned sub-human at age fifteen, only to re-emerge as real people at about age twenty two. That was especially true with David, who at an early age discovered that he could easily out-run me and that to avoid corporal punishment, all he had to do was to zig and zag and finally, I would give up.

That worked most of the time, even if I suddenly burst into his room to complain about his school work. In the summer, he'd leave his window ajar, and if I came in, he'd scramble out the window onto the porch alcove and drop himself down the gutter to the ground and get away. But one winter evening two inches of snow covered the ground—and the porch alcove. I was especially angry with him for something (he was always into some grief), so I opened the door suddenly. He was expecting me. His window was open, and he leapt out expecting to scramble down from the alcove as he always had before. But this time the snow greased his exit, and he flew out the window across the alcove and into midair, landing in the snow—one story below. I screamed for I thought I'd killed him, and I ran downstairs and outside, hollering, "David, David, are you ok?"

Fortunately, he landed flat on the snow-caked ground and simply had his breath knocked out. When I helped him up and could see that he was fine, well then, I really wanted to clobber him. But it was more bark than bite. Now that the years have passed, David has a son and daughter of his own. And the Good Lord indeed has a sense of humor, for after all the harassment David gave his mother and me, his kids, Barklie and Allie, are giving it right back to him. And it sure is fun to watch.

Shep, my oldest, was easier. When he and I had issues, he'd pack his knapsack, take lots of candy bars and peanut butter and go down the block to the woods beyond the cul-de-sac to run away. That usually lasted at least an hour.

And when our teenaged middle son, Richard (bless his soul!) was mad at me, he developed a habit of punching holes in the wall board in our unfinished basement. A ping pong table, weights, and some crude exercise machines were down there, so that area was his refuge. By the time he went away to college, there were holes every six to eight inches in the wall just above the hand rail all the way downstairs to the basement.

Each of my boys would occasionally be a pain in the neck (or other parts of the anatomy), but none of them ever caused us any significant problems. They drank infrequently, but that never really got out of hand. And I can thank God and the nuns at St. Michael's Elementary School that drugs were never an issue in our house. Once, while Rich and David were still in school, another kid was caught with some marijuana. When he was confronted and asked where he'd gotten it, he pointed out my boys. The nuns swooped down on both of them like a pack of wolves and they threatened my guys with expulsion. Despite our repeated inquiries, the school refused to tell us who the accuser had been. The boys were tried, convicted, and suspended from school for a couple of days without any evidence save the other boy's statement.

As it turned out, the kid had gotten the stuff from his brother, and rather than turn him in, he fingered my boys, who were appalled that their denials were not believed. Bonnie took each of them to a doctor and a psychologist, and it was determined that not only had they never distributed the stuff but they had never used it either. Eventually, the truth came out. The nuns never apologized, and I didn't find out who the boy was who'd raised the allegations until years later. But the lesson was taught to my sons in capital letters. Even though some of their friends later became pot-heads and in one instance, brain-fried on LSD, drugs (other than chewing tobacco) never became a habit with any of my boys. In fact, my oldest son, Shep (Robert III), after earning both BA and MBA degrees, is now a full time DEA agent and an evangelist on how drugs can destroy lives and families.

All in all, Annandale, Virginia, was a terrific place for my kids to grow up. While my life was anything but normal, Bonnie was a wonderful mother, and they grew up as regular American kids with football and soccer games, good friends, and decent schools. They never caused us any serious difficulties that other parents have to contend with, and my only regret is that I didn't spend the time with them that a non-political father might have done.

We didn't have a lot of money, but we lived comfortably on my salary. Once, in the early '80s, the *Wall Street Journal* did an article depicting us as a stereotypical Congressional family with the wife at home with the kids. It noted that we had an old station wagon with a rusted out floor board in the back seat. Bonnie placed a cookie tin over the hole in the floor so the kids wouldn't put their feet through it. The article ran over the country, and when I went home to New Orleans and gave a speech to some constituents at Texaco, Fred Palmer, Texaco's government relations person, thanked me for my speech and said, "Bob, we saw the article, and we wanted to do something nice for you. We thought about buying you a new car but we couldn't afford that, so we got you a new cookie tin!"

These days, the Rules of the House would have prevented me from accepting the cookie tin for fear that as a member of Congress, I might trade my vote for such a gratuity! Give me a break! Clearly, members could then and can now be corruptly influenced by people seeking special favors, but in the name of reform, the Rules have become mindlessly restrictive. Today, they are so restrictive that members have become isolated from their constituents. The constitutionally empowered right to petition one's representative is unnecessarily impaired.

But when I was in Congress, it was not unusual for folks from back home to come to DC and take Bonnie and me out to dinner. One time, some friends took us to the Rive Gauche, a very expensive French restaurant in DC. The waiter was the type-casted snooty French waiter who looked down his nose at me as I struggled to understand the French menu. He proceeded to explain the "specials of the night," and included a listing of *poisson,* or fish. "Monsieur, we have ze rockfish, ze sea bass, ze flounder, and ze fish from Fraunce." I was curious and asked, "What's the difference between the American fish and the fish from France?" He sneered and replied, "About $35.00."

Meanwhile, life progressed in the Congress. Midway into my second term in 1979, Dave Treen vacated his seat on the Merchant Marine Committee to make a second run for Governor of Louisiana. His ambition and drive were just amazing. He had run unsuccessfully three times for Congress and once for Governor, and now in his fourth term in Congress, he was running for Governor once again. Edwin Edwards was term limited and was prevented from serving a consecutive third term, so Dave entered the heavily contested race for the open seat.

In his absence, I made a case to Bob Michel, who had succeeded John Rhodes as Minority Leader, that since the seat on the Merchant Marine Committee had been held by my friend and colleague from Louisiana, and because the issues were of so much importance to the Port of New Orleans, I should be assigned to the committee. Bob agreed, but with one condition: that I agree to serve on the Ethics Committee. Most people in their right mind had no desire to serve on the committee to judge their own colleagues, and I was no exception. But Bob was insistent, so I took the assignment, adding it to Merchant Marine and, of course, Public Works, on which I remained.

The Merchant Marine Committee was one of the most interesting assignments I was to have in my early years in Congress, even though it was very short lived. The chairman of the committee, Jack Murphy (D-NY), West Point graduate and decorated Korean War veteran, had been a roommate at West Point with Nicaraguan strongman Anastasio Samoza Garcia. Jack was a great guy with a tough no-nonsense approach to his duties on the committee. Unfortunately, he was later charged, convicted, and sentenced to serve eighteen months in prison on a bribery charge. But I never saw that side of him, and frankly, I thought he ran the committee fairly and with all of the dignity required of a committee chairman. He studied and understood the issues within his jurisdiction; he could articulate his positions clearly and with authority; and he was comfortable allowing challenge from any quarter without resorting to personal ad hominem or unfair tactics.

The Offshore Energy Act of 1978 was the principal issue on the table within the committee, and I was fairly treated by the chairman as I tried to shape the issues from the perspective of a member from an energy producing state, despite my minority status in Congress. Eventually, the issue was taken from the Merchant Marine Committee and placed in an "Energy Task Force," but that didn't work out well. Congressional price controls were levied and led to a distinction between "old oil" and "new oil" over my strong opposition. As I had predicted, it later proved to be not only a total failure, but since oil is as fungible as cash, it became fertile opportunity for scam artists who bought the cheaper "old oil" and sold it on the market as if it were the more expensive "new oil."

As I've noted, the Ethics Committee, officially titled, "Standards of Official Conduct Committee," was one that few members wanted since it meant sitting in judgment on your fellow colleagues for infractions, both large and small. But some members like Floyd Spence (R-SC) served on the committee for many years, and I guess that was a good thing, but I never fully understood it. I didn't want the assignment, but Bob Michel had made it clear that if I wanted to keep the other assignments, this was the deal.

My experience as a criminal prosecutor was useful background for service on the Ethics Committee, and I suppose it was one reason why I was drafted. Once ensconced, I found myself surrounded by senior members like Chairman Charlie Bennett (D-FL), Jack Murtha, (D-PA) and Morgan Murphy, (D-IL). Sometime later, Jack Murtha would vacate his post for an uncharged involvement in the "AbScam" scandal that erupted during the term. Jack survived the allegations unscathed, and he enjoyed a successful career in Congress for many years afterward. He was replaced on the committee by Speaker O'Neill with "Good Time Charlie" Wilson (D-TX), a bigger than life and truly unique character. Charlie became one of the more famous of all the people I served with, but more on that later.

Morgan Murphy (D-IL) also had to leave the committee after being officially reprimanded for casting votes in Congress at the very same moment that he gave a speech in Chicago. The Rules required that a member of the House cast his/her votes in person, and Murphy found it impossible to explain how he could be in two places seven hundred miles apart at the same time; hence the reprimand. Murphy chose not to run for reelection at the conclusion of that term.

Lou Stokes (D-OH) and Wyche Fowler (D-GA) were also on the committee. Lou was subsequently named chairman of the Ethics Committee and, still later, the House Intelligence Committee. Wyche was later elected to a single term in the U.S. Senate.

On the Republican side, there were future luminaries as well. Long before he became Vice President under George W. Bush (43), freshman Dick Cheney (WY) was appointed to the committee, as were new members, Bill Thomas (CA) and Jim Sensenbrenner (WI). Once we took over as majority of the House in 1995, Bill became chairman of the Committee on House Administration and later, the

Ways and Means Committee; and Jim assumed the chairmanship of the House Judiciary Committee.

From the beginning, we Republicans supported and encouraged Ethics Committee Chairman Charlie Bennett (D-FL) to set an aggressive tone and run the committee in an honest and straightforward fashion. Ongoing standing complaints had been lodged against a few members, including flamboyant Dan Flood of Pennsylvania, who wore a cape and sported a curly "Oil Can Harry" moustache. But in the midst of the ongoing routine investigations, "AbScam" hit the press and became the scandal *de jure* for months to come.

AbScam evolved as an FBI sting operation during which the Bureau video-taped various officials in a DC hotel room. FBI Agents covertly spread the word that some rich oil "sheiks" were available to do business with elected officials. Through intermediaries, they enticed several men, mostly members of Congress, into the room to meet an alleged sheik. In the course of the conversation, a request for legislation and an offer of cash for services was made. Several members fell for the charade and some took the cash, while others did not. Larry Pressler (R-SD) categorically rejected the offer and left. Jack Murtha (D-Pa) refused to take the cash, but engaged in conversation that led to further investigation and embarrassing video tapes that were later released, but no formal action was ever lodged against him.

Jack subsequently became chairman of the Defense Appropriations Subcommittee, arguably the most sought-after subcommittee in the House, and he was a key advisor to Speaker Nancy Pelosi until his untimely death in February 2010. Charlie Wilson had long since retired from Congress when he passed away two days after Jack died. Both men served with me on the Appropriations Committee for many years and were extremely effective members despite their notoriety. Notwithstanding our political differences, they became good friends and I truly enjoyed working with both of them.

Most of the other members involved in the AbScam Scandal were reprimanded or censured for their participation. But Ozzie Myers (D-PA) was actually expelled from Congress on the recommendation of our committee. Ozzie's defense that he took the money because "Everyone did it!" wasn't of great comfort to sitting members, so he was ousted. Former Florida state judge and Congressman Dick Kelly

(R-FL) was taped stuffing his pockets with cash and later prosecuted for his role. He defended himself by contending that he suspected that the "sheiks" were criminals and that he was participating in his own "sting" in order to catch the crooks. But he couldn't fully explain why he'd put all the money in his car glove compartment . . . except for some he'd taken out for personal incidentals. He was convicted and was forced to resign from Congress before he went to prison.

Dave Treen for Governor

While I was wrestling with the processes of the Ethics Committee and tending to business on my other Congressional Committees, Dave Treen ran and won a hard fought race for Governor of Louisiana. Because we were as close as we were, I felt responsible to do all in my power from DC to see to it that Dave's tenure was successful. That turned out to be difficult.

Dave's key advisors, Billy Nungesser and John Cade, were the same two people who had guided him through his bids for Congress, and both had been invaluable to my own political success. The problem was that the gregarious Billy and the thoughtful and quiet John could rarely agree on anything, and the governor, who usually heard them both out before deciding which action to take, always had difficulty deciding between them.

Honest to the extreme, Dave Treen was one of the finest, most decent people ever to run for public office. He was kind, generous, and principled. Methodical, brilliant, but often frustratingly dilatory, he always thought about issues from every vantage point. Sometimes he would give so much thought to an issue that he'd come to a conclusion that was out of step with his district, the state, or his own political interests. No one who knew him could ever question his sincerity nor, for that matter, his integrity. But his thought processes were so thorough that he sometimes opened himself up to ridicule. He and Edwin Edwards faced off against each other for Governor of Louisiana more than once. Always master of the quip, Edwards once said of Dave, "Dave Treen is so slow, he takes an hour and a half to watch *60 Minutes*!"

It was true! I spent timeless hours speaking with people who wanted to work for or be of help to the new Governor. I spoke with hundreds of people, and I'd apply my best judgment and provide personal evaluations, both favorable and unfavorable, on job applicants to the Treen administration. They were candid appraisals of people that could advantage or harm the ostensibly reform-oriented Treen administration.

In the beginning, Treen's tenure was viewed as a breath of fresh air following two corrupt terms under Edwards, who had been formally charged with illicitly selling hospital licenses. He was tried twice and ultimately acquitted by a jury of his peers. (We know that they were a jury of his peers since when the trial was concluded, the hotel in which the jury was sequestered billed the government for $600 in stolen towels.)

I loved having Dave Treen in the Governor's Mansion. He was personally generous with his time and supportive of my own political efforts. But in reality, the sum of Dave's term was a disappointment for me and for many of his most ardent supporters. If anyone read my notes on applicants, they certainly didn't act on them. Loyal Treen supporters were ignored or insulted or both, and people hostile to Treen were often cultivated and rewarded. Appointments of the wrong people were not unusual.

Nungesser and Cade often couldn't agree on actions of importance to the state and key decisions languished. Phone calls weren't answered. In the end, the gubernatorial term of Dave Treen, a lovely, honest and decent person, lasted only four years. On election day in 1983, Edwin Edwards, who had conspired with his cronies to undermine the Treen administration throughout the length of Treen's term, was restored to the Governor's Mansion. He had been so sure of victory that shortly before Louisianans went to the polls, he declared, "The only way I can lose this election is if I'm caught in bed with either a dead girl or a live boy."

Despite the failure of Dave to win reelection, those years were good ones for me. His gubernatorial tenure overlapped the entry of Ronald Reagan to the Presidency of the United States. Former "B" actor and TV host of Borax's "Death Valley Days" and "General Electric Theater," Reagan had placed himself on the map as a serious politician as far back as 1964 when he delivered a brilliant and rousing speech to the Republican Convention on behalf of Barry Goldwater. Subsequently elected Governor of California, he unsuccessfully challenged Gerald Ford in 1976 for the Republican nomination to the Presidency, and in 1980, he launched a vigorous challenge for conservative support against George H.W. Bush (41).

As a candidate for Congress in 1976, I was elected a delegate to the convention in Kansas City and again in 1980 to the Detroit convention as a sitting Congressman. In each case, I was a relative newcomer to politics, so the last thing in the world I wanted was to be drawn into internecine battles between Reagan and Ford or Bush. Reagan easily carried my district in the primaries, and I was elected as a Reagan delegate in both instances. But when the conventions tied up in arcane rules disputes, my political career could have been nipped in the bud at either juncture. I survived them both.

President Ford took the nomination in 1976, and Reagan was a good soldier until Ford was defeated by Jimmy Carter in the general election. But in 1980, Reagan went "all in" and won the nomination. He toyed with putting former President Ford on the ticket as Vice President, but common sense prevailed and Bush was nominated as VP. Somehow, I managed to finesse the rules dispute and emerge unscathed sufficiently to stay on good terms with both men, and I became a strong supporter of the ticket.

Serving in Congress under President Jimmy Carter for three-and-a-half years and enduring what I thought to be his abysmal conduct of domestic and foreign policy, I had no reservation about doing what I could to bring about his defeat. When things went sour because of Carter's inability to lead the nation, he charged that the American people were guilty of "malaise." Much like Obama in more recent years, he possessed a wholesale inability to understand that the decline of country was heavily correlated to his inadequate leadership.

His energy policies led to shortages of supplies of fossil fuels and long lines at the gas pump. Energy prices skyrocketed, so he urged Americans to turn down their thermostats and wear sweaters in the winter. His successful victory over President Ford in 1976 had been due in large part to his coinage of the term "misery index" that added the rate of inflation to the level of unemployment. But by his own measurement, the economy declined precipitously during his term. The "misery index" jumped from an aggregated 13.6 in 1976 to an astounding 20.5 in 1980.

Inflation:	**Unemployment:**	
1976	**5.8%**	**7.6%**
1977	**6.5%**	**6.9%**
1978	**7.7%**	**6.0%**
1979	**11.3%**	**5.8%**
1980	**13.5%**	**7.0%**

(Source: Statistical Abstract of the United States)

Carter's foreign policy was even worse. His appeasement led to a Soviet invasion of Afghanistan, Communist gains in Latin America, and the humiliation of America by Iran's capture and imprisonment of U.S. Embassy personnel for 444 days. In 1980, the people voted for a different approach and opted for Reagan. Moreover in 2016, the belligerence and hegemony of Russia, China, Iran, and North Korea following eight years of Obama were proof positive that history does repeat itself.

Reagan in 1980

Reagan easily defeated Carter, and on the bitterly cold Inauguration Day in January, he was sworn to the Presidency, the clouds parted, the sun shone through, and the hostages were released from captivity by Iran.

But Reagan wasn't isolated in his victory. His coattails brought a lot of Republicans to Washington with him at the same time. Twelve Republicans were added to the Senate to put the majority in Republican control for the first time in since 1954. And while the R's remained in the minority in the House under Speaker O'Neill, we gained thirty five seats, thereby significantly increasing our proportion of R to D seats on the various committees; so much so that my own future in Congress took a major turn for the better.

On election evening in November 1980, Bonnie and I were invited by Tommy Boggs, son of the late Hale and by then Congresswoman Lindy Boggs (D-LA), to watch the election returns at his home. In 1972, Hale had risen from House Majority Whip to Majority Leader and was likely to become Speaker when on a campaign trip in Alaska, the plane that he shared with Freshman Congressman Nick Begich disappeared and was never found. His wife, Lindy, who had virtually run Hale's office for several years, was easily elected to fill his New Orleans Congressional seat. Lindy was a masterfully gracious politician in her own right, and by the time I was first elected, she had established a solid seat on the Appropriations Committee.

Her son, Tommy, once ran unsuccessfully for Congress from his home in Maryland but he was defeated, so he set about creating and growing one of the most successful law and lobby shops in the District of Columbia and beyond. A heavy hitter in the Democratic Party, he raised funds and supported candidates around the nation. But he was pragmatic enough to understand that his party wasn't the sole repository of intelligence in Washington, and both he and his firm occasionally supported Republicans, especially if the doors were open to pleas on behalf of their clients.

When I came to Washington, I knew that I was not sent there solely as a Republican. I was a conservative, but so were thousands of

Democrats in my district who had voted for me. Beyond that, I also knew that if I didn't work for *all* the people of my district to as great a degree as possible, I was not likely to be reelected. Even if I had been, I would have been very uncomfortable with myself. I knew that my votes would not be to the liking of all my constituents, and there was no way that I could be all things to all people. I was philosophically conservative and with few exceptions, that's the way I voted. I generally earned an 80 percent to 85 percent rating on the conservative polls, and zero to 20 percent rating by the more left wing assessments.

But I also felt that my office should be open to everyone from Louisiana regardless of their party affiliation or whether they had supported me or my opponents. Hence, my staff was instructed to fit in anyone from my district who wanted to see me during regular office hours whether in DC or back home on weekends or longer breaks. I made it a point to go around to as many gatherings, council meetings, Elk's and Rotary gatherings, farmers' pig roasts, and inner-city town meetings as my schedule would allow. If I was in the neighborhood and there was a meeting, I would show up, invited or not.

If a businessman or labor union had a request that I deemed legitimate, I supported it, at least if I thought it was in the best interest of my constituents. If there was competition between two businesses or entities of any sort within the state of Louisiana, I generally demurred, saying that if they were pitted against any group outside the state, I would likely support them. But I wasn't going to take sides between constituents, even if one had supported me and the other had not. I had seen other elected officials get themselves in trouble by supporting their friends in competition with other competent and even superior bids, and I didn't like it. I believed then as I do now, that in a fair and free market, competition is the best way to sort out the best person or business to prevail.

When government officials get involved to slant the market to their own ends, the system breaks down. I'm vehemently opposed to allowing corporations or banks to become "too big to fail," and I find the "corporate fascism" and "crony capitalism" of today... the practice of government bail-out and/or ownership of targeted companies... to be positively frightening. Government has little capacity for proper judgment to choose winners and losers between private sector competitors and when it tries to do so, it usually skews the market unfairly...or worse. That doesn't mean that it doesn't make the attempt. It does in almost every facet of our economy, sometimes with disastrous results. Even if intentions are to benefit large numbers of Americans, political judgment superseding economic reality usually ends up badly.

For example, in the name of making housing available to the poor under the Community Reinvestment Act (CRA) of 1977 as revised in 1995, Congress demanded that banks make loans to people who couldn't possibly have repaid them, thereby sowing the seeds for the great financial collapse of 2007-2009. Learning nothing from history, the Obama administration renewed the very same policies. But then that administration was never shy about picking winners and losers. Unfortunately, far too many they picked were losers! Solyndra was exhibit number one, but there were hundreds of examples.

So there we were on election night, 1980, in Democratic lobbyist Tommy Bogg's house, anticipating a normal election in which even if Reagan were to beat Carter, the conditions of Democratic domination of Congress would continue as they had for most of the preceding thirty six years. We were surrounded by Democrats, including my good friend and lobbist Duffy Wall, with few if any other Republicans around. As the returns started flowing in, the Democrats grew quietly subdued, and despite my prodigious consumption of Tommy Boggs's liquor, I started to realize that something profound was happening. Reagan was not only winning; he was thrashing Carter. By the time the polls closed in the eastern third of the nation, the TV networks began predicting a Reagan landslide, and that news discouraged Democratic voters on the west coast who had not yet voted from going to the polls at all. In consequence, Congress changed appreciably as Republicans voters turned out and Democrats stayed home.

The news hit the crowd in the Boggs home like a birthday party in a mortuary, so Bonnie and I offered our thanks and she drove us home whereupon we immediately turned on our television. Maybe it was the booze, but I recall us laughing and crying, tears streaming down our faces as we jumped up and down in our living room. I had run for office to help change the face of traditional liberal politics in America, and the American people were awakening to make that change possible. Carter's appeasement of Communist gains around the world;

his misbegotten coddling of criminals by appointing liberal judges in courts engendering increased violence and hardcore crime; his foolish manipulation of energy markets resulting in long lines at the gas stations; and his blaming of rising unemployment and runaway inflation on the "malaise" of the American people—all these were about to change for the better under a new and very underestimated President whose opponents derided him as a dumb "B" grade actor.

When the dust settled the next day, Republicans had captured a new majority in the Senate and historically improved the House of Representatives.

I returned to business in the House, but as we were still in the minority, I didn't expect my own situation to change to any degree. I was fully content with my committee assignments except for service on the Ethics Committee. Even though I hadn't enjoyed it, we had worked extremely hard to make the committee work and bring the AbScam malefactors to task. So I felt that I had earned my ticket off the committee. Otherwise, I enjoyed my tenure on both Merchant Marine and Public Works, where with the help of my legislative aide, Paul Cambon, I had taken an active interest in port and waterways issues on the Water Resources Subcommittee.

The Merchant Marine Committee was rumored to have outlived its usefulness, but since it allowed me to work closely with the maritime industry and the Seafarers International Union (SIU) headed in New Orleans by my friends, Lindsay Williams and Gerry Brown, I had no desire to see it disappear. I had even taken my two oldest boys, Shep and Rich, to visit the Seafarers' getaway in Piney Point, Maryland. It was unfortunately a cold winter day when we visited so we didn't get much opportunity to take advantage of the resort by way of fishing or sailing, but we appreciated the hospitality and natural beauty of the area.

In one of the few times when he did listen to me, Governor Treen acceded to my request and reappointed Lindsay Williams to the Louisiana Boxing Commission. That solidified my tenure in Congress since without the SIU, the other unions were never able to unify the AFL/CIO against me.

So when Reagan won, I was happy just to have been on the winning team and I didn't give much thought to changing my committee assignments. My happiness intensified when the skies parted and the sun shown on Governor Reagan as he was sworn in to become President Reagan. Hours later, we heard the news that Iran had released our 444 U.S. Embassy hostages and it truly was a perfect day.

The Reagan victory changed the proportion of seats in the House from Democrat to Republican, so each committee had to be readjusted in favor of the Republicans. I had already begun to appreciate that my seniority on committees was to be substantially advanced. But a few days later, my friend, colleague, and adjoining neighbor from the southwest District of Mississippi, Trent Lott, caught me in the Republican Cloakroom and advised me that he was running for "Whip" in the Republican Conference. I quickly signed on to support him.

Trent won the race by a single vote over Ed Madigan of Illinois. Ed was a nice guy and had a lot of friends among the older members, but the younger among us teamed up and asserted our presence as a new force in the "Reagan Era." The passivity of a compliant Republican minority was waning, and Young Turks like Newt Gingrich and Bob Walker were given opportunities to be heard that they might not have enjoyed in earlier times. Jack Kemp, whose "supply side" philosophy formed the genesis for "Reaganomics" was readily embraced by the younger members, and he provided the vitality of new ideas for which the country seemed so hungry.

Trent provided teamwork and organization needed to back up Minority Leader Bob Michel. I was part of the team and served as Trent's Regional Whip over the growing southeastern section of the country. Together, we projected a significant alternative to the Democratic majority led by the colorful Speaker, Tip O'Neill. Until Dave Treen and a few others were elected in the early '70s, Republicans were scarce as hen's teeth in the South. But that had begun to change in the mid-'70s and '80s. Democrats leaned more and more to the left with increasingly liberal policies affecting both war and peace, and Republicans made inroads among the generally conservative center of the country, especially in the South. The population began shifting southward as well, and Republicans began to gain strength in areas with growing demographics, while losing strength in the shrinking North East, North Central, and in due time, the far Western regions of the country.

As he prepared for his post as Minority Whip, Trent suggested to me that I take one of the five seats soon to be open on the Appropriations Committee. Frankly, I hadn't paid much attention to committees other than my own, and I was comfortable where I was. I liked the issues I was dealing with and was content to accept the increase in seniority in those committees. In fact, I wasn't even sure what the Appropriations committee did, and I told him so and said I wasn't interested.

Fortunately, Trent didn't take "no" for an answer. He told me to go back and confer with my staff and check out the role of the committee. A couple of days later, after conferring with Paul Cambon and Allen Martin, my relatively new "AA" (Administrative Assistant, now called "Chief of Staff"), I wisely changed my mind.

Appropriations Committee

Since my colleague, Democrat Lindy Boggs was already on Appropriations, it may have looked like overkill to have two people from New Orleans on the same committee. But with Trent's help and that of Henson Moore, who had gotten appointed to the Republican Steering Committee, the intra-party committee in charge of slotting members to committee assignments, I won a seat on Appropriations and voluntarily gave up my slots on Merchant Marine, Public Works, and Ethics. In fact, I eagerly gave up the Ethics post. New Orleans and Louisiana were big winners in the move.

With no money or recent family political lineage, it was clear that my first election to Congress had beaten the odds. But I was willing to throw all my waking hours into both the campaign and my service in Congress, first because of my commitment and belief that the country was deserving of change, and secondly because I believed I was the very best person to provide that change. I'd read *Atlas Shrugged* by Ayn Rand, and I was inspired to apply all my energies to prevent a slide by the United States into socialism. Throughout the late '60s and early '70s, I'd witnessed the erosion of common sense by politicians, mostly Democrats but with the cooperation of many Republicans as well. The American belief in the power of the individual to manage life on his own to as great a degree as possible was waning, and too many politicians seemed committed to approaching all the problems of the world with government solutions and additional layers of bureaucracy. Others simply believed that in any confrontation, the best way to overcome a problem was through capitulation or procrastination.

Whether the issue at hand was the withdrawal of troops from Vietnam; the capitulation to unions by major corporations (planting the seeds of collapse of major manufacturing companies like General Motors years later); the withdrawal of support for police in the inner cities leading to an overly lenient judiciary and rampant crime sprees; or a burgeoning Federal Government displacing the roles of the states in taxation and regulation of education, energy, commerce, and every other function of human interaction; all these and so many more led me to believe that someone had to assert the need for a smaller, less intrusive government. Nixon's abuses in "Watergate" had cooled my idealistic jets, but when the opportunity arose to run for Congress, they were reheated to peak intensity.

I really believed then and still believe the admonition that "Government is best when it governs least!" No matter who said it first, Thomas Paine, Thomas Jefferson, or Henry David Thoreau, it makes sense to me. The frequent instances of corruption arising from south Louisiana did little to dissuade me from the belief that the government closest to the people is the most responsive to their needs. And when I was appointed to the Appropriations Committee, I began to realize an opportunity to employ those beliefs.

But I wasn't without conflicting motivation. I was not an anarchist or even a libertarian. While I believed that government should NOT do those things that the states or the people could do for themselves, I also believed strongly that government should do what the people could NOT do for themselves. Therein lay the seeds of conflict.

Clearly, the making of war and the need for a strong national defense; the administration of a safe environment in which to live and prosper; and the building of highways, airports, and other infrastructure, police protection, etc., are all legitimate functions of government. But I also believed strongly in the concept that that which the government does, it should do honestly, efficiently, and frugally. In more recent years, this thought seems to have been forgotten by Republicans and Democrats alike.

As I assumed my role as member of the minority on the Appropriations Committee, all these feelings were uppermost in my mind. Having served as an enlisted man in the Navy, I was very concerned for the welfare and encouragement of the American Serviceman. As a former criminal prosecutor, I was a "law and order" guy who wanted tough but sensible penalties for criminal offenders, particularly for those who preyed on innocent victims. Victimless crimes were not high on my agenda, but equal application of the law for all our citizens was very important. I'd never heard of nor imagined the concept of "hate" crimes that sought out specific classes of "victims" that would be more protected than the populace at large. I had always been taught in law school that motivation was not at issue . . . only intent. Intent to batter, rob, rape, or to murder—this was all important. Who one battered, robbed, raped, or killed, or why one did it was not at issue unless it was considered for the purposes of determining sentencing.

Today, we have "hate" crimes proliferating on the books to empower select victims over others. It's a fool's errand. I'm reminded of the words of George Orwell from *Animal Farm* in which he asserts, "Some pigs are more equal than others." I believe we should abandon "hate crimes" altogether. Common sense demands that we return to strict punishment for crimes against all innocent people without favoring classes of victims.

My years on the Public Works Committee embedded in me a belief in the need for adequate infrastructure. Many states simply don't have the resources to provide for an interstate highway system, accessible waterways for waterborne commerce, or a national air transit system. National rather than local planning is essential to maintain safe access to personal and commercial traffic and to prevent natural disasters from inflicting undue harm on large populations. But invariably, spending on infrastructure projects inspires opposition from parts of the country that do not receive tangible benefit from them and the environmental community (now categorized as "Greens") raises perpetual hell about virtually every project on the books. With the increase in litigation and the growth of the "Trial Bar," lawsuits are filed almost every time a project is conceived, thereby adding immeasurably to the cost of even the most worthy projects. Add in the ubiquitous bone of the "Davis-Bacon Act" of 1931 thrown to appease construction unions requiring virtually every federal project in the country to pay top union wages, and one realizes why the federal government is so inefficient and costly in its development of needed infrastructure.

As a result, Democratic and Republican administrations alike have allotted insufficient funds for infrastructure, and we now find ourselves with failing bridges and navigation structures and clogged highways and airports. The problem intensifies with age, and apart from crowing with empty "shovel ready" rhetoric in its trillion dollar "Stimulus" bill, the Obama administration did little to meet the structural needs of the country. In 2009, the Democratic chairman of the House Public Works and Infrastructure Committee, Jim Oberstar, was eager and ready to rebuild our infrastructure, but Obama placed him on hold for the first two years of the administration and time ran out on him. He was defeated in the 2010 election and he died in 2014. The size of Obama's government grew astronomically, yet relatively few private sector jobs of significance were created and infrastructure is still in gross disrepair. All this is despite that in the eight years of the Obama administration, he nearly doubled the already outrageous $10.625 trillion dollar debt left by the George W. Bush (43) administration to a new total of $19.95 trillion. On his watch, national unemployment topped out at 10 percent, not counting all the people who just gave up and stopped looking for work. When he left office, the official unemployment rate was 4.9 percent, but if those people were counted as well, the unemployment number was really much higher.

But I digress. In January, 1981, I assumed my duties as an Appropriator with these simple motivations. I became the "The Man in the Arena" as described by President Teddy Roosevelt:

> It is not the critic who counts: not the man who points out how the strong man stumbles or where the doer of deeds could have done better. The credit belongs to the man who is actually in the arena, whose face is marred by dust and sweat and blood, who strives valiantly, who errs and comes up short again and again, because there is no effort without error or shortcoming, but who knows the great enthusiasms, the great devotions, who spends himself for a worthy cause; who, at the best, knows, in the end, the triumph of high achievement, and who, at the worst, if he fails, at least he fails while daring greatly, so that his place shall never be with those cold and timid souls who knew neither victory nor defeat.
>
> ("Citizenship in a Republic," Speech at the Sorbonne, Paris, April 23, 1910.)

It was slow going at first. Silvio Conte of Massachusetts was our ranking Republican on Appropriations, meaning that he was the senior Republican and, as such, was in charge of subcommittee assignments. He was well known as a blustery liberal Republican, and he had served in Congress for an eternity. Some twenty-plus years older than me, I gave him a wide birth until I got to know him better. Sil initially assigned me to the Health and Education Subcommittee governing issues that were not close to my heart, but it was his own favorite assignment. I'd almost flunked high school biology and have always been uncomfortable with issues in the health arena. As much as I believed that American education was failing students across the nation in inadequate public schools, I'd seen how hostile the system was to competition through education vouchers, and I just didn't see much hope for improvement there in years to come. So I wasn't very keen on those issues either.

Nevertheless, I pitched in and engrossed myself in committee activities, and I guess I must have impressed Silvio, for we gradually became good friends, notwithstanding our regional and philosophical differences. We stayed that way until his death in the early '90s. Silvio was an incredible human being. He had enormous energy and a zest for life like few people I've ever met. He was a lousy golfer who loved to play golf; a fisherman who had no shame claiming someone else's trophy fish; and a hunter who once shot a guide dog. He once campaigned with me in New Orleans when he knew he was dying of cancer, but he wouldn't give in to it. In a single day, he fished, played a round of golf, and attended a campaign party for me in the French Quarter. I'll never forget his opening remarks using the very same joke that Dave Treen had told in almost every speech I'd heard him give for the preceding fifteen years. Dave was in the audience along with all the people who had heard Dave tell that same joke hundreds of times before. The audience roared, and Silvio was delighted.

The only time that Silvio and I crossed swords was once in the mid '80s when I'd been particularly frustrated with losing a conservative vote on the floor, and I stood up in the Republican Conference and blasted our "moderate" Republicans for not adhering to party line. Silvio followed me out of the room afterwards and told me, "You broke my heart!" I'd learned a great lesson about the "big tent" that would carry me far later on. I apologized to him and always tried to avoid repeating recriminations of people on my side with whom we depended to provide our strength in numbers. It takes a diverse crowd to make up a majority.

I think of Silvio frequently as I have watched Republicans self-immolate from time to time since my departure from Congress. "Heritage Action" and "Club for Growth" have become enforcers of ideological purity, and their members give that kind of speech all the time. Talk-radio eggs them on incessantly. That's OK for very conservative districts. But for primaries in moderate Republican districts, that group often weighs in for truly conservative candidates against more viable but moderate incumbents and candidates in open seats. Frequently, the committed conservative will beat the more moderate or even liberal Republican in the primary under the banner, "No more RINO's (Republican in Name Only)!" Then the conservative is deemed out of step in his district and gets beaten by the Democrat in the general election. Now, maybe I'm missing something, but wouldn't it be better to have a person in office that votes Republican some of the time, rather than a Democrat who *never* votes with the Republican?

Frankly, I'm in full agreement with the late William F. Buckley who said, "The wisest choice would be the one who would win. No sense running Mona Lisa in a beauty contest. I'd be for the most right, viable candidate who could win." Before 2010, we'd lost almost all our potential Republican seats in the northeast when we put up less qualified but more conservative candidates. Fortunately, 2010 was a better year, and Republicans came back to win several of those seats.

How are conservative causes advanced by Democrats, most of whom lean harder to the left than ever before? Purity is no substitute for majority. Silvio never served in the majority, but I know that he would agree with me when I say that given the choice between majority and minority, a majority is better. The majority sets the agenda and calls the shots. It runs the Congress, while the minority gives noble speeches. Conservative speeches are great! As a conservative myself, I usually agree with most if not all they espouse. But it takes numbers to maintain a majority, and not all of those numbers will be in ideological lockstep. Conservative groups may console themselves by being "right," but what good is that if they have no control over the agenda? It's virtually impossible to govern from a "small tent."

Silvio also put me on the Appropriations Foreign Operations Subcommittee. Being an unapologetic anti-Communist, I was deeply interested in international issues. I soon learned that the subcommittee really only dealt with funding issues in foreign policy, leaving large policy issues to the Foreign Relations Committee. But since that committee could rarely if ever pass a bill through the Congress, I found that for all practical purposes, our subcommittee provided primary influence on foreign policy. Foreign aid, a bugaboo in the conservative community, was a prime issue of contention, but through foreign aid we exert control over attitudes of the rest of the world toward the United States. The trick was to see the aid spent judiciously with U.S. interests at heart, rather than willy-nilly dispensing taxpayer funds without regard to the needs, desires, and security of the American people.

The perception around the country has always been that our dollars in foreign aid constitute about 30 percent to 40 percent of the U.S. Budget. In fact, it rarely exceeds 1 percent of the budget. But it was never popular in conservative commentary, and being on that subcommittee wasn't a plus for my folks back home. It generated zero campaign support, and it provided some interesting moments in my district town meetings when "John Birchers" like my nemesis and always vocal constituent, Leo Champagne, would stand up and attack me as one of the spendthrifts in Washington. I took it in stride, but just being on the subcommittee usually gave me very bad marks on the Birch scorecard that he handed out to my constituents before every town meeting.

One of the greatest benefits from my service on the subcommittee came from my friendship with the vociferous, indomitable, and larger-than-life Congressman, Jack Kemp. I only knew Jack as a fellow Congressman, and I had little recollection of his athletic career other than the fact that he had been a successful quarterback in the NFL. It was only later that I learned about his thirteen years in the National, Canadian, and American Football Leagues during which he was captain of both the San Diego Chargers and the Buffalo Bills. He set many career passing records and was named the AFL's Most Valuable Player in 1965 following two championships. He appeared in the AFL's All-Star game seven times. He co-founded the AFL Players Association and served as its president five times.

Be they rich, poor, black, white, Hispanic, or Asian, Jack had friends everywhere. He was keenly interested in everything, most especially the economy, the gold standard, the application of U.S. foreign aid to underdeveloped nations, and race relations in the United States. He was loved by African American football players like Roosevelt Greer and Ernie Ladd with whom he'd played football and that always inspired him to pitch for broader outreach by the Republican Party to the minority community. Since I and others like Ed Bethune of Arkansas and Mickey

Edwards of Oklahoma had sought and obtained sizable blocks of black votes in our districts, Jack urged us to push the RNC to support an increase in budgets for minority outreach within the Republican political machinery. Gradually, we made inroads that began paying dividends, only later to be largely abandoned by subsequent RNC leadership.

It was Jack's "supply side" rhetoric that inspired Ronald Reagan to win the Presidency in 1980, and I'm convinced to this day that as Reagan employed Jack's ideas to substantially cut taxes, the Carter recession gradually gave way to one of the greatest economic booms in our history. Time passed, and Jack attempted a run for the Presidency on his own in 1988, but it went nowhere against the sitting Vice President, George H.W. Bush. My own race for governor of Louisiana in 1987 kept me from committing too much time or resources to Jack's campaign, but since I openly supported him in his short-lived primary bid, I was never one of the chosen ones in the Bush White House.

But President Bush (41) wisely appointed Jack as Secretary of Housing and Urban Development, where he championed increased home ownership for the poor and under-privileged. In 1996, Jack ran second on the Presidential ticket with Senator Bob Dole, only to be trounced by the Clinton-Gore machine. He and I remained friends over the years, and I never ceased to be amazed at the spirit and vitality of this truly wonderful guy. In 2004, years after we were all out of office, I joined Jack, former Speaker Newt Gingrich, and former California Congressman, Attorney General, and unsuccessful candidate for Governor of California, Dan Lungren, at the same garden party. When Jack spotted the rest of us, he declared, "My, this is certainly a gathering of well-known has-beens!" Dan subsequently returned to California and won a Congressional seat that he held for several more years.

Shortly after Thanksgiving, 2008, Jack developed a pain in his hip. He went to the doctor for a checkup and discovered that he had bone cancer. He underwent treatment, but it didn't take, and in July 2009, Jack F. Kemp departed this earth. He was truly one of the very few people I've ever known who was "bigger than life itself." I'm proud to have known him, and I was so pleased that my friend and colleague, Vin Weber (R-MN) and I had a chance to meet and talk politics with him for an hour or so at his office a week before his death. Apart from his hairless head and a voice more raspy than normal, he looked hale and hearty. But a week later he was gone.

(As I actually wrote this section, his oldest son, Jeff, called me on the telephone to tell me of his foundation to promote marriage and families in the military. With the same raspy voice, Jeff sounded exactly like his dad. At first, I felt as if I were speaking to Jack, and I've have rarely been so shocked by such "coincidental' timing in my life.)

Assuming the Presidency in 1980, Ronald Reagan named Max Friedersdorf as his chief legislative counsel for the House. Max looked as if he had stepped from central casting into the role of a pilot in the German *Luftwaffe*. He was tall, handsome, gregarious, well liked, and effective. Our Whip Team under Trent Lott and Max worked with the Senate Republican majority and the White House to combat the intransigent Democrats and provide effective alternatives to the Democrat agenda for the first time in many years. We beefed up the nation's defenses in stark contrast to the Carter years; we cut taxes and we held down the demands by our opponents' for ever bigger government. Even so, government spending demanded by the Democratic House of Representatives rose faster than the rapidly increased revenues that flowed from a growing economy.

When Reagan began his term as President, the United States was in a recession, and in his first two years in office, unemployment and inflation were running out of control. Reagan brought in Paul Volcker to chair the Federal Reserve, and gradually Reagan's emphasis on "supply side tax cuts," restraint on the growth of government, and tight lending policies brought down inflation and generated prosperity for the next twenty years by re-igniting the engine of private investment. None of this was easy, but it worked and it stands in great contrast to the more recent actions of the Obama administration to go "Keynesian" by throwing money at our problems.

My favorite recollection of our Whip Team during the early days of the Reagan administration was when we were all invited over to meet with the President and his Cabinet in the Oval Office of the White House. We sat around the long cabinet table as the President presided at one end. He made some preliminary comments from note cards, and then he sat attentively as each of us (fifteen or so) offered our own input about how to enhance the country and/or prepare for coming battles in Congress. Discussions of that sort were always fairly predictable and repetitive, yet Reagan was constantly polite and gracious. But when this very special first meeting was over, the President invited us to rise and walk out to the Rose Garden where we would have our picture taken with him and Vice President Bush. I remember walking out along beside President Reagan and patting him on the shoulder. He was incredibly fit; it was as if I was slapping a brick wall!

Once outside, the President and Vice President stood in the front center of our group, and we gathered around them. Reagan turned to David O. Martin, a former Marine pilot from upstate New York, who was on his far right.

"You picked the very best spot!" he said.

"Why is that, Mr. President?'

"Oh, my old friend, Wallace Beery always picked that spot because he knew that when the picture hit the paper, his name would be the first one listed!'

We all chuckled in agreement. But he wasn't finished.

"But he had another trick. Back in those days, he could see the photographer's finger on the camera's shutter trigger. Just before the guy would push the trigger, Wallace would shout, shake his head, and smile at the camera as if nothing had happened. The cameraman would shoot the picture, and when it was developed, everyone else in the picture was looking in shock at Wallace while he was smiling calmly at the camera."

We roared! And it was the first of many little stories that Reagan would tell to endear himself to friend and foe alike.

Even Speaker Tip O'Neill liked Reagan, and they would speak regularly. That was in stark contrast to O'Neill's relations with Jimmy Carter. Not only did they not speak any more than was absolutely necessary, but at one point, O'Neill threw Carter's legislative assistant out of the House with orders not to come back!

But Ronald Reagan was liked by everyone—John Hinckley being a noted exception. Three months after Reagan entered the Oval Office, in an effort to impress actress Jodie Foster, Hinckley opened fire on the President and his entourage as they were leaving the Washington Hilton Hotel. Secret Service agent Timothy McCarthy, police officer Thomas Delahanty, and Reagan Press Secretary James Brady were all wounded; Brady, critically. The President himself was struck by a ricocheted bullet and spirited to George Washington University Hospital with what they initially thought was a superficial wound to his chest. In fact, Reagan was fortunate to have survived. He was operated on immediately upon his arrival, and before they put him under, he queried the doctors, "Please tell me you all are Republicans!" Regardless, they were great professionals and literally saved his life.

Reagan frequently beat the odds. Later, the National Air Traffic Controllers Association walked out on strike. The press predicted that Reagan wouldn't have any choice but to capitulate to their demands. But the President, himself a former president of the Screen Actors Guild, felt the unauthorized strike was a threat to commerce and the safety of the American people, so he calmly told them to get back to work. They disregarded his warnings, so he fired every last one of the striking union members. They tried every imaginable way to overturn his decision, both legally and politically, but to no avail. They stayed fired, new controllers were hired, and the issue was resolved.

He gradually convinced Congress to work with him as he built up our military defenses, and he refused to back down to the Soviets and our other adversaries. When the elite of Western Europe wrung their hands and worried with most Democrats in Congress about strengthening our missile presence there, he disregarded all the naysayers and raised the ante by installing updated Pershing missiles. "Peace through Strength" was not just a slogan, but a promise in the Reagan administration under Secretary of Defense Caspar Weinberger and Secretary of State George Schultz. When it came down to negotiating with the Soviets, "Trust but Verify" was Reagan's mantra. He ignored the hand wringers and pundits, and he did what he thought was right. Opponents painted him as a naive B-grade movie actor. Yet we know now that he read incessantly, that he wrote or edited most of his own speeches, and that his really big declarations were of his own making. The phrase "Mr. Gorbachev, tear down this Wall!" was struck by State Department types more than once, but Reagan both restored and delivered it in his speech at Brandenburg Gate in Berlin. Because of his efforts with the assistance of British Prime Minister Margaret Thatcher and Pope John Paul II, we will celebrate the thirtieth anniversary of the fall of the Berlin Wall in 2019.

One of the most tragic blights on his Presidency happened in 1983 in Beirut, Lebanon, where he had committed troops to help quell the fratricide that was inflaming that once beautiful country. Our efforts fell short. Two hundred forty one American Servicemen, mostly Marines, were killed together with fifty eight French soldiers when terrorists blew up the inadequately defended barracks. Some three weeks earlier, I had traveled to Beirut on a CODEL led by my friend and colleague, Jack Murtha (D-PA), and we had visited our troops and slept in those very same barracks. The attack was the deadliest single incident suffered by American troops in many years and the President's response was to immediately pull our troops out of Lebanon. In retrospect, the withdrawal emboldened the Islamic extremists responsible for the bombing. They learned that cowardly acts of terrorism offered promise to ultimately defeat America or as they call us, "The Great Satan." Over time, similar acts have occurred with greater frequency, peaking on September 11, 2001, when Islamic lunatics flew commercial airliners into the "Twin Towers" of the World Trade Center in New York and the Pentagon in Washington, D.C.

Reagan was determined to reverse the successes enjoyed by the Soviets and their Communist franchises during the Carter administration. When Maurice Bishop threatened to turn the small Caribbean Island of Grenada into a Soviet submarine base, Reagan sent our troops in to invade the island. Despite communications glitches prompting a soldier to use a pay phone to get orders from the Pentagon, Reagan cleaned out the nest of subversives and restored the island to liberty. I daresay that if President Reagan had remained alive and in office, the ignorant despot Hugo Chavez of Venezuela could not have imposed the catastrophe he later created in the name of socialism in Latin America.

Reagan's genius was manifest when he embraced Dr. Edward Teller's concept of Strategic Defense Initiative (SDI) and put the pieces in place to begin engineering and design for missile defense. The Soviets and the U.S. "Peace Now" crowd disparaged the program as "Star Wars," and they howled that it was a mindless escalation of weaponry that couldn't possibly work. They claimed that it could only result in devastating antagonism between the Super Powers. In point of fact, it created a technological boom for the U.S. and pushed the Soviets to the brink of bankruptcy. Their controlled economy was simply incapable of creating the wealth and infrastructure needed to keep up with the U.S. and its improved defenses.

If Reagan's opponents had had their way, we would have been stalemated indefinitely by Soviet domination of much of the globe. But because of Reagan's fortitude, the seventy-year-old Soviet Empire collapsed altogether. And to the chagrin of its detractors, "Star Wars" does work. Missile defense offers great hope that we may one day save Americans from nuclear conflagration, notwithstanding President Obama's decision to cancel planned deployment in Poland and the Czech Republic and his systematic curtailment of the program in the defense budget.

The Democrats were frustrated at every turn by the decency and common sense of Ronald Reagan. But they were determined to bring him down, and they almost did. At some point, he denied that he would ever trade with the Iranian leadership that had imprisoned our Embassy people during the Carter administration. His intention was to deny trade with and/or weaponry to Islamic dominated Iran. But the policy was apparently breeched in his zeal to support the Freedom Fighters or "Contras" against the Communist Sandinista government in Nicaragua.

Carter turned a blind eye to Communist intrusion in Central America, but for years, Reagan tried to topple the Sandinistas by supporting the anti-Communist Contras who operated out of El Salvador and Honduras. Tragically, some of the right-wing groups he supported went rogue and killed some Catholic priests and Nuns. That was enough for Tip O'Neill, whose "liberation theology'" Catholics in Massachusetts convinced him to close down the Contra operation. O'Neill and his roommate in DC, Eddie Boland, added a rider to withdraw funding in an Appropriations Bill and funding for the Contras ultimately dried up.

Not all Democrats supported Tip's failure to support the Contras. One of the most vigorous and eloquent supporters was eighty-plus year old Claude Pepper. "Senator" Pepper served in the Florida House of Representatives and after one defeat was elected to the U.S. Senate in 1936, where he served until 1951. In those early years, having once met with Joseph Stalin, he was a Communist sympathizer and gave a number of pro-Soviet speeches. He evidently experienced a philosophical metamorphosis, for when he was later elected to the U.S. House of Representatives in 1962 where he remained until his death in 1989, he became a staunch anti-Communist.

He never lost an ounce of mental vigor in all his years. He was short of stature and in his waning days was far less mobile than he had been in his youth. But although he often spoke as if he had marbles in his mouth, he could still deliver a stem-winder of a speech without notes at the drop of a hat. His speech in the House in 1983 on behalf of the Contras was better than any given on the subject by anyone on either side of the issue. The Congress was filled to capacity that evening and when his twenty minute oration was over, both sides of the aisle rose and gave him a standing ovation. Few members ever received such acclaim!

Likewise, when my Louisiana colleague, Gillis Long, a Democrat on the House Rules Committee chaired by Pepper passed away at far too young an age, Claude was on hand to eulogize him in Louisiana along with then Speaker Jim Wright, Majority Leader Tom Foley, Governor Edwin Edwards, and others. Claude led off with a wonderful ten minute speech sans notes but complete with a quote from the Bible. Jim Wright also gave a very fine eulogy that he read in part. When it was Edwards' turn to speak, the usually loquacious Edwards had written out his entire speech. That alone was fine, but coincidentally, he had included the very same Biblical quote that Claude had recited by heart. Edwin was clearly uncomfortable reading it again, but he had no choice, and it just highlighted the remarkable ability of the talented old man from Florida.

An inland waterways public-works project bisecting the state of Florida was begun and supported by Claude in the early days of his first Senate term. The project was begun with a groundbreaking on the site with Senator Pepper on hand. Fifty years later, when environmentalists won a law suit and caused the closure of the project, Claude Pepper was both present and in opposition to the project. He'd opened it under President Franklin Roosevelt and he closed it under President Jimmy Carter, and he took credit on both occasions.

One day, the old gentleman pulled me aside and told me that my forebear, Chancellor Robert Livingston, who had co-authored the Declaration of independence, sworn in our first President, George Washington, consummated the Louisiana Purchase, and contributed otherwise to the foundation of our nation, had been the subject of discussion between himself and President Roosevelt. He said he had a project back in the '40s that required Presidential approval. He tried for months to get an appointment with Roosevelt and it was only after pulling out all the stops that he was successful. He said that on the appointed day, he showed up in the Oval Office eager to tell the President about his project. Upon entering, Roosevelt greeted him with a hearty welcome and invited him in.

Before he could get a word out, Roosevelt asked him if he had ever heard about the exploits of Robert Livingston. "No, Mr. President, I don't think so." "Well, then, Claude, come over here!" Pepper said the President took him over to a corner of the room and showed him a picture of Livingston and gave him a twenty minute lecture on the exploits of Robert Livingston.

Then the President guided him by the arm to the door and showed him out. "Thanks for coming by, Claude," he said, "It's been great seeing you." So the visit was over and Claude told me he never was able to tell the President about his project.

President Reagan was committed to maintaining U.S. support for those who were willing to fight for their own freedom, so he encouraged his administration to look for alternatives to Speaker O'Neill's withdrawal of financial support for the Contras. Marine Colonel Ollie North was Reagan's point man at the National Security Council, and he took it upon himself to keep that support flowing. The covert operation worked well until it blew up in the press, and it surfaced that the U.S. had allegedly furnished arms to Iran in return for financial assistance from Iran to the Contras. The Democrats in Congress flew into frenzy, and Reagan's Attorney General, Ed Meese, named former Judge Lawrence Walsh as Special Prosecutor.

Few Special Prosecutors have ever been appointed that didn't exceed their authority, and Walsh was no exception. He lived like a king with offices and excessive staff and he did all he could to bring down the Reagan administration. He convicted Ollie North and National Security Advisor Admiral John Poindexter, but those convictions were later reversed. He indicted Defense Secretary Caspar Weinberger on two occasions, once just before the 1992 elections, but the indictments were suggestive of an attempt to politically influence the Presidential election and went nowhere. However, his excesses bore sufficient weight to help throw the election away from then President George H.W. Bush (41) to then Governor Bill Clinton. In short, he accomplished little more than embarrassment for Presidents Reagan and Bush (41), but at an incredible cost to the taxpayer. I was so upset with him that I put a bumper sticker on my car that read "Impeach Walsh!' My friend and colleague on the Appropriations Committee, Jim Walsh (R-NY), didn't appreciate that very much even though he was of no relation to the Special Prosecutor.

We should have picked up seats throughout the Reagan years, but by 1986, we Republicans had successively lost seats in the House in every election since 1980. We were raising more and more money each year, but we were getting little or nothing for our investment. When we looked carefully at our losses, a few of us decided that the National Republican Congressional Committee (NRCC) which had been responsible for electing House members had become a self-licking ice cream cone, a grab bag for specially connected people to fatten their wallets, but had done little to grow Republican presence in the House. The more we looked at it, the worse things appeared. So we decided to challenge the incumbent, Guy Vander Jagt (R-MI), for the chairmanship of the committee. Guy was well liked by all of us who had been elected in his tenure, myself included. But directly or indirectly, he was ultimately responsible with for the failure of the committee and lack of progress in building our team.

This wasn't an easy decision since Guy had virtually created the NRCC, and he had certainly assisted me in my election almost ten years earlier. But several of us thought it important that the challenge be made. Then Congressman (and later, Governor) Don Sundquist (R-TN) agreed to be the token candidate, and I became his campaign manager. Together, we started digging into the information we could find on the NRCC. We found a lot. Management personnel and select field workers had formed outside businesses to supply the NRCC with all its needs. We found companies providing the NRCC with paper, printing, mail order services, polling, and other needs vital to campaign organization, some of which were owned directly by inside people or others who mysteriously and repetitively won contracts with the NRCC over less favored competition. This was no small venture. Lots of money traded hands with little or no supervision. We developed voluminous information and evidence of questionable activities and much of it made its way to the press.

Younger members were convinced that a change was needed in leadership, but older members couldn't accept that a change was necessary so the Republican Conference was heavily divided. When it came time to vote, Newt Gingrich, who had developed a good following among younger more conservative members, threw his considerable political heft behind Vander Jagt and turned the tide in his favor. Guy was re-elected to the chairmanship of the NRCC. But the following election year he was defeated in the Michigan primary by Pete Hoekstra, who subsequently became chairman of the Intelligence Committee and more recently, an unsuccessful candidate for Governor of Michigan. He currently serves as Ambassador to the Netherlands.

Don Sundquist later left Congress and was elected to two terms as Governor for the State of Tennessee. Bill Paxon was elected to lead the NRCC, after Guy's primary defeat by Hoekstra, and I provided Bill with a list of seventeen rules to govern the NRCC without conflicts or sweetheart deals. Bill incorporated them as part of his governing charter for the NRCC and he built it into a much more productive, competitive, and successful organization.

After two years on Appropriations, I exchanged subcommittees, moving away from Labor, Health and Education issues to concentrate on Defense and Foreign Policy. I had worked diligently on my committee assignments and was delighted when the ranking committee Republican Silvio Conte assigned me to the much sought-after Defense Subcommittee. Better yet, Republican Minority Leader Bob Michel assigned me to the Select Committee on Intelligence. These provided me a platform to study in depth the strategic and tactical needs of our armed forces in both open and classified special programs. I gradually became knowledgeable about the quality of life needs of our service personnel; military construction of housing and bases; and the maintenance and procurement of weaponry and equipment. And the committee assignments provided me a platform to espouse my strong but ultimately futile support for the Contras and "Freedom Fighters" who were fighting the Communists in Nicaragua.

While much of my time was spent on the Contras, I didn't immediately understand that our colleague, Charlie Wilson (D-TX), had reached a quiet agreement with Speaker O'Neill to support efforts by the rag-tag Mujahideen against the Soviet Army in Afghanistan. Charlie began slowly and effectively, and he gradually convinced our defense colleagues to back him in his efforts to support those "freedom fighters" on the other side of the world, even as O'Neill was withdrawing support from the Contras in Central America. As I grew increasingly supportive of Charlie's efforts, he invited me on two separate occasions to travel with him on trips to the Khyber Pass. Charlie passed away in February, 2010, and I have always felt a lingering regret that I didn't accept his offer.

But I did support his sporadic requests for unusual weaponry to be used by the Mujahideen. They were losing their legs and lives with regularity in minefields strewn by the Soviets across the Afghan landscape, so Charlie asked for help to mitigate the damage they were suffering. Working with the CIA, we developed and funded a gun that shot detonating cord some one hundred yards across an open field. Once on the ground, the cord would explode and detonate the land mines in its path so that the terrain could be crossed safely by Afghan soldiers. Likewise, when they showed that they could stand up to their far better equipped and technically more capable enemy, we armed them with "Stingers," the shoulder mounted short range missiles that became lethal against Soviet Helicopters. The Soviets had owned the skies until that point, but the stingers were so effective that Russian pilots grew fearful to operate anywhere close to known Mujahideen forces. We knew that it was dangerous to provide Stingers to the Afghans for indefinite periods of time for fear that the weapons wouldn't only be used against the Soviets. So the Stingers were equipped with "poison pills" rendering the weapons inoperable after a period of time. That ultimately proved to be a wise move.

One day, Charlie walked into my office accompanied by a tall, rugged Mujahideen fighter with bandoleers crisscrossed on his chest. Charlie said he was there to thank me for my support, and they handed me a heavy leather belt with a scabbard and bayonet on one side, and an empty gun holster on the other. There was a large brass buckle with a hammer and sickle embossed on the front. I looked at the belt thinking that I couldn't accept the gift. "Oh, I can't accept that! Someone will need it!" They both broke out laughing, "Oh no, Bob. The guy who had this won't need it anymore!"

The book and movie *Charlie Wilson's War* were pretty close to the truth. With Charlie's help, the Mujahideen ran the Soviets out of their country. My only objection to the movie came at the end when a character on the Appropriations Committee named "Bob" refused to approve financial support for Pakistan, the implication being that his refusal led to emergence of the Taliban. Actually, that was Hollywood's improvisation. In truth, I was the only "Bob" on the committee, and I strongly supported Charlie in his efforts to keep the U.S. involved with Pakistan so as to keep the good Mujahideen on our side. It was the Democrat liberals in Congress who interrupted assistance to Pakistan in order to thwart her expressed intent to develop nuclear weapons. Just as their closing down of our assistance for U.S.-backed troops in Vietnam brought about the collapse of freedom in that country in 1974, the Democrat, majority in Congress withdrew financial support from Pakistan. The rest is unhappy history, as our absence led to the abdication by the U.S. in Afghanistan in favor of the Taliban and Al-Qaeda, thus enabling Osama Bin Laden's attack on the United States on 9/11.

Long after he'd left Congress and after the publication of the book and movie, I invited Charlie on more than one occasion to speak to friends and associates. When health and schedule permitted, he accepted the offers and delivered a spell binding account of his adventures. One of my favorite stories of his was when Tom Hanks bought the rights to "Charlie Wilson's War," he approached Charlie to ask if he thought that he, Tom Hanks, could effectively play Charlie in the movie. Charlie, knowing that Hanks was a rather straight-laced and proper sort of boy scout entirely unlike himself, demurred. "Well, I don't know," said Charlie who stood several inches taller than Hanks. "Can you say 'mother-fucker?' " Tom turned red and exclaimed, "Well, I never have, but I guess I can try!" Tom was good in the movie, but he wasn't quite as colorful as the original Charlie Wilson!

I frequently combated liberal attempts to promote peace through disarmament of the U.S. Had the liberals had their way, Congress would have adopted a "nuclear freeze" with the Soviets in the 1980s, thereby ensuring permanent arms parity and enabling the Soviets to maintain hegemony over Europe indefinitely. But President Reagan led Republicans and conservative Democrats to invest in American defensive technology, and he broke the economic backs of the Soviets. They couldn't keep up with us on any score, and Reagan's determination to develop a strategic missile defense was the ultimate straw. When they could no longer absorb and pillage the wealth of captive nations, they virtually imploded.

As a supporter of the President, I am most proud that I was among those assisting him to stop the Soviets' Empire in it's tracks. We could never have done it had we listened to the liberals. Granted, they enjoyed some successes. Indeed, as noted above, they fought Reagan's Strategic Defense Initiative ("SDI") with every resource they could muster. Since they held a majority in the House throughout Reagan's two terms and in the Senate for the last two years of his Presidency, they did succeed in delaying development.

Despite my consistent advocacy for developing a capable "ASAT" or Anti Satellite weapon, my liberal friend, Les AuCoin (D-WA) relentlessly garnered the votes to beat me in the Defense Appropriations Committee, and we didn't fund it. But in the twenty-five years since, several satellites have disappeared without public explanation, and we know that the Chinese have developed ASAT capability and the Russians have come a long way as well. Did we make a mistake?

I was successful in my support for both airborne laser and Naval-based missile defense for I believed then as I do now that expensive fixed-based defense systems are not as capable and responsive as lighter and more mobile systems. We now have the technology to successfully deploy these advanced systems, but until recently, we haven't developed the political will to provide much more than lip service. President Trump views the need for a strong defense far more favorably than did his predecessor, so I can only hope we don't wait until it becomes too late.

One that we do deploy with great success is the development of a weaponized UAV or Unmanned Aerial Vehicle or drone. It was a project with few adherents in the late '80s. Nevertheless, I vigorously supported it in my role as a member of the Select Committee on Intelligence, and it's now a critical component of our defense structure. The "Predator" and related drones have enjoyed great success in Afghanistan, and they've saved countless American lives as they quietly and efficiently scout and attack cowardly non-uniformed terrorists. And by the way, they were initially developed because I and others inserted entries (read "earmarks!") into the budget to get them started. I'm proud to say that in so doing, we added much maligned but much needed earmarks to the budget that were originally opposed by both the administration and the Pentagon.

On the lighter side, in 1974 my friend, Henson Moore (R-LA), was the second Republican from Louisiana elected to Congress since

Reconstruction. He represented a district inclusive of Baton Rouge and parishes east to the state line bordering Mississippi, in essence the trunk of the "boot" of Louisiana. In the early '80s, Jon Hinson (R-MS) was elected to the House to succeed Thad Cochran of Jackson, Mississippi, who had just been elected to the Senate. That district encompassed the western central sector of Mississippi, bordering on Henson Moore's district in eastern Louisiana.

Primarily because of his pretty wife and family, Jon Hinson's election overcame some unfortunate rumors about his sexual preferences. Once elected, Hinson could have put that behind him, but his secret nature got the best of him and one day he was arrested "in flagrante delicto" in a Longworth Building men's room with a guy named Larry Moore. The arrest immediately hit the wires and was the scandal *de jour* called the "Hinson-Moore" affair. Needless to say, all of Henson Moore's constituents were appalled, and Henson had to spend much of his time that year saying, "It's not me!" Fortunately, it all died down when Jon Hinson left Congress soon thereafter, and Henson Moore could breathe more easily.

In 1986, Henson ran for the Senate against then Congressman John Breaux. Henson led the pack throughout the race and it looked like he was going to win, but one day he delivered an excellent speech on foreign policy. When he'd finished, Ed Anderson, a reporter at the New Orleans newspaper *Times Picayune* approached him and asked, "Henson, if you don't win this race, will you run for Governor?"

If ever there was a time to demur to avoid a response to a hypothetical question, that was it. But Henson missed the cue and answered, "Yes, I guess if that were the case, I probably would." The newspaper ignored his fine speech and ran the story with the headline, "Moore contemplates run for Governor!!" That unnerved Henson's supporters and gave John Breaux an opening to claim that Henson really wasn't interested in the Senate race, but that the race was just a stepping stone to the State House. It hurt Henson badly. Then, when it was discovered that his campaign operatives had purged dead people from the voter registration lists, the Democrats successfully fed the press the idea that the Republicans were weaning black voters from the rolls. Henson never recovered; he lost narrowly, and John Breaux, who had been preparing for private life, succeeded the venerable Senator Russell

Long in the U.S. Senate.

Richard Baker, a veteran of the state legislature from Baton Rouge, was elected to Congress to succeed Henson, and roughly two months later, I announced that I was running for Governor of Louisiana in the off-year election in 1987.

Governor's Race - 1987

Because it was an off-year election, it was a free shot so I didn't have to give up my Congressional seat. But to this day, I'm not really sure why I decided to run for Governor. My interests had always focused on national issues and I'd had little interest and even less experience in state politics. I felt Edwin Edwards was emblematic of everything I wanted to change in politics. But I learned too late that if you don't have a burning desire in your gut to make a political race, you'd be better off not making it. I had that desire when I ran for Congress, but it simply wasn't there in the gubernatorial race. I guess it was simply a good windmill to chase.

The race was a challenge for me. As a former prosecutor and federal legislator with no experience in the state capitol in Baton Rouge, I had to learn the issues from scratch, and I don't think I ever became comfortable with them. My head told me that with ten years of success in Congress, I could most certainly be a good Governor. My heart had yet to be convinced, but I threw myself into the race and crisscrossed Louisiana with vigor reminiscent of my early races for Congress. I was one of nine candidates, including my Congressional colleagues Billy Tauzin and Buddy Roemer, State Commissioner of Insurance Jim Brown, sitting Governor Edwin Edwards, and six-foot, nine-inch insurance executive, Butch Baum.

Since I was the only Republican in the race, I rapidly gained support of the growing state-wide Republican organization. Under revised campaign law, we weren't confined to party primaries. Instead, we all would appear on a single ballot in the first primary and the top two vote getters would be thrown into a run-off regardless of party. Edwards had served two terms (1972-80) before Dave Treen was elected, and he had just completed his third term (1984-88) after defeating Treen in his bid for re-election. That third term had not been a fully happy time for Edwards as he was indicted, tried, and acquitted for manipulating hospital certificates. Yet he still was nonetheless popular in the black community, and that support guaranteed that he would run at least second in his race for a fourth term. So the challenge for the rest of us was to see who could fight their way into the runoff with Edwards with a presumption that anyone who made it would defeat the tainted former governor.

My Republican and conservative Democratic support placed me first from the beginning of the race until the last two weeks of the campaign. The issues facing state government were largely new to me. Moreover, the more I saw of the state legislature, the less comfort I had that I was the right person to deal with them. The state was not in good condition. Edwards had served as a quintessential populist, and he had screwed the state budget up beyond belief. I heard tale after tale of his corruption and how his shake-down of legitimate businessmen had discouraged investment into the state. That infuriated me, and I really wanted to put an end to the acceptance of corruption affecting the long term prosperity and viability of the state. But my lack of comfort with state issues prevented my projection of confidence to the voters, notwithstanding our development of a first class political organization all over the state.

Meanwhile, Buddy Roemer, heavy on self-confidence but almost devoid of organization or ability to lead anyone, was possessed of an appearance of braggadocio confidence that trumped virtually everyone else. Billy Tauzin, who had grown up under the wing of Edwin Edwards and had served in the state legislature during Edwards's earlier terms before he was elected to Congress, was convinced from the time he was five years old that he was destined to be Governor of the State of Louisiana. In my opinion, he was an Edwards re-dux and would simply have been more of the same.

Billy and I had a mixed relationship. We got along when we had to, but we fought over the re-apportionment process in the early '80s and the waters were frequently unsettled between us. I took great pleasure in beating him in a crawfish-eating contest that year. I was so determined to win, he being an authentic Cajun from the heart of Cajun country, that I stuffed the crawfish, shells and all into my mouth and chewed them up and swallowed them. It wasn't the most comfortable way to eat crawfish, but I did win the contest.

In the nine months of campaigning between January and November of 1987, there were a plethora of memorable incidents. Halfway through the campaign, our opponent, insurance magnate Butch Baum, flew in his own plane from Baton Rouge to Shreveport late one evening. But the next day his plane and body were found crashed in the wilds of Arkansas. We assumed he had fallen asleep. Shortly thereafter, Jim Brown flew in a small plane piloted by a friend to meet us all at a Watermelon

Festival in north Louisiana. For some reason, he accidentally bumped his door on the side of the plane and it fell off into a field below. Jim was fortunate that he didn't go with it.

Toward the end of the race, when Dave Treen was traveling with us on a wide swing around the state, Bonnie and I were returning to New Orleans in an RV that was loaned and driven by our friend Mike Cenac of Mandeville. It had been a long trip over several days, and we were all exhausted. I recall riding over the twenty-six-miles of two-lane Causeway across Lake Pontchartrain bounded by nothing but short concrete railings and miles of water on either side. Dave and I were swapping stories late into the evening while Mike was driving, and Dave had me laughing uproariously at some comment about someone he'd met in Lafayette. I laughed and yelled out to Mike, "Mike, did you hear that one . . . ? Mike . . . ? Mike . . . ? MIKE!!!!!!"

Mike was sound asleep, slumped over the wheel on his elbows as he drove along the Causeway at about sixty miles per hour. Only with the hand of God had he kept us on the road! He immediately woke up and we made it home, but I still can't fully understand how we avoided catastrophe.

The race itself was exhausting. Yet I maintained the lead in the race until about three weeks before election day. But as we came down to the stretch, I showed up at the final debate with all the candidates. Tired and over-prepared, I lost my train of thought while answering a question about halfway through the event. My stumble was lethal. Roemer immediately contacted all the newspaper editors and publishers in the state. He glibly persuaded them that I wasn't ready for prime time and that he would be a better governor. I'm convinced that the publishers collaborated for on the same Sunday a couple of weeks before Election Day, all the major papers endorsed Roemer for Governor. He was lifted overnight from fifth place to first. Edwards placed second, and I slipped to third. And that's the way it ended. I lost.

Tauzin couldn't believe he could lose, but he came in fifth. Brown fell even further when he unleashed a last minute attack on Roemer with some questionable information provided him by the Edwards campaign. They shopped the information with us, but I had turned them down. Brown used it, but the voters had begun to hate nasty tactics and he lost ground overnight.

A few good things happened during the campaign. The first was early in the race in the summer of 1987 when my participation in the Appropriations Committee was less active than it had been in previous years. My committee colleagues and friends, both Republican and Democrat, tried to assist me by funding more projects for Louisiana than I'd ever had funded in the past. Louisiana benefited, but it didn't work for me.

Closer to home, my wife, Bonnie, turned out to be a much better campaigner than I had been. She traveled the state, and everyone who met her absolutely fell in love with her. She was still a full-time mother and the kids needed her attention, but in retrospect, I should have probably stayed home with them and let her campaign. Fortunately, the race for Governor was an off-year election so when it was finally over, Billy Tauzin and I still held on to our Congressional seats.

So I lost the race. Bonnie was distraught, but I think I was less so. I had marshaled our resources and finished out of debt, but Billy had thrown caution to the wind and overspent himself by about $2 million that he owed with little ability to repay. I now look back on those days and wonder why I did it, but I felt sorry for him at the time. I signed letters to help encourage people to help him pay off his debt. He had run against me as a Democrat, but not long afterwards when we had both returned to Congress, it served his purposes to maintain his committee seniority so he switched parties and became a Republican. Anyway, had I the choice to do it again today, I might not be as likely to help him, but I did then, so that was that.

Roemer moved to the Governor's Mansion, but he failed to live up to the hopes of those who had supported him. Buddy's personality was mercurial and he had a hard time engendering support and friendship from even those who wanted to like him. He dealt with the Legislature with difficulty, and half way through his term, he too switched parties and became a Republican. His personal life suffered a crisis when his wife left, and late in his term a guru publicly advised him to snap rubber bands on his wrist to remove negative thoughts. I guess he didn't snap them hard enough, for despite endorsements of most "good government" types, my own included, he ran a dismal race for reelection in 1991, thereby matching his unimpressive four years in office. Buddy finished third in the open primary against Edwin Edwards and David Duke.

But his ambition wasn't thwarted in the least. In 2011, he announced his candidacy for President of the United States, but fortunately nobody noticed.

The choice between Edwards and Duke was a low-water mark in Louisiana politics. Edwards had been tried and acquitted for selling hospital certificates, and people had no illusions about his integrity in office. In fact, he was later convicted for irregularities involving gambling licenses and he spent about eight years in prison. But in the first primary in 1991 when he beat Roemer, he was opposed in the run-off by the notorious David Duke, Klansman, racist, and con-artist. Louisianans realized they had no choice! "Vote for the Crook; it's Important!" became the most popular bumper sticker in America! The race inspired the legislature to dump the state election open primary process they'd passed after my early Congressional races. Better qualified but lesser known candidates had been defeated in favor of the two most outrageous people the state might have nominated. But the old primary process wherein a person can be compelled to run three separate races is expensive and burdensome to the state and the candidates, so the debate on the best approach continues to this day.

Duke had served a single term in the state legislature after beating, of all people, Dave Treen's brother, John, in a special election in 1989. John was nothing like his brother, and although they were very close, John is known to some people as being a mean spirited, small minded, control-freak. He rode his brother's coattails and was a fixture in Dave's politics and in the management of the Louisiana Republican Party. No asset, he often cost his brother vital support from people who were fond of Dave but couldn't stand John. He could be so nasty that it was rumored that in his race against Duke, a Jewish family in Metairie, voted for the rabid racist and anti-Semite because they personally knew and despised John Treen.

The state legislature gave Duke a national platform for his foul tirades. He used it effectively, not just to spread his message of hate, but allegedly to pad his pocket by hiring his own public relations company into which he would pour campaign contributions and pay himself a salary. He ran for the U.S. Senate in 1990 and in 1996; for the U.S. Presidency in 1988 and in 1992; and upon my retirement, for my U.S. House seat in 1999. But his closest unsuccessful race was when he managed to parlay his support to gain a slot in the 1991 gubernatorial run-off against Edwards. In that context, it was inevitable that the nefarious Edwards beat Duke to win a fourth term as Governor of Louisiana.

Presidential Race - 1988

Even though the 1988 race for President wasn't on the calendar until a year after my own gubernatorial race, Vice President George H.W. Bush came to New Orleans in the midst of the gubernatorial campaign in 1987 to hold a major fundraiser for his Presidential campaign. Like all my opponents, I was scrambling for resources to run my own campaign, so I was none too pleased to see him raising money in my back yard. Ours was one of very few races in the country that year, so I felt that he could go anywhere else around the country to raise campaign funds. Mitch McConnell (R-KY) had been elected to the Senate in 1984 and was doing advance work for the VP in New Orleans. He asked for my help for a fundraising event. I let him know that I was unhappy with their timing and demanded that they split 50 percent of the proceeds with my own campaign. I didn't get it, but I think it did earn me a spot on the VP's blacklist. That was only compounded when I endorsed my friend, Jack Kemp, for President.

The Kemp campaign didn't get off the ground, and George H.W. Bush easily won the nomination for President at the 1988 Republican Convention in New Orleans. Since I was back in the House of Representatives following my futile race for Governor, I threw all my organization into making the convention in our home town a successful one. I chaired the Defense Subcommittee on the Platform Committee, and I think that I enjoyed no more than roughly eight hours of sleep during the entire two weeks of the convention. But I was wide awake for George Bush's acceptance speech and was only fifteen feet in front of him when he uttered the "Read my Lips" assertion that he would never raise taxes, thereby convincing his Reaganite supply-siders that he was one of them. In fact, he was not and at one point he'd even referred to Reaganomics as "voodoo-economics." This, together with the choice of my friend, Dan Quayle, who was immediately derided and vilified by the mainstream press, as his vice presidential running mate proved quite difficult for him in the long run.

But when in a TV debate his opponent, Massachusetts Governor Michael Dukakis couldn't decide if he would be angry or not about a hypothetical rape and murder of his wife, he subjected himself to public ridicule for laxity against criminals. That was characterized by "Willie Horton" ads, which belittled a lenient sentence imposed by one of his judicial appointees upon a cold-blooded killer in Dukakis' home state. Then when Dukakis allowed himself to be photographed in an overly large Army helmet while driving a small tank, he looked foolish and was ridiculed for the remainder of his candidacy. Moreover, Bush (41) benefited tremendously from the military buildup and improving economy left by his predecessor, Ronald Reagan. He won the race handily.

The U.S. economy was emerging from rampant inflation and unemployment in one of the most sustained and dramatic periods of growth in history. The Berlin Wall collapsed when the Soviet Union could no longer compete with U.S. technology. Nor could the Soviets justify their totalitarian dominion on their client colonies in Poland, East Germany and beyond. Historical revisionists now try to credit the Soviet collapse to the last of the Soviet Dictators, Mikhail Gorbachev, but in fact, Gorbachev tried everything in his power to keep the Soviet Union intact. Ronald Reagan prevented him from forcing any more countries under the Soviet orbit, and the disastrous Soviet Afghanistan campaign against U.S. supported Mujahideen (Thank you, Charlie Wilson) virtually imploded their economy. Their Potemkin village fell like a house of cards when the Berlin Wall collapsed.

America declared a "peace dividend," and we thought that would be the end of our international problems for years to come. But In December 1989, Bush (41) launched "Operation Just Cause" in which our Marines and Special Forces invaded Panama to rid the world of tin-pot dictator and drug trafficker, Manuel Noriega. More on that later.

In August 1990, Saddam Hussein invaded Kuwait. To his credit, Bush (41) did not permit the takeover to stand and he launched "Operation Desert Storm" led by General Norman J. Schwarzkopf. With careful planning and the support of the international community, the Reagan-Bush reinforced American military accomplished the quickest and most lopsided victory the world had witnessed in five hundred years. In hindsight, it's too bad that President Bush (41) did not permit our troops under General Barry McCaffrey to extend the successful "Left Hook" attack all the way to Baghdad to wipe out Hussein and his corrupt regime. Instead, he stopped short of total victory, leaving the evil Iraqi leader empowered to continue his tyranny for another ten years. Ironically, his son, President George W. Bush (43), was forced to finish the job with far less domestic or international good will and support than had been enjoyed by his father.

I traveled to Saudi Arabia twice during the first Gulf War. It is perhaps the most unusual culture in the world. I didn't mind being there as a man, but if I were a woman, I sure would hope to live elsewhere. Once outside, women had to walk everywhere in Burqas that covered them from head to toe in a virtual sack. Today, Muslim fundamentalism has become so pervasive that you might see Burqas in the United States and you could even buy a "Barbie in a Burqa" at Toys R' Us until they closed shop. Not for my grandchildren, thank you! But at the time of the first Iraqi war, they weren't seen often out of Saudi Arabia, and it was a shock for me to see them wherever I went.

In fact, if a woman in that country were seen on the street without full covering, a mullah would accost her and hit her with a stick until she remedied her "indecent exposure." Arms, legs, and even ankles were likely targets. A woman couldn't work in jobs other than in hospitals and schools, and she wasn't allowed to drive. While I was in Riyadh, a fellow pointed out three apartment buildings that had been built five years earlier by an American developer, but he said they had never been occupied.

"Why not?" I asked.

"Because they each only have one elevator!'

"I don't understand."

"Well, clearly, men and women in this country don't ride in the same elevator!"

A couple of years after the war, I was campaigning in Folsom, Louisiana, and ran into a friend I'll call "Joe," who had been both a Deputy Sheriff in St. Tammany Parish and an officer in the National Guard. He'd been called to active duty during the Gulf War, and they put him to work using his law enforcement experience. Joe told me a story about having been ordered to Germany with a colleague to pick up three terrorists who were wanted by the Saudi Arabian government. He was to escort them on a plane from Germany to Riyadh for trial.

Joe said that when they arrived in the palatial airport in Riyadh, they were met by Saudi security forces who took control of the prisoners. They escorted them together with my friend and his buddy to a large chamber in rear of the airport where he said the prisoners were summarily arraigned, tried, and convicted. They were sentenced to die the next morning, and the executions by decapitation were to be carried out in that same chamber at dawn.

He said they invited him to attend the executions, and while reluctant, he relented and was on the scene when the prisoners were led to the chamber the next day. A broad cloth was spread over the floor with a block placed in the center. Joe said the first prisoner was brought out in chains from an anteroom and bent over the block as a hooded, heavy chested executioner towered over him with sword in hand. Joe said he was nauseated and frightened by the scene, so he put his hands over his eyes just as he heard a loud "Whack!" as the sword found its target.

He said a cleanup crew came in, and in a matter of minutes, they had removed the body, the block, and the broad cloth. A new cloth and block appeared and the second prisoner was brought out. Joe said his curiosity got the best of him so this time he still covered his eyes, but at the appropriate moment he said he couldn't resist and peaked through his fingers.

Evidently, he got used to the ritual because when they finally brought out the third prisoner for execution, Joe said he asked the officer in charge if he could have a turn with the sword.

When "Desert Storm" was over and the Iraqi Army was decisively defeated, President Bush (41) enjoyed a 90 percent positive popularity rating. But while his foreign policy triumphs provided his boost in the ratings, his domestic policy ran into trouble. I was determined to do my part to support him and his administration. But because I had had my collisions with his campaign staff and had supported Jack Kemp in the Presidential primary, I think the word was spread among his legislative agents to treat me as less than a full member of the Bush team.

Tradition had it that a member of the House of Representatives in the President's own party was given deference when it came to filling judgeships and U.S. Attorney's positions, especially if there were no members of the party in the Senate. Louisiana had not yet elected a Republican to the Senate, so I assumed that as the then ranking Republican from our State in the House, I would determine the next U.S. Attorney for the Eastern District of Louisiana. I intended to reappoint my friend, John Volz, who himself had been appointed by President Reagan in 1984 following the retirement of my former boss, Gerry Gallinghouse, after a very successful fourteen years in office. Volz had generated opposition to his reappointment by virtue of his unsuccessful prosecution of Governor Edwards for manipulation of hospital certificates, but I felt that he had taken the hard road and deserved to be retained in his office.

But with my support during his bid for office, Baton Rouge attorney and Louisiana State Representative Richard Baker was elected to succeed Henson Moore in the Sixth District of Louisiana. While I was running for Governor, Richard had time on his hands, so he signed up to become the Bush State Election chairman. When Bush won the nomination, Richard became the favored Louisiana son in the eyes of the Bush administration.

That was fine with me until Richard intruded onto my political turf by ignoring my pick for U.S. attorney for the Eastern District of Louisiana, John Volz, and naming his own candidate. Years earlier, we'd created the Middle District of Louisiana at the urging of Senator Russell Long, and as that district was centered in Baton Rouge, I felt that Richard should have been content to fill vacancies in that district. But Richard moved into my territory, and I didn't like it a bit. We quarreled about it for several months. But at Richard's request, Bush ultimately denied my choice for U.S. Attorney and appointed Richard's choice, Harry Rosenberg. Harry also happened to be a longtime friend of mine, but he wasn't my choice for the post. He replaced Volz as U.S. Attorney and he did a good job, so the dust settled and peace was restored to the land.

Richard and I subsequently resolved our differences, and I helped him through his somewhat rocky relations with his own district. He endured some real squeaker elections until he ultimately retired but as we renewed our friendship, I supported and assisted him in his reelections.

I gradually became a Bush loyalist, but when he reneged on his commitment to not raise taxes and passed a large tax increase in his concession to Democrats in the 1990 Budget Agreement, I should have heeded his quip at the New Orleans Convention, "Read my lips! No new taxes!" and voted "no" in good conscience. But I reluctantly voted for it, and in so doing, I cast what was among the worst votes of my twenty two years in Congress.

That bill cost Bush his support among his base, and as the economy receded in the latter days of his Presidency, it fueled demand by the public for someone new.

Bill Clinton, the young and untested Governor of Arkansas, accompanied by a cracker-jack campaign team, rose from a bland pack of Democratic contenders. James Carville was pardoned from living in his car to became a political adviser and confidante to Clinton. He coined the phrase "It's the economy, stupid!" and together with his mean and nasty partner, Paul Begala, perfected the political attack on all Clinton opponents, real or imagined. Rumors emerged about Clinton's consensual and non–consensual relationships with various women who had the temerity to question his ethics. The Carville/Begala team jokingly dismissed them as "bimbo eruptions" and successfully distracted the press from charges that today would doom any candidacy. More on that later.

Special Prosecutor Lawrence Walsh's politically motivated re-indictment of Caspar Weinberger only added to the discontent with the President. Furthermore, President Bush (41) had done himself and his campaign no favors by constantly appointing his friends to high office, regardless of their qualifications. He, like his son years later, had a blind eye when it came to demanding loyalty over competence, and if the two were in conflict, both invariably opted for the former. George H.W. Bush (41) named his friend, Robert Mosbacher, as his reelection campaign chairman. Mosbacher had been a fine Secretary of Interior, and he was an especially adept political fundraiser. But he was ill equipped to be a campaign chairman, and he was caught flatfooted by the juggernaut of organization that evolved between the Clintons, Carville, Begala, the American press, and most of Hollywood.

By this time, I had acquired a relatively significant degree of seniority on the Appropriations Committee. Many of the more successful members tried to specialize in areas of jurisdiction that rendered them a degree of expertise in those areas. With twelve years on the full Appropriations Committee, mostly on the Defense and Foreign Operations Subcommittees, and six years on the Select Committee on Intelligence, I had become one of the more senior members in defense and foreign policy. During the Republican Convention in New Orleans in 1988, I co-chaired the Platform Subcommittee on Defense and wrote the defense plank with Bay Buchanan, whose brother Pat later ran unsuccessfully in 1992 for President in the Republican Primary. Subsequently in 1994, I was to write the Defense plank in the "Contract with America."

In those years, I didn't hesitate to take advantage of the opportunity to travel and learn my trade. Most of my trips were to war zones under the guidance and leadership of my Democratic friend, Jack Murtha. Jack was close to ten years older than I. He'd served valiantly in Vietnam as a young Marine officer, and he'd been elected three years before me in 1974. He was not a knee-jerk liberal like many of his colleagues, but he was very much a street-savvy deal maker. He wasn't cynical about his duties. He really cared for the welfare of the troops, especially his Marines. But he'd had a near scrape in the "Ab-Scam" scandal in the late '70s, and his ambition and desire to help his friends was to earn him a reputation as poster-child for what was wrong in Congress in the new millennia.

Throughout the 1980s and early '90s, Jack led a number of CODELS to war zones around the world. I felt privileged to travel with him on several of them. Despite the bad publicity he generated for himself from time to time, I have to say that when I knew him best, Jack Murtha was a good member. He would run a tight ship, and there was little time on his trips for foolishness. We visited the troops in all corners of the globe, and our main goal was to see that they had the resources to do their jobs properly. If we found deficiencies, we made sure to report them and, if necessary, return to Congress and assure that funds were appropriated to remedy the fault. While on the trips, we would get up early, work hard all day, and retire late at night, and get up and begin again. Murtha was punctual and he expected everyone to meet his standards. He was the first one on the bus and if anyone was late, they would hear about it.

Contrary to conventional wisdom about CODELS, we did not travel in luxury. When we went to El Salvador during the Contra wars against the Nicaraguan Sandinistas, we marched all night through the jungles of Honduras on a mock raid with American and Salvadoran Special Forces. A State Department official at the Honduran Embassy was assigned to accompany us. Thinking it was a typical CoDel, he showed up in a white linen suit with Gucci loafers. We had borrowed Army fatigues, but he'd turned them down for "protocol" reasons. He stayed with us all night, and by the end of the trek through the jungle, his clothes were ruined. I later heard he'd caught malaria and nearly died.

We traveled to Beirut right after Reagan sent the Marines in to relieve the Israelis in the Lebanese War of 1983. After a long day of talking with the troops and checking on their welfare, we turned down an Embassy offer to stay in a secure hotel and instead slept in sleeping bags on the floor in the Marine Corps barracks. A few weeks later, the same building was blown up taking the lives of 299 American and French Servicemen, including 220 U.S. Marines, eighteen Navy and three Army personnel.

The devastation from war in that once beautiful city of Beirut was unimaginable. We gained full perspective of the violence in a quick Jeep tour through the war-torn city. Later, we stood on the deck of one of our Navy vessels anchored offshore, and we looked back at the coast of Beirut. Standing there, we saw a puff of smoke and heard a loud "boom" as another building was blown apart in the distance.

We also visited Grenada right after the U.S. invasion of the Communist base, but our troops had done their job and there wasn't much that we could do to be of help, other than to insist on better intermodal communications. In the midst of the battle, a young marine found that he had no adequate radio to call into cross-service leadership for support from artillery. In desperation, he searched for and found a public pay phone. He put a quarter in the machine and called the Pentagon. Somehow, he got through and ultimately received the artillery coverage he needed. But the incident highlighted how intense planning falls apart in war time.

We Americans enjoyed good relations with Egypt after President Carter hosted Egyptian President Anwar Sadat and Israeli Prime Minister Menachem Begin at Camp David in September 1978. I was fortunate to have been invited to the Rose Garden for that ceremony when they signed the accord and shook hands. Since then, there have been joint exercises between American and Egyptian troops known as "Operation Bright Star." Jack Murtha led more than one delegation to review the troops, observe the operation, and help cement warm relations between the Egyptian government, their military, and many of our political and military leaders. I have a wonderful memory of my standing in a field during a training exercise as hundreds of paratroopers, Egyptian and American, jumped out of low flying cargo planes only to land in the field all around me.

I think it was during the Gulf War of 1991 when a Murtha CODEL stopped in Cairo, Egypt, to confer with the Ministry of Defense. While I'd been to Egypt at least once before, I had not taken time to visit the pyramids. I told Jack, and he agreed to take a quick trip out to see them one afternoon. But by 11:00 a.m. that day, it began to rain. Now it only rains in Cairo a few days a year, but when it does, it really rains. So as the streets began to flood, we scrapped the pyramids in favor of waiting out the storm in a local restaurant. There were about ten of us, including the Egyptian security guard who was assigned to us.

The restaurant was well over one hundred years old and was reminiscent of Rick's Cafe in the movie *Casablanca*. Slow moving ceiling fans circulated the air within high dark walls topped with long thin windows that looked like they hadn't been moved or washed in decades. The windows were built to open to the inside from the top, but it must have been a rare event if in fact it had ever happened. They loomed about ten feet over our heads and were encased in transoms with sills broad enough for large ornamental urns to have been placed solidly in front of the windows. The ten of us gathered around a long table with enough room for four people to sit with backs to the wall under the transoms.

As the storm intensified outside, I squeezed into my seat with my back to wall on one end of the table, and the security guard sat on the same side at the other end. We ordered something to drink and the security guard rose from his seat to go to the bathroom. He hadn't been gone thirty seconds, when a brutal gust of wind blasted outside the restaurant and the transom encased window popped open immediately above the security guard's seat. It slammed into the urn on the sill in front of the window, and the urn toppled down onto the vacant seat with a fearsome crash. We all jumped out of our skins, but fortunately, no one was scratched. As the waiter rushed over to check on all of us and begin cleaning up the mess, the security guard, who'd heard nothing of the incident in the bathroom, returned to take his seat at the table. As he approached the table, he spotted the dirt and debris tossed everywhere by thirty pounds of smashed and broken pottery in his vacant chair. He looked up at the open window and vacant spot left by the urn, turned absolutely white and ran back to the bathroom.

When Bush (41) grew weary of warning Manuel Noriega to quit his nefarious dealings with drug runners and other enemies in Latin America, he authorized plans to topple the regime. I had some Panamanian contacts in my Congressional district and at their insistence, as the time for action grew near I decided to travel to Panama in hopes that military action might be averted. My contacts told me that they thought Noriega could be convinced to leave Panama and retire peacefully in Spain or elsewhere. He was clearly a thug who had encouraged the transit of cocaine through his country, but I just didn't feel that it was worth the expenditure of American lives on a mission to depose him. I traveled to Panama on a Murtha-led CoDel and met with a number of people claiming influence over Noriega. They understood that if he didn't get out of there the U.S. forces would eject him, but he was not yet convinced of the fact. They claimed they were trying to convince him, but implied that his reticence was simply a matter of settling on a price and a suitable place to retire with security.

I called some contacts at the National Security Council and told them what I had learned. I continued the dialogue with Noriega's intermediaries and reported my progress to the NSC in several conversations over a couple of days. In the meantime, our Armed Forces began moving forward with their invasion plans. When we couldn't reach a definitive agreement, my contact in the NSC told me to discontinue all negotiations and get out of Panama. I relented and followed his direction, and "Operation Just Cause" began a couple of days later. It was no surprise that we took Panama in a day. But several days elapsed before they finally found Noriega hiding under his mistress's bed somewhere in Panama City. He was brought to the United States, tried, convicted, and sentenced to serve forty years in a U.S. correctional facility. But in the process, twenty-three American troops died, and another 325 were wounded. I still believe we could have bought him off and that the invasion might have been avoided.

Golf

One of the few ways to get away from the constant political routine was to hit the golf links. Before all the ethics debacles, it was routine for charities and political organizations to throw tennis and golf tournaments. They were bi-partisan events, and in the old days, companies would contribute booty . . . golf bags, tickets to the theater, gift certificates to the golf shop for $50 to $100, golf shirts, balls, tees, towels, hats, bottles of wine, etc.

I didn't play tennis at all, but I enjoyed hitting a golf ball a few times a year. The most I ever played in a single year was about fifteen times, and that particular year was the only time in my life in which my golf score actually broke one hundred. I shot a ninety two and was ecstatic!

But there were other times when my performance on the links was less worthy of superlatives. In fact, I won the dubious "highest score" prize in more than one tournament. It reminded me of my school days when I was the last kid to be chosen for football scrimmages.

Worst of all was my experience one year at Tantallon Golf Course in Maryland during the first week of November. The day was quite chilly, overcast, and blustery, and as one who only liked to play golf when conditions were perfect, I didn't have my heart in going to the links in the first place. But my friend, Mel Goodweather, encouraged me to ride with him to the course so that we could play together. Mel was one of the few lobbyists I enjoyed playing with, since he was almost as bad as I was. Mel was more than ten years older and about a foot shorter than I and we were a great team. We both cared a lot more about the jokes we told than the quality of our game.

But this was not to be a good day. Fall in Washington is generally nice as the season changes. But on a rather cold and windy day, the leaves blow all over the ground, and it's not a very fun time for a bad golfer to hit . . . or find . . . his ball.

Mel and I had lost a collective twelve to fifteen balls by the fourteenth hole, and my own sense of humor had declined through the day. Mel was off looking for his ball in the leaves of the forest, and I grew tired of waiting for him. We were on the top of a hill overlooking a large pond and my ball was at the edge of the pond at the bottom of the hill.

I yelled at Mel to tell him I was going down to hit my ball. I climbed into the topless cart, turned it on and drove it to the edge of the hill. As I started down, I began to pick up speed. I was half way down the hill when I realized I was going a little fast, so I attempted to hit the brake to slow down. Unfortunately, I missed the pedal and instead hit the accelerator as I stared at the pond looming ever so quickly before me.

Driving straight for the pond at full speed, I knew I was going headlong into the water if I didn't do something fast. I yanked the steering wheel as hard as I could with my left hand, whipped the cart into a ninety degree turn, and hit the water broadside at about twenty miles per hour. The cart stopped abruptly, but I didn't. I flew out of the cart into the air with an ever so perfect flip, landing in the middle of the pond. I didn't notice until later that my left hand had been locked on the steering wheel as I departed, nor that I'd broken a couple of small bones in that hand as I flew free.

Well, the water was very dirty . . . and very cold. As soon as I hit and submerged, I practically reversed the film and flew back to shore. A lobbyist standing nearby saw the whole thing and ran to the edge of the pond. "Congressman, Congressman, let me help you!"

He reached down, grabbed my hand, and pulled me out. And there I stood on the shore, drenched, muddy, smelly, and shivering from cold as I stared at my golf cart that was jammed sideways in the mucky bank lining the water. My clubs had stayed with the cart, and it looked like such a nice place to park until someone could extract it from the mud onto dry land.

Mel ran down the hill and asked what I wanted to do. Did I want to dry off and finish the tournament? "I want to go home!" I hollered.

At that moment, a young, Arian-blond male golfer dressed in a beautiful plaid shirt, exquisitely creased tan golf slacks and two-toned golf shoes walked up, looked me up and down, and said, "Wow! I've never seen anything like this! Look, I've got a plane to catch. Do you mind if I play through?"

If I'd had my putter in hand, he'd have played on but with fewer teeth. I left the cart where it stood and had Mel drive me home, filthy, wet, and miserable.

During the term of Bush (41), the seventy year old Soviet Union finally collapsed and the Cold War ended. Bush had won a lopsided and magnificent victory over Saddam Hussein's Revolutionary Guard in Iraq. He had also conquered Panama in a day, ridding the Western Hemisphere of the thuggish Manuel Noriega. He should have cruised to reelection. But then he reneged on his commitment not to raise taxes and to reduce the size of government. Ignoring the wishes of his once solid political base, he was perceived as emptying the arrows from his campaign quiver.

Enter Ross Perot, Naval Academy graduate, entrepreneur, billionaire, organizer of an expedition to rescue some of his employees held captive in Iran in 1979, and now, third-party candidate for President. Perot was viewed as a quixotic hero with an odd appeal to those who felt disenfranchised by the leading candidates and their parties. No one gave Perot a chance to win, but when the dust settled, he'd captured 18.9 percent of the vote, thereby becoming the most successful third party candidate since Theodore Roosevelt in 1912. So despite Bush's vast record of experience as World War II hero, Congressman, Ambassador to the United Nations, Emissary to China, Director of the CIA, Vice President, and finally, President with 90 percent favorability eighteen months before the election, he lost in 1992 to little known Arkansas governor, William Jefferson Clinton.

As the country shifted from twelve years of leadership by two WWII-vintage Republicans in the White House to a new and charismatic "baby-boomer" Democratic President, the Congress did not appreciably change. The fossilized House committee leadership was as deeply entrenched with Democratic roots as it had been for almost forty years, and though the Senate had experienced intermittent Republican control under Senator Howard Baker in the early '80s, it too was strongly controlled by the Democrats. Now that party had it all, both Houses of Congress and the White House, and they did not hesitate to stamp their mark on America.

Hiking in the Appalachians; (left to right) John Oudt, Jimmy Conner, John Wolfolk, Johnny Bolles, me, and Howard "Nep" Smith, 1959.

Burning anti-Vietnam War propaganda, with Jimmy Conner, 1966; photo from *Tulane Hullabaloo.*

Bonnie and me with "Shep," 1967.

Bonnie and me with the boys, Rich, Dave, and Shep, during the first campaign for Congress, 1976.

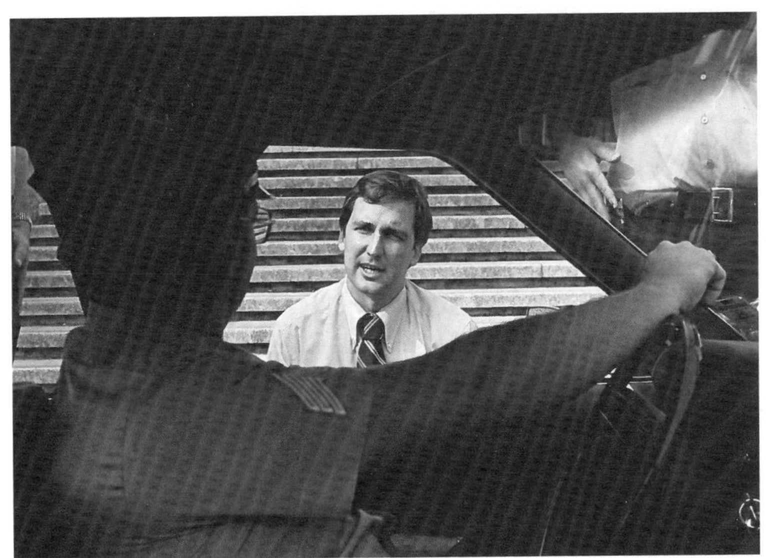

"Law & Order" campaign shot, 1976.

Me and the boys out for a run on the levee with Rascal, 1976.

Celebrating my arrival in Congress with fellow Louisiana Republicans Henson Moore (left) and Dave Treen (right), 1977.

Tip O'Neill swearing me in with Bonnie, Dave Treen, Minority Leader John Rhodes, and Henson Moore, 1977.

Bonnie and me with the boys and the recent addition to the Livingston family, Susie, 1981.

The Livingston family with President Ronald Reagan on his last day in office, 1988.

With Vice President George H.W. Bush during my campaign for the Louisiana governorship, 1987.

Bonnie and me with President George W. Bush and his wife Laura at the White House for Christmas, 1999.

Congressional leaders watch as President Bill Clinton signs the first balanced U.S. budget in over four decades, temporarily ending the era of big government, 1996.

Golfing with President Bill Clinton, 1996.

Exchanging the gavel with outgoing Speaker Newt Gingrich, 1998.

Robert L. Livingston Jr., United States Congress, 1977-1999.

Clinton Presidency

Bill Clinton, a savvy young governor from Arkansas rode into the Presidency amid a tide of enthusiastic southern pride and liberal optimism. His wife, Hillary, a non-southerner, was an aggressive lawyer who, with a coterie of canny friends in politics, Hollywood, and the media manipulated the press from her White House "war room" and maneuvered around a plethora of rumors, scandals, and outright criminal accusations. From "Whitewater" to "Travelgate," missing files from the Rose Law firm, and worst of all, political abuse and control of FBI files on private persons, she and her Carville-Begala goon squad successfully evaded all incoming charges and counter-attacked anyone who challenged the Clinton administration. "Bimbo-eruptions" emerged as women voiced pleasure and/or alarm at the attentions, welcome or forced, paid them by the boy-president. But like Teflon on pots and pans, "Slick Willy" oozed effortlessly from the stories, and his accusers were returned to obscurity, at least until the latter days of his second term.

It became evident that Bill Clinton was a consummate politician, not given to any ideology other than his own ambition—and desire for self-gratification. Hillary on the other hand appeared committed to a leftist agenda and was in full accord with the left's desire to ridicule anyone in the military, denigrate the United States role as purveyor of democracy and peace in the world, and promote greater government control over healthcare and other daily functions of American life. In short, she was a product of the '60s in every sense of the phrase, a flower child who while in Yale Law School, allegedly acted as support counsel to the Black Panthers on trial for murder in Connecticut and who supported leftist causes through most of her early professional life.

With Hillary's persuasion, Bill appointed left-wing activists to various ranking posts, especially within the Justice Department. Their new Attorney General was Janet Reno, later declared the "hero" of Waco, Texas, where, in order to rein in the weird activities of David Koresh in 1993, she directed an attack resulting in the burning of the Branch Davidian cult headquarters and the death of fifty four adults and twenty one children. Later at her command, the child Elian Gonzalez, was ripped from his relative's arms in south Florida to be returned to a life of subservience under Cuban Communism.

Prior to a spate of "empire building," the FBI was incontestably the premier domestic law enforcement agency in the world. While it had an international role, the Bureau of Diplomatic Security (DSS) effectively performed the role of investigating most crime beyond U.S. borders while the CIA's role governed all intelligence matters abroad. Members of DSS often complained to me that under Director Louie Freeh, the FBI pushed DSS aside to expand FBI responsibility around the world notwithstanding a limited ability to speak foreign languages. Regretfully, the Bureau spread itself too thin, and its effectiveness was diminished under his leadership. The failings of the Bureau in recent years can be traced back to failure of direction by Director Freeh in the 1990s.

In 1996, the FBI Laboratory was found to have fabricated forensic evidence under his watch. Richard Jewell, an Atlanta security guard, was erroneously tagged by the FBI as the perpetrator of a bombing in Centennial Olympic Park. The Bureau withheld evidence in the Oklahoma bombing case against Timothy McVeigh. Special Agent Robert Hanssen, a twenty-seven-year veteran of the FBI, was arrested on espionage charges on his watch. Critics say Freeh resisted a recommendation for regular polygraph tests that might have rooted out evidence of Hanssen's espionage. And Freeh attempted unsuccessfully to promote Larry Potts to the number two position in the FBI, despite Potts's wholesale lapse of judgment when he'd directed the disastrous shootings by federal agents of fugitive, Randy Weaver, killing his wife and son on their property in Ruby Ridge, Idaho, in 1992. In April, 1993, Potts also had been involved in the disastrous assault on the Branch Davidian compound.

FBI's Howard Shapiro was a frequent visitor to the White House in the latter '90s. As Chief Counsel to Director Louie Freeh, he controlled hundreds of personal FBI files on private citizens that mysteriously and coincidentally were discovered in the White House in the hands of a flunky named Craig Livingstone (no relation), whom no one could remember hiring. How strange! When it was discovered that Shapiro was in fact the top official in charge of "Filegate," an outrageous scandal involving wrongly distributed and misused FBI files in the White House,

Freeh refused to fire Shapiro until he'd landed a job almost a year later.

Scandals and embarrassing revelations were daily fare at the Clinton White House. Perhaps Clinton's worst hire, presumably at the insistence of Hillary, was Jamie Gorelick as Deputy Attorney General in the Justice Department. In her official role, she denied that terrorism was anything more than a criminal act so she constructed a firewall to prevent the CIA and FBI counter-terrorism sections from collaborating on international threats. Hence, the United States was eventually caught wholly unprepared for the attacks in New York and Washington on September 11, 2001, despite several separate terrorist incidents occurring throughout the 1990s. President Clinton repeatedly threatened retaliation after the first bombing in the World Trade Center in New York in 1993; the bombings of the Khobar Towers in Saudi Arabia in 1996; the two American Embassies in Kenya and Tanzania in 1998; and the USS Cole in Yemen in 2000. But in the words of former National Security Advisor Zbigniew Brzezinski in a defense meeting after 9/11, all he really ever accomplished was flying "a missile up some camel's ass" in the desert.

Gorelick's firewall prevented sharing of intelligence to support a unified attack on terrorism, and President Clinton failed to appreciate the threat posed to the nation by Osama Bin Laden and Al-Qaeda terrorists despite abundant evidence of their intent to kill Americans. But when the CIA finally did make the case on Osama Bin Laden for his responsibility for several attacks during his presidency, Clinton only simulated retaliation. Instead of hunting down Bin Laden to find and kill him, he ordered the military to fire off occasional cruise missiles into the region to convince the American people that he was doing something about the problem. Apart from using a technique in the DeNiro movie *Wag the Dog* to cover his own indiscretions when the proverbial "kitchen" grew too hot, Clinton rarely accomplished anything beyond generation of a flurry of headlines in the American press.

In fact, Clinton became so consumed with his personal problems with Monica Lewinsky that he pulled the plug on the CIA operatives' plan to kill Bin Laden and inadvertently sowed the seeds for the most disastrous foreign attack on American soil in history. Thus on September 11, 2001, nine months into the term of his successor, George W. Bush, Al Qaeda terrorists commandeered and flew two commercial jets into the twin towers in New York City. In response, knowledgeable observers were left breathless when President Bush (41) mindlessly appointed Jamie Gorelick to the 9/11 Investigation Committee to assist the development of "lessons learned." The best lesson might have been never to appoint her to anything of substance ever again. Unfortunately, that wasn't to be.

Gorelick left bankruptcy and devastation in her wake wherever she went. Despite her utter lack of significant business experience, she was appointed in 1997 to serve as vice-chairman of the Federal National Mortgage Association (Fannie Mae) with former Clinton's Office of Management and Budget Director Franklin Raines. Over the next few years, they fomented a $10 billion accounting scandal that served as catalyst for the worst financial collapse the nation had suffered since the "Great Depression" of the 1930s. Yet by the time she'd left Fannie Mae in 2003, it was reported that she personally had been paid almost $26.5 million! It is arguable that 9/11 was a foreseeable result of the firewall imposed by Gorelick at Justice, yet Bush appointed her to the 9/11 commission to study "lessons learned!"

The fox was appointed to see why the chickens were disappearing and nothing of substance came out of the hearings, short of another unnecessary layer of bureaucracy known as the Directorate of National Intelligence (DNI). Its role was to force communication between the intelligence sectors of the FBI and the CIA. Yet in December 2009, the nation was once again surprised by and narrowly escaped tragedy from the near success of the "Christmas Crotch Bomber" (a.k.a "Underwear Bomber") who tried to blow up the passenger jet on which he was flying as it approached Detroit. In truth, the moron failed to accomplish more than setting his own underwear on fire, but had he succeeded, hundreds, perhaps thousands of people could have been killed. He had been known to intelligence circles for weeks earlier when his own father turned him in, but for unknown reasons, the CIA, the FBI, and the other agencies had not communicated with one another. So why do we have an extra layer of intelligence bureaucracy?

Back in early 1994, Hillary's attempt to nationalize health care led the country to question the wisdom of unleashed Democratic control of government. Foreshadowing the even larger, more successful yet disastrous attempt in late 2009 by Democrats to socialize the country by forcing one sixth of the American economy into ObamaCare, Hillary made an energetic run to convince the nation to turn its back on free market health care. But she was countered by Minority Conference chairman Dick Armey, who read and deciphered her complex proposal. He and his team designed a chart that illustrated the absurdity of interconnecting agencies and departments with imposition of regulations and taxes. The chart was widely publicized, and it enabled Republicans to successfully challenge and mock the unrestrained power grab by the Democrats. It was not for nothing that the American people soundly rejected the effort . . . that time.

Her failed ploy enabled Republicans to highlight their message under the battle flag of the new Minority Whip, Newt Gingrich, who succeeded Leader Bob Michel. House Republicans unified under a cry of opposition to ever bigger government, and we began to think in terms beyond those permitted us by the rules of the perpetual minority in which I'd served for the previous seventeen years. In August 1994, Dick Armey and I went fishing one Saturday, and I recall him saying, "If we win . . . I'm running for Majority Leader." When Newt and Dick dreamed up the idea for a "Contract with America," we knew we were on onto something big. We gathered our top forces, parceled out a bunch of assignments, and gradually created a list of clear and unequivocal principles of lesser government, lower taxes, and strong national defense. I personally drafted the Defense plank. Once we'd condensed and published the platform, the "Contract with America" rapidly caught the attention of the country. While it listed the goals that we as Republicans would assert if we were to take control of the House, it served us well in contrast to the Clinton mistakes, their leftist agenda, and all their scandals. When the dust settled, we'd motivated the people to substantially change the course of government in the 1994 mid-term elections.

The New Majority

Republicans won a decisive victory in 1994. The final tally had us winning a majority in both chambers so Republicans now controlled the agenda in each House. In the House, we won 230 to 204 seats for the Democrats, and in the Senate, which had not really given much credit to our "Contract with America," we captured a majority of fifty three seats to the Democrats' forty seven. We were ecstatic! While the Senate had enjoyed Republican control for a few years in the early '80s, it was the first time Republicans had controlled the House in forty years.

Within days after the election, we began to organize our majority, and that meant new assignments to committees and election of officers and committee chairmen. Since the changes determined the political future of virtually every elected member of the Conference, it was a very tense but important process. Newt Gingrich, who had been our Minority Leader, was virtually uncontested as the new Speaker-elect. Dick Armey fulfilled his pledge to run for Majority Leader, and he won the race by the skin of his teeth. Tom DeLay sought and won the post of Majority Whip, and his organizational skills in that job proved so great that it wasn't long before he was awarded the nickname "The Hammer" to depict his significant ability to capture votes in favor of the majority agenda.

By this time, I'd served on the Appropriations Committee for fourteen years. I had especially enjoyed my role on the Defense and Foreign Operations Subcommittees together with my six years on the Select Committee on Intelligence. I had a broad depth of service on Appropriations but not so much when compared to Joe McDade (R-PA), John Myers (R-IN), Bill Young (R,FL), or Ralph Regula (R,OH). Each of them was senior to me, and each wanted to become the new chairman of the Appropriations Committee. The odds were that one of them would indeed win the seat.

But Joe McDade had run afoul of a scalp-hunting prosecutor in Pennsylvania, and he had been fighting to defend himself against an indictment for alleged bribery since 1992. A very bright and gregarious man, he was the logical person to succeed the departing Chairman David Obey (D-WI), who himself had only held the seat for the preceding nine months. But no matter how ill-founded, McDade's legal entanglements convinced Newt that he could not name Joe to the chairmanship. The next most senior member, John Myers, thought he had the post locked up. But John had not played much of a role in helping to capture the new majority and had not been viewed as much of a team player. So once the leadership decided to jump one member in seniority, I felt that they could jump more than one. I made my pitch to the Speaker about being a conservative team player, and after all was said and done, he chose me to become the next Appropriations chairman.

Actually, I didn't make this jump because of my good looks. In fact, when we won the majority in the '94 elections, I didn't think it was possible. I had begun making plans to run for the Republican Conference chairmanship. I started lining up votes and was half way through the process when John Boehner (R-OH) came to me and told me he was thinking of running for the conference chairmanship. That wasn't a problem in my mind, and I figured we'd have a good race and see who won.

But then John asked, "Wouldn't you really prefer being chairman of the Appropriations Committee?" I can't say I hadn't thought of it before but because of the seniority of those other members, I hadn't given it much thought. Yet when John said he would go to bat for me for the post, I immediately agreed. He was right. I did want that chairmanship more than the other position.

John followed through. He lobbied Newt, Armey and others, and I began stirring the pot as well. We convinced Newt to offer me the job, I accepted, and then I began pushing John Boehner for the Republican Conference chairmanship. He won, and I was delighted.

Obviously, Joe McDade was crushed, but he couldn't overcome the circumstances that had caused him to be passed over. The indictment was devastating to him and his family, and it lingered over his head like the Sword of Damocles for eight long years. The charges were both petty and frivolous, and most of us who followed it felt that the case should have been dismissed at the outset. The federal trial judge apparently despised elected officials, Republicans in general, and Joe in the specific, and he gave Joe absolutely no quarter. So the case went to trial and lasted for three or four days. I enthusiastically testified as a character witness for Joe at the conclusion of the trial. The case went to the jury, and with little more than fifteen minutes of deliberation, they returned a verdict of "Not Guilty!" Joe and his wife, Sarah, were thrilled, but the case had taken a terrible toll on Joe's health and on his family, and none of them ever fully recovered from the experience. It had been a terrible miscarriage of justice.

John Myers was so demonstrably unhappy about my appointment that he hardly spoke with me afterwards. He retired from Congress the next year. To the best of my knowledge, he rarely if ever returned to Washington before passing away in 2015.

Bill Young and Ralph Regula took the news of my appointment like soldiers and both served admirably as chairmen of their respective subcommittees, Defense, and Health, Education, and Welfare. Later, when I resigned from Congress, Bill succeeded me as chairman of the full Appropriations Committee. They are both gone now, but each of them remained good friends to the end.

So as the 104th Congress of 1995 convened, I assumed the chairmanship of one of the most significant committees in the United States Congress! It entitled me to a very large staff, a lovely office in the U.S. Capitol, and jurisdiction over the entire discretionary portion of the U.S. budget which at the time amounted to over $500 billion a year!!!

In the preceding seventeen years, I dared to enter the private office of the Appropriations chairman on only one occasion. Prior to David Obey (D-WI), who as mentioned earlier held the seat for only nine months, the chairmanship was held by Bill Natcher (D-KY), and before him, Jamie Whitten (D-MS), who was first elected to Congress in 1941, two years before my birth. Whitten became chairman in 1979 and held it until he fell ill in 1993. His friend and colleague, Bill Natcher, first elected to Congress in 1953, was chairman for no more than fifteen months when he too fell ill and was replaced by Obey. The longevity of his predecessors might have convinced the fifty-six year old Obey to assume that he might hold the gavel for another thirty years. But the Republican takeover interrupted his plans . . . at least until the Democrats retook control of the House in 2006 when he would reclaim his seat until his retirement in 2010.

A longstanding joke was told by Mr. Natcher about his career that ran parallel to that of Mr. Whitten's. Both moderately conservative

Democrats served on the Appropriations Committee together for decades, and both gradually scaled the ladder of seniority at a time when seniority really mattered. Being a few years senior in both service in the full House and on the committee, Whitten always got the first shot for subcommittee chairmanships and eventually for the full committee. For almost forty years, Natcher would walk into a subcommittee or full committee meeting and spotting Whitten sitting there ahead of him, and simply ask, "And how are you feeling today, Mr. Chairman?"

Notwithstanding his brief service as full chairman, Natcher was a consummate presiding officer in the full committee and on the House floor. He was always polite and fair, and I can hardly recall an instance in the near twenty years I served with him when he was not the ultimate gentleman in demeanor and impartiality. He was a Democrat first and foremost, but he honored the rules of decorum in the House for courtesy and compromise. I tried to pattern my own conduct as chairman after Bill Natcher and I think I succeeded. Unfortunately, these days that attitude has been far too rare in both Parties.

As a junior member in the minority, when I first visited Chairman Whitten in his office in the Capitol a few short steps across the hall from the House floor, I was struck with its history and beauty. But as I assumed the office as the new chairman of the Appropriations Committee, well, this was really something! Dave Obey and I had always gotten along well with one another despite our political differences as well as our respective reputations for verbal outbursts. David was an institutionalist, meaning that though quite liberal, he knew the Rules of the House and he respected anyone who tried to make the House do its business in regular order. Dave and I had known one another and had served together as chairman and ranking minority member of the Foreign Operations Subcommittee. We were philosophically miles apart, but I had learned to deal with him. I knew he hated surprises but that most of the time he was willing to meet and negotiate with those who treated him fairly.

Once he became chairman, he began a renovation of his new office with fresh furniture and curtains, and he had even had a Wisconsin state seal embossed over the entrance to the chairman's office. With the sudden disruption of his nine month old accession to the Appropriations chairmanship, one would have thought David might have begrudged me the right to replace him and that he might have been angry and petulant about my takeover.

In fact, he couldn't have been nicer. He kept to the rules and I was not permitted into the office until the 104th Congress was actually sworn in on January 3, 1995. But once done, I entered the office, sat down at my new desk, and surveyed my surroundings. There on the desk was a note instructing me to look in the lower right hand drawer. I pulled it open and found it empty but for another note and a bottle. I open that note and read:

"Dear Bob, no one should take over a new desk and empty office without some furnishings! Sincerely, David Obey"

He had checked to see what my favorite booze was at the time, and he'd left me a full quart of J&B Scotch. It was a warm and friendly gesture that I will always treasure. So many years have gone by, and I rarely ever drink hard liquor any more. In fact, I hate scotch these days, but I can't look at a scotch bottle without thinking fondly of David.

I really didn't have to do much in the way of office renovation once I moved in. Certainly, Obey's Seal of Wisconsin was short-lived, and I changed some of the portraits, but otherwise I was ready to go. Among those I kept was one of Thaddeus Stevens (R-PA), the first Appropriations Committee chairman. I might have taken it down but for that distinction. Stevens was a tough club-footed northerner who had been the chairman of the Ways and Means Committee well into the Civil War. But the committee was in charge of both raising revenue via taxes and paying expenses of the war. The federal budget ballooned so exponentially during the War that others in Congress decided that his chairmanship was just too powerful and all-encompassing to remain in the hands of one man. So in 1865, they divided the committee, created the Appropriations Committee, and gave him his choice of which committee to chair. He chose Appropriations.

Later, with the defeat of the South, Stevens contended that President Andrew Johnson wasn't sufficiently tough on the South so he led the effort to impeach him. Failing that, he continued to advocate the harshest of penalties on the defeated South, demanding conditions during Reconstruction that thwarted Southern development for generations. I kept his portrait up solely for its historical significance.

Also in my office was a magnificent portrait of James Garfield (R-

OH), the only former Appropriations Committee chairman (1871-75) to have been elected President (1880). Garfield, a Major General in the Civil War, was said to have been so scholarly and ambidextrous that he could write in Latin with one hand while in Greek with the other. Unfortunately, with only six months at the White House, he was assassinated by a disgruntled job seeker as he was about to board a train.

A portrait of John Taber (R-NY) hung on the wall behind my desk. Taber was the last Republican to chair the committee before me, vacating the office in 1955. I also kept a "pen and ink" drawing of Bill Natcher (D-KY), whom I so admired for his demeanor as a presiding officer, as well as a photograph of my Appropriations Committee mentor, Silvio Conte (R-MA), who by then had passed away to cancer, but who had been such a vital moderate force among Republicans in the Congress. Philosophy aside, these men taught me the meaning of pride in the job and effectiveness in office.

Congress is a place where ideologues can always be right from their own point of view, but they don't necessarily win. Having a political philosophy is extremely important, but if you can't win you are wasting precious time. If you are convinced of the righteousness of your position, but you can't garner the votes to enact it into law, why bother? It's far better to win and enact 60 percent to 80 percent of an agenda than to insist on 100 percent and enact little or nothing.

That means that from time to time, you have to concede some victories to the other side. I learned how to do that with Dave Obey, and we Republicans won many victories over the following four years. We scaled back the size and cost of government and ultimately balanced the budget. We lost a few battles, but we won far more than we lost. In retrospect, we did a lot better than the Republicans of the mid-2000s or for that matter, the Democrats of 2007 to 2010. (Of course, in his 2016 bid for the presidency, John Kasich claimed full credit for having balanced the budget, but anyone familiar with the process understands that it was the Appropriations Committee that controlled the discretionary purse, not the Budget Committee of which Kasich was chairman during my own chairmanship.)

For sure, the majority matters. The majority sets the agenda for each committee throughout both houses of Congress. As a fully committed conservative on most issues, I'd rather win many or most of my battles in the majority than few or none in the minority. But to do that, one must understand that it takes many people of different philosophies and concerns to make up that majority. Expecting everyone to walk in lockstep with every single issue is both asinine and unproductive. And it's contrary to the Constitution, which provides for compromise if results are to be had. This is a lesson that both Republicans and Democrats of today would do well to go back and relearn.

Appropriations Chairmanship

So, after seventeen and a half years in the minority in the House of Representatives, I found myself not only in the majority, but now the chairman of what in my mind was the most significant committee in Congress. But how was I to run it? No Republican had held a chairmanship of any House committee for forty years.

I could have swept out every last sitting Democratic staff member, as did most of my Republican counterparts. "They treated me like dirt, and by God, I'm going to treat them the same way!!" was not an unheard sentiment among incoming chairmen. The problem was that Republicans had labored in the minority for so long that they had no idea of how to run their own committees, let alone the House of Representatives. Even the new Speaker, who had spent much of his time strategizing for the takeover, had relatively little experience in actual committee meetings. He was singly the most responsible person for our new majority. He'd proven to be a great revolutionary, but now he had to show that he could actually run this great institution of 435 members and the 25,000-plus staff people in the House of Representatives.

I was only one of thirteen separate committee chairmen. But for my part, I actually had given thought to the problem of running the place. Fortunately, I reached a solution that worked out perfectly for the Appropriations Committee and ultimately was quite helpful to the Speaker himself. Taking control of the committee as the first Republican in forty years, I knew I couldn't run the committee by myself. There were no trained Republican staff who had any idea of the intricacies of committee business. My top Legislative Aide on the committee, Paul Cambon, had mastered the legislative agenda during our almost eighteen years of service together, but he didn't know how to actually manage the committee. So after some deliberation and consultation with Paul, I approached Fred Mohrmann, the Democratic Chief Clerk of the committee who'd served under Jamie Whitten, Bill Natcher, and David Obey. I knew Fred and on one occasion had even traveled with him and his wife, Jan. I knew him to be a loyal Democrat, but I also knew him to be relatively conservative and a totally honest and committed civil servant in the finest sense of the words.

With some trepidation, I approached Fred and asked him if he thought he could assist me in breaking in the committee under a Republican majority in a fair and unbiased manner. After a discussion about how I viewed my own new job, he thought it over and accepted my offer. I caught a lot of crap about that move from conservatives and Republicans for two or three years afterwards, but it was the best decision I could have made. Fred was a walking encyclopedia on the history of the committee, and he was loved by all the professional staff that I kept on board. And yes, that was the other decision that was more than heavily criticized, but it was absolutely the right thing to do.

I gathered all the staff people who had served the committee and who were still aboard in the aftermath of the elections. My message to them was very simple. I told them I was the chairman and that as such, I would preside over the committee. I said that I considered that every member of the staff would answer to me and would serve on the committee and subcommittees at my pleasure. But then I told them that I believed them to be professionals and that I would treat them as such so long as they performed their duties in a straightforward and professional manner. I said I would not inquire about their political affiliations, but that I could not keep them if they truly believed that their Democratic loyalties would interfere with their professional judgment. I then invited them all to take a day or so and consider whether in good conscience they could abide my wishes and serve as professional staff to the full committee and to me as chairman. Many left. But of those who remained, I asked Fred, who knew each of them personally, to interview them and ascertain first that they were capable and competent and secondly to avoid keeping any "ringers" or people who would be in any way disloyal to me or the Republican leadership. When Fred completed his interviews, about half the staff remained. Then he went about the process with my concurrence of hiring new applicants, most of whom but not all were Republicans.

With Fred's incredible help and assistance, we named the Chief Clerks for the various subcommittees, filled out the rosters of staff in the central office, the subcommittees, and the "S&I" Team, officially known as "Surveys and Investigations Squad," a group of retired FBI, CIA, and GAO (Government Accountability Office) personnel who assisted the majority in investigating the worthiness of existing government programs we were tasked to fund. I found these people fulfilled a vital role of oversight that I deemed so important to an often ignored responsibility of Congress, especially when we couldn't always depend on Executive Branch agencies to provide unvarnished truth about controversial issues.

When the committee staff was fully constructed, I began to feel sufficiently comfortable in my role to control the committee and lead it in a fiscally constructive manner. Fred, who told me from the start that he wanted to retire to his farm in Kentucky once he had gotten me up and going, helped me select his own successor. We considered a large number of people, but after full consideration, we landed on Jim Dyer, a former Appropriations Committee staffer to Joe McDade from Pennsylvania. Jim can be a crusty curmudgeon who gets grumpier with the passage of time. But he is a dear friend to this day, and he turned out to be the perfect choice for the job. He's very bright, and he has an excellent grasp of the legislative agenda. He's moderately conservative but not overwhelmingly so, and his somewhat cynical sense of humor made him a perfect complement to my own too often trusting, more conservative nature.

Fred brought Jim in and trained him to assume the role as Chief Clerk of the committee. With both Fred and Jim at my side, I waded through the Republican members on the committee and prepared my list of more senior members to serve as the respective subcommittee chairs. Knowing that I had some disgruntled senior members to accommodate, I had no difficulty in assigning Bill Young, Ralph Regula, and John Myers as chairs of their preferred subcommittees. And while less senior members were a little harder to satisfy, I finally worked it all out and they were by and large pleased with the outcome. Unfortunately, Joe McDade was still on the sidelines as he fought through his legal battles. Once I'd made all the assignments with only a few unhappy souls, I obtained confirmation of my assignments from the Republican Steering Committee, of which I was a member due to my chairmanship. Ultimately, the full Republican Conference approved my appointments. We were ready to go.

The first thing we did was to call all the new staff together and give them a pep talk. I told them how I viewed my role as chairman to run the committee and to make sure that to the degree possible, I wanted to reduce the redundancy, waste, fraud, and simply unnecessary programs and that I would need their assistance. I admitted that I was a novice and that I would make mistakes along the way, but I reiterated that I considered them each to be professionals and that I expected them to make sure that I didn't show my behind to the world. I needed them, and I didn't hesitate to let them know that they needed me. We would work as a team, but I left no doubt about who worked for whom. It was the right tact and for the four years that I served as chairman, I never felt that I had anything other than the utmost respect and loyalty from the committee staff. I'd known a good many of those folks before we took over, but I became personal friends with many of them then and since. We were a team and with their help, we did manage to pare down spending and ultimately create a climate for a balanced budget. But it wasn't easy, and it was often over the objections of the Clinton administration, many Democratic members, and even some Republicans.

I recall my first meeting in the full committee. After speaking with my own personal office team headed by Allen Martin and Paul Cambon in Washington, and Rick Legendre, my district representative in New Orleans, I took a large paper bag into the full committee room for my first address to the Republican and Democratic members of the committee. The meeting was somewhat historic so it was recorded on CSPAN. After some introductory remarks preceded by a generous introduction and the handing of the gavel to me by outgoing Chairman Dave Obey, I began to outline my thoughts for our role to reduce the federal budget. I explained that I hated "across the board" budget cuts favored by so many members, both Republican and Democrat. I told them I had no difficulty increasing outlays for meaningful and necessary programs, so long as the money for a program was in the best interest of the country and was being well spent. But I said that wasted money should NOT be spent and that the only way to tell the good from the bad was to provide competent oversight and use good judgment and discretion.

Once we sorted out the good from the bad, I said that wasteful, redundant, and unnecessary programs should not be continued in force as long as other options were available. Freezing all or parts of the budget is a last resort, but it simply isn't a sufficient tool to actually cut the budget. There will always be some parts of government that really should be increased under selective conditions. Defense in wartime or law enforcement in times of great crime are examples of required increases. But to truly reduce the budget, judgment should be exercised to scale back and if possible eliminate unneeded programs.

I tasked the members and Staff to seek out and cut those programs so that we could reduce the burden on the taxpayer. To do that, I said, we'd often need a scalpel. And with that I reached in the bag and pulled out a very sharp alligator skinning knife that we called a "Cajun Scalpel" obtained from a friend on the West Bank of Jefferson Parish, Louisiana. I then said if a program was really wasteful, we might have to use something larger and I produced a "Tennessee Toothpick" commonly known as a "Bowie Knife." Finally, I said if we're still not doing enough to core the budget down to size, we might have to use the heavy artillery and with that, I produced and waved a large machete from El Salvador. That picture made the papers around the country. Today, it might have been seen around the world on YouTube, but I was pleased with the coverage we received. The point was made and the tone for the new majority was cast in stone.

By the time Fred Mohrmann was prepared to retire, Jim Dyer was fully armed to take over, and indeed, the transition took place without a ripple. Fred had become a good and loyal friend. He had done his job for me, and he retired to his farm in Kentucky with his wife, Jan, and family. Sadly a few months later, Fred suddenly and tragically collapsed and died of a heart attack. We were all devastated that he didn't have time to enjoy the retirement he'd worked so hard to earn!

At the outset of the new Congress in 1995, it was a darn good thing that we had the experienced hands within the Appropriations staff that we did. Virtually all the other Republican staff were new and "on the job training," and there were very few people on the new majority staff who knew how to handle House business. For the first few months, my team provided expertise for the Speaker's Office and other offices to assist them in running the daily routine of the House.

Even so, it took a while for each of us as members to make the transition from minority to majority. We wanted to be efficient, to reduce spending and trim the size of government, and to provide adequate resources for the defense of the nation. But we also had to show that we could govern, that we could "make the trains run on time," and that we deserved the majority entrusted to us by the American people. That proved to be a constant source of tension, not just with the Clinton people, but among our own members and our supporters. Obviously, many of our supporters wanted all of our conservative agenda and the "Contract with America" enacted immediately.

The day-to-day activity on the committee was always interesting. I'd begin the day in my regular district office in the Rayburn Building, but once the House began business for the day, I'd usually shift over to my Appropriations office in the Capitol. From there it was a one-minute walk across the hall to the floor of the House, and if one of our bills was on the floor, I'd bounce back and forth between the two. Since, as chairman, I authored all of our Appropriations bills plus "Continuing Resolutions" to extend time between deadlines so that we could get our work done without shutting down the government, I probably was the lead author on more bills in the four years of my chairmanship than any of my colleagues.

But before the bills ever got to the floor, they would have to be "marked up" in subcommittee, debated in full committee, and then once approved by a majority vote of committee members, they'd go to the Full House for debate and a vote. I would preside over the full committee debates, amendments, and final passage of the bills, but my "Cardinals" (subcommittee chairmen divided by issue jurisdiction) handled the bills in subcommittee from hearings to "mark-up" before sending them to the full committee. Each of them was assisted by committee staff, who again were hired by me as the full committee chairman. That was important so that I could keep control over the process.

Before the bills were assigned by Majority Leader Dick Armey for debate on the House floor, they had to be processed in the Rules Committee chaired by my friend, Jerry Solomon (R-NY). Generally, we tried to make Appropriations bills ready for floor debate under "Open Rules," meaning that any debate on an amendment to strike or to raise or lower the cost of a particular line item would be subject to a specified period of time with reduced restrictions on the House floor. But when sticky political issues arose, they might be awarded a "Closed" or "Modified Closed Rule," so that sensitive amendments could be restricted or barred from debate to prevent unwanted delay or controversy. With the passage of time and subsequent takeover of the Democratic majority in 2006, almost all of the bills brought to the floor by the Democratic majority (2006 – 2010) were limited or fully closed so as to reduce or circumvent input from the minority. That's a practice to be avoided, and I was pleased to hear the more recent Republican majority express intent to return to the old practice of open debate on as many bills as possible. Unfortunately, it became better expressed in intent than in practice.

"Regular Order" required that once a bill passed the Full House, it was sent to the Senate for similar but not identical action. There were inevitable differences between two completed bills on the same subject, and those differences would be hashed out in Conference between key Senate and House members from the respective committees. Some of my favorite memories arose from those Conferences. For example, in the early '80s when Senator John C. Stennis (D-MS) presided over a conference of Defense Appropriators, he enjoyed a very close relationship with his Republican counterpart, Senator Ted Stevens (R-AK). Joe Addabbo (D-NY) chaired the Defense Subcommittee for the Democratic majority on the House side, and Joe was far more liberal than either Senators Stennis or Stevens. I was a junior minority member of the subcommittee back then, but I fondly recall watching Stennis, who was well into his forty-one-year career in the U.S. Senate, sitting ram-rod straight in his wheel chair with full military bearing all day long each day during a three to five day conference. Much of the work was handled by members and staff, but when there was a difference of opinion between the more liberal Addabbo and his Senate counterpart, Addabbo would make his case and both Stennis and Stevens would listen attentively. They would then confer with each other in whispering tones and would reach an agreement between themselves. Stennis had a throat ailment that prevented him from speaking loudly, so Ted Stevens would bark out, "The chairman says, 'No.'" And that was not an infrequent occurrence.

Later, when I was chairman of the full House Committee and Ted Stevens was chairman of Senate Appropriations, there were many times when we'd hash out the differences between our sides. While Ted was predictably protective of his native Alaska, he also was a patriot with whom I enjoyed many productive discussions. As a young man, Ted flew missions against the Japanese from Burma during WWII, and still later, he'd been instrumental to the effort to make Alaska a State. He was a wonderful human being, and I thought the Bush Justice Department treated him poorly when they indicted and convicted him a few weeks before his 2008 election. He was defeated in that election, but the conviction was overturned only a few months later. The prosecutors were cited for deliberately and unjustly manipulating the evidence, but nothing of consequence ever happened to them. Yet this wonderful man who gave so much of his life to his state and to his country was no longer to serve in the Senate.

Ted and his family were involved in a plane crash in Alaska in 1978. He survived, but his wife, Ann, did not. Ironically, after remarrying and establishing a family with his second wife, Catherine, Ted was among the victims of a subsequent plane accident in Alaska on August 9, 2010. This time he did not survive.

Senator Robert Byrd (D-WV), was the longest serving U.S. Senator at the time of his death in June 2010. In his day, he was a walking encyclopedia on Senate Rules, and he was also a published authority on the legislative history of the Senate of the Roman Republic. When Senator Byrd delivered a speech, his voice would theatrically resonate in stentorian tones throughout the Senate Chamber, and he could speak for hours on subjects of interest. When Republicans took control of the Senate in 1995, he lost his chairmanship of the Appropriations Committee to Ted Stevens, but he quickly acclimated to his role as ranking minority member. In those days, Senate Republicans and Democrats often aligned together against the White House for intrusion into Congressional prerogatives. One such occasion involved President Clinton's Office of Management and Budget (OMB). Senators Byrd and Stevens joined my ranking Democrat, David Obey, and me in my Capitol Appropriations office. I outlined the problem and was delighted when Senator Byrd waved his right hand from left to right as he boomed, "I give the back of my hand to the administration!!!" Needless to say, we won that argument with OMB and wrapped up the final issues on our bills before adjourning for the year.

As we Republicans first began to pour over the budget in the spring of 1995, we searched for programs to cut. Our first victory was won when we produced a rescission package that significantly pared down

President Clinton's fiscal year '95 package passed by the Democrats before we took control in the fall of '94. By the end of 1995, we'd eliminated roughly 300 redundant programs entirely and reduced hundreds more, thus saving the taxpayer some $50 billion in wasteful spending. My friend, Jerry Lewis (R-CA) the chairman of the Subcommittee on Housing and Urban Development, provided the largest share of the cuts, but every one of my subcommittee chairmen, jokingly known as "Cardinals," pitched in and contributed to the savings.

That first year of my chairmanship set the tone for our frugality, and in the remaining years that I served as chairman, we used the Appropriations process to reduce the growth of spending in the discretionary portion of the budget. We kept earmarks to a minimum and prevented the Clinton administration from going wild with their inclination to spend ever greater amounts of public money. None of these priorities were easy to achieve, and we had many battles—some with the administration, many with the Democrats, and some with our fellow Republicans as well. But when the final tally was done as I left, we'd flat-lined spending in those four years and ensured a balanced budget, at least on the discretionary side of the equation.

The progress we made was not without controversy or strenuous opposition from the Democrats. They fought it at every turn, and we met their challenge. When we first took control, Leon Panetta, former Democratic Congressman from California, was Director of OMB. We were so effective in our attempts to cut the budget that Bill Clinton conceded in his State of the Union Speech in January 1996 that "The Era of Big Government is now over!" We continued to restrain spending in our bills, and Panetta had a difficult time dealing with us. But as time passed and Panetta handed the reins to his successors, Franklin Raines and Jack Lew, the Clintons grew more effective at manipulating the budget by spending on their own priorities and underfunding Congressional favorites like water resources infrastructure and defense projects that they knew we in Congress would restore. The battles over the Budget and Appropriations grew tougher, yet we still won most of them. But in the last year I was there, Speaker Gingrich and then Senate Majority Leader Trent Lott assumed control of negotiations over the remaining unresolved line items, and we began to lose ground. Clinton gradually managed to increase spending. Still, by more recent standards, those increases amounted to little or virtually nothing. The accumulated cuts we achieved between 1995 through 1998 enabled us to balance the budget, provide confidence to investors, and maintain growth and affluence throughout the country well into the next decade.

Unfortunately, once I was gone, our frugality was abandoned during the Bush (43) administration by Republicans and Democrats alike. Despite the excesses in spending by the Congress in his presidency, George W. Bush (43) vetoed only two Appropriations bills in his eight years in office, so he certainly shared the blame for the growth of the federal budget in that era. Of course, 9/11 and two wars contributed heavily to spending demands, but there was no visible spending restraint inside his administration any more than there was in the Republican-controlled Congress during his watch. When Republicans lost control of the Congress in 2006, the Democrats abandoned any pretense of frugality under Speaker Pelosi, yet Bush still signed most of their bills.

It now appears that without severe cuts in the budget comparable to those by the Coolidge administration in the early 1920s when federal spending was cut by 50 percent, another balanced budget will be unlikely in this century.

As chairman, I found myself constantly torn between my desire to enact our Republican agenda and acting on what I thought possible versus what I believed impossible to accomplish. Not all my efforts were appreciated by my own squad. In the early days, the Speaker left me alone, and as long as I delivered, he was relatively happy. But the Budget chairman, John Kasich, felt that as lead dog on the Budget Committee, he could override the Appropriations Committee with his own assessment of what was important to the country and what was not. He constantly tried to micro-manage the Appropriations Committee by dictating budget priorities of his own. We had an early confrontation in the Speaker's office, and I produced a copy of the enabling legislation that created the Budget Committee in 1974. It clearly stated that the purpose of the Budget Committee was to set targets for overall spending but not intrude into line items of the Appropriations process, especially so long as my committee abided the strictures of the overall Budget guidelines set by his committee and approved by the House.

Time is the rarest of commodities on Capitol Hill. Members are torn from constituent meetings, subcommittee meetings, political meetings, debates, or votes in committee or on the House floor, to receptions galore. They are always running hither and yon, and the more they allow themselves to be overloaded, the less effective they become. I felt strongly that committees and subcommittees ought to be kept to a minimum size, that members should be restricted to a single major committee and maybe a minor one. I felt that they should be assigned to a total of no more than five subcommittees so that they could attend meetings, digest the evidence from witnesses and staff, and learn to govern intelligently. With more than five assignments, the member certainly can't cover all activities at once, and he hardly becomes knowledgeable about the material in his jurisdiction. I also thought that if at all possible, major committees should each encourage an oversight subcommittee to dig down into the nuances of government in order to root out waste, inefficiency, and corruption.

The only way to keep down the aggregate number of assignments to members is to reduce the size of the committees to no more than fifty, so that too many members could not be assigned to any one committee. I managed to persuade the Steering Committee to go along with me for a while, but the leadership inevitably wanted to please some member by putting him on a committee of his choice, and Bud Shuster (R-PA), Chairman of Transportation, stretched that theory as far as he could. Bud believed that by stacking his Transportation Committee with over eighty members, he could use sheer numbers of votes to exert clout on policy decisions so that the leadership simply couldn't overrule him. The more members on a committee, the more autonomy a chairman had over the leadership, and that was not necessarily a good thing.

I thought holding each committee to fifty or fewer members was ideal in that it made the committee more manageable for committee and subcommittee chairmen, and I struggled to achieve that ceiling on Appropriations, as did Bill Archer (R-TX), chairman of the Ways and Means Committee. We weighed in with the Steering Committee to apply a universal limitation for all committees, but we never were quite able to whittle the numbers that low. Bud on the other hand was allowed to continue to add members to his committee. When an internal Republican dispute arose over the Transportation Trust Fund, he won the fight by simply rallying his many troops to his side in the majority conference. But it still wasn't good policy.

I was convinced that no junior member should be assigned to a major committee in his first term, and I tried to make that rule universal as well. When a member is first elected to Congress, his colleagues usually don't know him, and it takes a while to judge whether he's a flamboyant pop-gun, a work horse, a leader, or just a jerk. I thought it important to know that before assigning him to key committees to be sure that responsible people would be well suited to their responsibilities. I also felt that while I knew how to run my committee, I didn't want people on it who would countermand my own goal of cutting the budget. But when it was time to assign members to new committees, there were at least two occasions when my suggested practice was overruled by the internal governing authority, the Republican Steering Committee.

Mark Neumann (R-WI) was an exceptionally bright fellow who was terrific with numbers. But he came to Congress with the attitude that he was the only person there who was conservative and genuinely interested in scaling back the budget. He was convinced that everyone senior to him was a corrupt conniver who stood in his way to save America. After two previous losses, he'd won election in 1994, and Newt wanted to reward him with a seat on the Appropriations Committee despite my arguments that he was a freshman and needed some seasoning before becoming so assigned. My relations with Mark were rocky from the start, and they grew worse as we went along. He was so obnoxious that I finally had enough and ejected him from the committee. The Speaker conferred with him for about a half hour and then called and ordered me to take him back. I reluctantly did so, but then I opened an Appropriations slot on the Budget Committee and gave him to John Kasich just to get him out of my hair. I guess I shouldn't have been surprised when after a year on Budget, Mark developed his own budget that cut more than anyone thought possible, and he came very close to getting his alternative passed by the House. It was an extraordinary effort, and I acquired newfound respect for him. But I still didn't want him anywhere near me. And Newt learned that gratitude in politics is short lived. Neumann subsequently repaid Gingrich's support by voting "present" instead of voting for Newt for

Speaker in 1997.

The other notable affirmation of my policy to exclude freshmen from the top committees was Randy "Duke" Cunningham. Duke had become the only Navy "Ace" during the Vietnam War, meaning that he was the only pilot in the Navy to have shot down five enemy planes. He seemed like a nice guy, and he was a real hero in the minds of many people, especially his own. He won a seat to Congress in a close election, and when he arrived, he began maneuvering to get on Appropriations. Again, I lodged my objection to putting freshman members on the "big" committees like mine, Ways and Means, and Energy & Commerce. There were lots of other members waiting patiently to get on these committees, and it was unfair to them to reward newer, junior members with such assignments without first checking them out. But Duke played the "war hero" card and maneuvered to convince Frank Riggs (R-WA) to leave Appropriations to make room for himself. After all, he was an "Ace," so once again I was overruled, and Duke got the assignment.

No sooner had he won the new position, but he wanted an assignment to the Defense Subcommittee. I blew up. "Of course not!" I fumed. "The Defense Subcommittee is the most highly sought-after subcommittee in the House and people on the full committee have waited for years to be assigned to it!"

"But, he's an 'Ace,' Bob!" shot back the Speaker. So "The Dukester" as he was subsequently to name a boat we learned was bought for him by some lobbyist, soon became a member of the Defense Appropriations Committee. I wasn't finished. When I was instructed to put him on the subcommittee, I took him aside in a small room and told him in loud and explicit terms that he had circumvented the traditional process and that he had won a spot on a subcommittee sought by other members for years. I told him I was going along with the Speaker, but I wanted him to know that I was the chairman and when I needed his vote, I expected him to respond accordingly. Duke actually broke into tears and thanked me, saying, "Bob, I'll always be your wing man!"

Well, Duke spent the waning days of his career in Federal prison on an eight year sentence for bribery. But I guess he's still my wing man.

The size of the Federal Budget is of ever increasing concern, and in recent years, expenditures have vastly exceeded revenues. The shortfall has accelerated to such a degree that the country has reached the precipice and is finding itself incapable of meeting its obligations. History is replete with countries that failed to restrain their financial desires, and the ultimate result is financial collapse, impoverishment of its citizenry, and ultimate tyranny of a privileged few over the masses. People have worried about the problem throughout history:

> The budget should be balanced, the treasury should be refilled, public debt should be reduced, the arrogance of officialdom should be tempered and controlled, and the assistance to foreign lands should be curtailed lest Rome become bankrupt. People must again learn to work instead of living on public assistance.
>
> Cicero - 55 BC

The United States is still the most powerful country on earth, politically, economically, and militarily. We are by nature a free and independent people. But a significant financial collapse would undermine our strength and our freedoms. If we don't tend to business in a thoughtful and deliberate fashion in the near future, our children and grandchildren may not enjoy the independence that we and our forebears have enjoyed.

In short, over the last many years Congress has lost all restraint on government spending. When revenues were abundant, we spent more than we received, and as revenues declined, we spent even more. Most people look to a President to rectify such the problem, and by acknowledging the pressure imposed on him by a Republican Congress, President Clinton professed, "The era of big government is now over," and we made some significant strides in the right direction. But both Presidents George W. Bush (43) and Barack Obama ignored, or worse, aggravated the situation. While the Bush administration was remiss in fiscal control, the Obama administration was wastefully profligate. The national debt virtually doubled under Bush from $5 trillion when I left Congress in 1999, and it doubled again to $20 trillion under Obama. The first year of the Trump administration has boosted the debt by another trillion dollars, so we haven't yet made the correction we need.

Yet, fiscal restraint was never the intended concern of the Chief Executive. Instead, our forefathers invested the power of the purse to the Legislative Branch and specifically to the House of Representatives.

> The House of Representatives . . . alone can propose the supplies requisite for the support of the government. They [the House], in a word, hold the purse—that powerful instrument by which we behold, in the history of the British Constitution, an infant and humble representation of the people gradually enlarging the sphere of its activity and importance, and finally reducing, as far as it seems to have wished, all the overgrown prerogatives of the other branches of the government.
>
> This power over the purse may, in fact, be regarded as the most complete and effectual weapon with which any constitution can arm the immediate representatives of the people, for obtaining a redress of every grievance, and for carrying into effect every just and salutary measure.
>
> James Madison—Federalist #58

With this statement, Madison portrays his belief that divided responsibility is the single greatest check on natural growth of government that any nation could possess. But it can only be successful through the wise and attentive exercise of power by diligent members of the Legislative Branch. If Congress engages in a race with the Presidency to see which Branch can provide more benefits for the American people by spending ever more of their own money, the "check" is ultimately returned "NSF" and the system will inevitably fail. Concerned about that possibility, the Senator from Arizona and unsuccessful candidate for President of the United States against Barack Obama said it best:

> I take exception to folks saying that Bernanke, Obama, Reid, and Pelosi are spending like drunken sailors. When I was a drunken sailor, I quit spending when I ran out of money.
>
> Senator John McCain

I may have well been a drunken sailor across the same pier in Norfolk, Virginia, at the same time as Senator McCain, and I recall that I couldn't spend a nickel more than I had in my pocket at any one time either.

As noted earlier, when, in the midst of the Civil War, Congress created the Appropriations Committee, they did so because they were concerned about fraud and abuse as well as uncontrolled spending. They thought the rising cost of war conveyed too much authority to the same legislators charged with the country's taxing authority, so they took the spending side of the equation away from the Ways and Means Committee.

Since then, the power of the newer Appropriations Committee has undergone cycles of war and peace, affluent times and times of poverty with significant power of the purse and with more restricted power. When it was perceived as being too powerful, it was reined in by other members of Congress. When it was attentive to its own responsibility to frugally govern programs in its jurisdiction, it was permitted a freer hand. The Budget Act of 1974 was created in part to rein in the perceived power of Appropriators in reaction to the escalating costs of the Vietnam War. But the Act has been a disastrous failure. Try as they might to attack the Appropriations process, members have been unable to find any workable alternative to functional oversight and scrutiny over federal expenditures. Simply put, without proper oversight, the taxpayers' money will be ill spent. And whether in the hands of Republicans or Democrats, we've seen abundant evidence of this very trend in recent years.

The Federal Budget is made of two components, mandatory and discretionary. Mandatory programs are those specifically designated to provide regular benefits to designated classes of citizens. These are "entitlements," be they pensions and Social Security for the retired; Medicare for the elderly; Medicaid for the impoverished; benefits for the unemployed; or some of the lesser programs passed into law in the 1930s and expanded by the "Great Society" of the 1960s, or since. No matter their utopian intent, once created, such programs never go away! If a person is eligible under an entitlement program, he need only declare his eligibility, and periodic checks will be written against the federal treasury in his favor. The money is redistributed monthly from the U.S. Treasury to the newly qualified "entitled" person, and as more people become eligible . . . or "entitled," the cost to the taxpayer becomes ever greater. These entitlements are not subject to annual appropriation or review. In fact, while they are subject to the jurisdiction of an authorizing committee like the Ways and Means Committee, they may or may not be reviewed over a period of years. Once created and unless amended, such programs become a "mandatory" element of the budget for every eligible person at any given time. The government is thus mandated to make the monthly payment without further debate. In the aggregate, all mandatory programs plus interest on the debt (which is itself "mandatory") are approaching a disproportionately large share at 75 percent of the federal budget in 2020.

Discretionary programs on the other hand are comprised of those expenditures that must be affirmatively funded by Congress in each successive year. The many thousands of programs including defense, education, transportation, expenses of the White House, and virtually every other executive department, agency, etc., are rolled over and re-appropriated year after year. They each must be reviewed and accepted by Congress through the legislative process in the several annual Appropriations bills, or they will cease to exist. Congress must either legislatively approve or amend an appropriation for every discretionary item. If it fails to do so, an item will not be funded and will not be included in the Federal Budget for the fiscal year.

Various descriptive pie charts are available on the Internet, and I thought about including them here. While visuals help to understand how our budget situation has deteriorated, a few figures will suffice to show how our system needs a radical overhaul. The figures are stated in percentages of the entire federal budget since with the passage of time, inflation distorts an honest view in terms of dollars.

In 1960 as Jack Kennedy assumed the presidency of the United States, defense of the nation accounted for 55 percent of every dollar spent in the federal budget. Mandatory spending including pensions, social programs, and interest on the debt amounted to about 20 percent. All discretionary programs apart from defense were spread among the remaining 25 percent of the budget.

In contrast, today's American taxpayers are currently shelling out vastly larger sums for the cost of government than in 1960. In 2015, mandatory spending inclusive of interest on the debt accounted for nearly two-thirds of the total federal budget. Social Security alone accounts for over half of that amount. The remaining one third of the budget covers discretionary spending including defense, which amounts to slightly more than half of that one-third, or 18 percent compared to 55 percent in 1960 of the total budget. All of the other discretionary civilian items governing administration by the entire executive branch of government are squeezed into the remaining 15 percent of the federal tax dollar. So no matter how critical the issue might be—like law enforcement, immigration control or disaster assistance—when the money runs out, it runs out . . . unless we borrow it. In fact, that's exactly what we have been doing. As noted, the aggregate debt throughout our history was $5 trillion in 1999 when I left Congress. Now, two Presidencies and nineteen years later, it has quadrupled to around $21 trillion. This cannot continue.

Despite conventional wisdom that foreign aid consumes too much of the federal dollar, in truth it amounts to less than 1 percent of the federal budget. Since such assistance helps our allies stay out of the orbit of our enemies, it is mostly money well spent.

I must underscore the budget's impact on our defense capability. In 1960, defense represented well over half of every dollar spent. No one recalls it today, but after the Korean War, the country found itself in the midst of the Cold War and Vietnam hadn't yet become a problem. Yet defense consumed fully 55 percent of every federal dollar spent.

It now accounts for slightly over one-sixth of the federal budget, and we are too frequently reading that our planes are falling out of the sky and our ships are running into each other, so it's high time that both Republicans and Democrats woke up to the most significant responsibility the American government owes to its citizens. Without an adequate defense, we needn't worry about economics. But without fiscal integrity, we can't afford to defend ourselves. The two work hand in glove, and if we don't get our economic house in order, the future of this nation is in jeopardy.

Ordinarily, a President asserts his priorities in the Federal Budget on recommendations from his Office of Management and Budget (OMB) which is tasked with gathering and coordinating the requests for funding from all the executive departments and agencies. The Speaker and the majority leadership of each house of Congress then have *carte blanche* opportunity to change the President's budget as much as they wish before submitting it to their committees. One could characterize the President's entire budget as one big "earmark" since it inevitably proffers as many adjustments to federal expenditures as he cares to make. Likewise, the Speaker and the congressional leadership are not constrained from reshaping the President's budget to their heart's delight—again technically "earmarking" the process, except that neither the changes by the President nor the leadership are ever called "earmarks." They are simply statements of their priorities.

"Earmarks" in Appropriations bills are increases (or decreases) by individual members in the course of consideration of the budget. They have always been a source of concern for those who worry about the size of the discretionary budget. The press and fiscal hawks often point to earmarks as being emblematic of wasteful spending. In truth, earmarks can become a catalyst for reducing the budget. They were exactly that when we balanced the discretionary budget in 1999. Recent Congresses have outlawed earmarks blaming them for the escalating cost of government. No one can excuse fiscal abuse of wasteful and unnecessary spending. But if a committee is on the ball, an earmark can be published in advance of mark-up, vetted by committee staff and leadership, and finally authorized with full transparency by open vote of the membership. Such is inherent to the legislative process envisioned by James Madison. To assure that earmarks are properly weighed and scrutinized requires time, oversight, and intelligent judgment. It can't be had if members aren't paying attention, nor if they misuse the process for overtly political reasons. This was the case in the early 2000s, thus leading to the ban. But an arbitrary ban is no more than a denial of constitutional authority of individual members over the treasury as well as an abdication of authority from the Legislative Branch of government to the faceless bureaucrats of the Executive Branch.

Far too many changes offered by individual members of Congress to redirect spending in meetings of the Appropriations committee or subcommittees or on the floor of the House are now castigated as "earmarks" and are eschewed or mindlessly rejected regardless of merit. This is an absurd policy. A member may have a constituent come to him with a remedy to cure cancer or redirect traffic to save lives, or otherwise provide funds essential to a well-functioning government.

By today's rules, he is arbitrarily blocked from such action. If his "earmark" constitutes a request for money for a new program, more money for an existing program, or simply a programmatic change in the way government does business, it can be barred as an "earmark" despite how meritorious or worthwhile the idea may be.

It's not a popular theme, but there really are abundant examples of good earmarks, and I never hesitated to include them in Appropriations bills if I thought them to truly be in the best interest of the country. When liberals derided missile defense in the Reagan '80s as an illusory "Star Wars" program, I championed the concept and managed to help keep the program alive over strenuous opposition. Likewise, when on the Intelligence Committee, I provided the seed capital for Unmanned Aerial Vehicles (UAVs), which are now protecting America under numerous successful programs. Weapons systems of all kinds including submarines and aircraft carriers were allegedly initiated by "earmarks" when the Defense Department was for whatever reason opposed to the budget entry. My friend and successor as committee chairman, Bill Young (R-FL) created the National Bone Marrow Registry through an initial earmark, and tens of thousands of people have been cured of cancer as a result. Likewise, Senator Orrin Hatch used an earmark to create the National Cord Blood Registry to enable placenta blood to be registered and stored for retrieval in the event of subsequent serious illness. Today, a child might grow to adulthood, contract a debilitating disease and be cured with his or her own stem cells because of this worthy earmark. And some years ago, The National Federation of the Blind used earmarks to enable blind people all over America to read newspapers by simply calling assigned numbers on their touch-tone telephones.

In short, earmarks are useful tools to permit members of Congress to respond to their constituents for the betterment of the nation. If carefully evaluated by responsible members of Congress, they may play a useful role in the exercise of the "power of the purse" entrusted to them by our forefathers. Without earmarks, Federal spending is left to the whims of unelected bureaucrats in the executive branch. And they answer to virtually no one in the general public.

In my opinion, the cry of press and politicians to condemn "earmarks" is just mindless demagoguery. If members of Congress would exercise prudent and responsible judgment through due diligence and proper oversight to make sure that only good ones were allowed, earmarks would never be a problem. And members certainly shouldn't abdicate their Constitutional responsibility over the Federal budget to any President or his bureaucracy. Those eschewing earmarks are attacking straw men and are escaping hard and thoughtful analysis. In the process, discovery of truly wasteful and unnecessary spending is left on the back burner. There is more than enough waste in the Budget to be discovered and condemned by diligent souls. But taking the easy route won't find it.

Earmarks rarely if ever add to the bottom line since they merely redirect already budgeted spending from lesser urgent programs. Indeed, the sum and total of earmarks have rarely if ever amounted to much more than 1 percent of the discretionary budget, which again including defense is less than one-third of all government spending in a year. But they do provide the means through which individual members of Congress exercise discretion to change priorities that an Executive Branch bureaucracy would naturally overlook or worse yet, ignore. In sum, banning earmarks simply denies members their right to truly represent their constituents.

John Boehner initiated the ban on earmarks when he was Speaker of the House. He crowed that he had never asked for nor received an earmark. Of course, his Ohio colleagues on the Appropriations Committee never shrank from accommodating their state wherever needed, but Boehner's hands were clean. Unfortunately, implementation of the earmark ban has corresponded directly to the wholesale inability of Congress to pass most Appropriation bills since it was adopted. But as can be seen from the dearth of legislative product in recent years, far sighted legislative strategy may be in short supply.

I've argued that the Appropriations process can be used to cut the budget as well as increase it. We did exactly that during my tenure as Appropriations chairman. Remember, mandatory entitlement programs representing two-thirds of all federal spending have been out of control for decades, and they desperately need review and overhaul. Neither party has stepped up to the task. But the last time Congress balanced the discretionary budget was in 1999-2000; that was when earmarks were managed and allowed openly with discretion. Likewise, the last time Defense Authorization Act was passed within the time prescribed by law was 2005—the year before the earmark ban was adopted. Without earmarks, too many members have no reason to support worthy bills and blindly vote "no." The system is badly broken and is in dire need of improvement. The Senate is especially bogged down because of its archaic rules. Changes are desperately needed, and a rational earmark rule should be among them.

While I'm on the subject, the media loves to attack campaign contributions almost as much as they condemn earmarks. I will be the first to admit that if a member of Congress actually links action in Congress to financial support obtained from contributors, then his or her actions are wrong and probably illegal, and they should be sanctioned. Moreover, if money flows to the personal benefit of a member in return for legislation as it allegedly did for our former colleague, Randy "Duke" Cunningham, then it constitutes bribery, and as it did for him, the member risks criminal charges and imprisonment.

But the issue is not as clear when it comes to legitimate campaign contributions. Legally, a member is not permitted to convert such contributions to his own use. Every campaign needs lots of campaign cash to broadcast the candidate's message. In years past—long past—all a candidate had to do was stand on a soap box and speak to the voters. Town meetings, press conferences, and public debates provided limited opportunity to broadcast a message. Voters had little option to receive a candidate's message other than through personal observation of speeches, newspapers, and whatever other older media might have existed. But as technologies of radio and television evolved, campaigning became more expensive. When I first ran in 1976, money was required for media exposure, but not nearly in the quantities commonly spent in campaigns today!

Television, radio, newspapers, Internet, direct mail, telephone conferences, social media—the list is infinite, but it all costs money. No longer can a candidate give a speech while standing on the corner and expect to get his message out. He has to purchase media exposure. I have always thought it to be ultimate hypocrisy for the media to attack candidates for soliciting campaign donations, when in fact at least 80 percent of money raised goes directly to media to broadcast their messages. A candidate must raise money for his campaign, and he must spend most of it on the media. Under current law, if he converts it to his own use, he goes to jail. But when he pays the media, reporters attack him for raising the money in the first place.

Personally, I had no idea who contributed to my campaigns apart from meeting those who showed up at my fundraisers. I rarely looked at my contributor list, and I never imposed rules about connecting actions in my office to whether or not a person contributed to my campaigns. It didn't even occur to me to do so. I took action when I thought it best for my district, state, or nation, and I didn't if I saw no benefit for them. I certainly attempted to judge issues on merit, not who might or might not have given me a contribution.

Clearly, corrupt practices in the raising of campaign cash do exist. Some members will offer to engage in specific legislative practices in return for campaign donations. This is wrong and whether Republicans or Democrats do it, it should be stopped.

Some say the solution is to go to public financing, but I believe public financing is perhaps the worst possible solution. In 1992, racist and bigot David Duke, communist Lenora Fulani, and billionaire Ross Perot were among the candidates running against George H.W. Bush (41) and Bill Clinton. A publicly financed campaign would have required everyone to pay into a government fund, and each of these candidates would have received an equal amount of taxpayers' dollars to run their campaign. Personally, I would have been horrified if my tax dollars had been taken to support any of these candidates other than President Bush (41). But in fact, that would have been the case under a full-fledged public financing scheme. Adoption of such a system is just plain un-American and in my opinion, a violation of the First Amendment for the government to take my money to support a candidate to whom I'm vigorously opposed.

In fact, a mild version was adopted and implemented by Congress in 1966. Since then, tax forms have provided for a check-off donation of one dollar by a taxpayer to be matched by three dollars from the Treasury for a Presidential Campaign Fund. But evidently most people agree with me, since support for the fund has dwindled to the point of irrelevance over the years.

Until recently, I've felt that the best way to regulate potential corruption in campaign finance would be to follow the original intent of the Campaign Finance Law of 1974 by making full disclosure the ultimate governor of campaign contributions. We should still discourage different state rules in all federal elections so that national candidates need not hire lawyers and CPAs to decipher the nuances of law in each and every one of the 50 states. But I used to feel that we should require that all donors and funds raised be published on the internet within twenty-four hours of receipt. I would have barred straw men, perjurers, and foreign donors from contributing and also provided penalties to include lengthy prison sentences for ignoring the law. I felt that at least for all Federal elections, the rules should be clear, concise, simple, and uniform. If voters had all information on donors available to them on the internet, they could make up their own minds about the candidate and his supporters.

I still believe this would be the most ideal format in a peaceful and serene world. But our country has changed for the worse in recent years in that public discourse has become more difficult. Far too frequently, anarchists and thugs seek out contributors to causes or candidates they oppose, and they threaten them with political, financial, and even personal injury. This is not the America in which I grew up. It's a phenomenon that is ugly and harmful to a free society, and it must cease. Thus, while I wouldn't change current law requiring that most contributions be made public, there are some provisions like 501(c)4s in law that permit confidential contributions. I might once have abolished them in the name of full transparency, but large donors concerned about their safety do have an argument for confidentiality. The system should still guard against those who refuse to play by the rules, and the rules should be simplified well beyond the current spaghetti of law and regulation that so encumbers today's candidates for office. But people should feel confident that their contributions to candidates or causes of their choice will not place them in positions of peril.

Returning to my ardent desire to cut the federal budget, my forty-one years on the Hill have convinced me that the Congressional budget process created by Democrats in 1974 is simply far more complicated that it should be. When it's working, the Executive Departments and Agencies begin the process well in advance of each fiscal year. They funnel their requests to the Office of Management and Budget (OMB), which weeds through them and assembles a viable proposal for the President based on his political priorities. Once approved, the President sends the Budget to Congress shortly after his State of the Union Speech in January. Congress then has the responsibility to accept or reject whatever the majority wishes and then to offer up its own budget to guide the Appropriations bills for the coming year. In recent years, the whole messy process has collapsed so that too frequently, no Congressional Budget is passed at all.

Since the President doesn't ever sign a legislative budget anyway, the document has no force of law. It is really just a guide or roadmap for Congress to plan Appropriations and contain unnecessary spending. We've seen how well that has worked in recent years. In fact, it hasn't worked at all and one could make a strong case that the system is badly broken

I strongly believed that much of the budget process was wasteful, time-consuming and simply unnecessary. Both Houses often spend months debating the size and shape of the budget, thereby delaying the Appropriations process and the votes needed to appropriate funding for government to function. After all the debate on the budget, the two Houses often fail to agree so nothing at all is passed. In that event, they simply and far too frequently refer back to the previous year's agreement to pass a Continuing Resolution (CR). That's the worst possible fiscal action a Congress might take, since it doesn't reduce waste or enhance worthy programs. A CR simply takes what was done the year before with little or no change and adds more money to cover inflation. Legislative initiative, discretion, and oversight are postponed entirely for another year.

Rather than spend all that time on a meaningless document, I've often said the Budget Committee could convene for no more than a day or two to listen to economic forecasters explain what they saw in the previous year versus what they expect to see in the coming year. Then the Budget Committee could determine four numbers to pass onto the Finance and Appropriations Committees:

1) How much did the nation raise last year;
2) How much did we spend;
3) How much do we anticipate raising this year; and
4) How much of that (or how much over) do we want to spend?

The roles of the House Ways and Means Committee and the Senate Finance Committee are to assess the need to raise or lower taxes, and clearly, the Budget Committee would play an advisory role with them. But assessing changing needs of the country from year to year shouldn't take more than a few days to accomplish. When completed, the answer to number four above should be passed to the Appropriations Committee which would be compelled to live within the prescribed allotment. Appropriator's first priority should be to cut wasteful and redundant spending, and with proper oversight, they could pass as many or as few "earmarks" as they like. But if they spend a dollar over the number provided by the budget, their bills should be voted down by the House and/or Senate and, at the very least, vetoed by the President.

Eliminating months of debate on the budget would provide members with far more time for Congressional oversight of the President's budget proposals and the ongoing administration of government by existing agencies and departments. With greater oversight, a practice far too rare in today's Congress, duplication, waste and fraud can be more easily uprooted and exposed, leading to reduction of much of the wasteful drain on taxpayers.

Once in the majority in 1995, John Kasich enjoyed his position as Budget chairman and certainly didn't want to change the process to dilute his own influence. Instead, he frequently used his job as a bully pulpit to assert his views on how the government should spend taxpayer funds. Being moderately conservative, he generally advocated positions with which I agreed, but some of his agenda was either implausible or beyond what I thought prudent. For example, he joined with Ron Dellums (D-CA) in 1996 to successfully kill the B-2 bomber, one of the most effective defensive weapons in our arsenal. I thought he was wrong and voted to keep it. But he prevailed and cut the 132 authorized planes down to just twenty one, one of which crashed a few years ago. In my mind, John killed one of our most effective weapon systems, but I never heard him brag about it in his futile race for President in 2016.

When President George H.W. Bush (41) sent his budget to the Congress, Senate Majority Leader George Mitchell would declare with great fanfare that the President's budget was "DOA" (Dead on Arrival).

The Congress then totally ignored it and wrote their own budget. As a loyal Republican, I didn't like it at the time, but this is not really a bad thing! As noted above, Article One of the Constitution bestows the Congress, *not* the President, with the power of the purse.

Article 1, Section 8, Clause 1 of the U.S. Constitution states:

> The Congress shall have Power To lay and collect Taxes, Duties, Imposts and Excises, to pay the Debts and provide for the common Defense and general Welfare of the United States; but all Duties, Imposts and Excises shall be uniform throughout the United States.

Clearly, the President and his Executive employees do not possess a monopoly of wisdom for the good of the country, and since they also do not have the power under the Constitution to mandate spending priorities, it is important for the Congress to debate and legislate those priorities. Committees in both Houses, if they do their duty, may come up with very different priorities than the President, and it is their Constitutional right, nay, their Constitutional responsibility, to offer them through the Appropriations and/or Authorization bills.

As long as Congressional revisions have merit, they should not be discouraged!! They should be scrutinized, weighed, and evaluated. Members on the Appropriations Committee or a subcommittee, and even those not on the full committee, have the responsibility to assure that a change is justifiable, that it is not an abuse of the Treasury, and that it does not constitute an illicit expenditure of money. But a good idea should not be discouraged or denied simply because the President, his bureaucracy, or even the leadership of the Congress have not thought of it.

While I am quick to defend the right of an individual member to offer improvements to the Federal Budget even if they constitute additional spending, I was (and still am) convinced that once Congress has the votes and the will to *cut* the budget, it should do so with intelligent planning. I am a conservative; I believe in restraint of government, and I believe it imperative that we balance the budget as soon as practically possible! In so doing, we must discriminate between the truly wasteful, redundant, and fraudulent programs so that the important and needed ones might be adequately funded.

As chairman of the Appropriations Committee, I took my stand to impose frugality, and America briefly acquired and enjoyed a balanced discretionary budget in the latter years of my tenure. But the events of September 11, 2001, diverted our attention from fiscal rectitude, and since then, the nation has gone astray. The national debt is spinning out of control, and we have no choice but to amend our ways.

As noted above, Congress is empowered by the Constitution with the "power of the purse." So if the President overreaches in any way through his department chiefs, Congress has the Constitutional authority to rein him in by simply not appropriating money for policies with which there is disagreement. If there are wasteful programs, they need not fund them. Moreover, Congress has the power to sanction a Department Secretary or Agency Chief who is found to have performed in an arbitrary or capricious manner. Congress can use the Appropriations process to cut off funding for his operations and even for his staff. If the majority of both House and Senate members vote to sustain the punishment, the offending official can find himself incapable of paying his employees unless he is able to prevail on the President to overrule Congress and veto that Appropriations bill.

In an instance when Congress might have acted, the Obama administration vastly overstepped its power by entrusting delegated powers to unelected "Czars" who operated outside the Departmental structure and were unresponsive to Congressional oversight. In an Editorial Opinion Letter in *Investors' Business Daily*, Svetlana Kunin, a Soviet Union civil engineer until 1980, now living in the United States, said in early 2010:

> Of course, it is not fair to compare our current American Democratic leaders with the Bolsheviks. Yes, they both use the same slogans in their speeches. Yes, they both stir up envy and class warfare to distract from their failures. Yes, both political movements sought control of the banks as the foundation for their new egalitarian vision. And yes, they are both opposed to free speech, as was made clear by the reaction of American leftists to the recent Supreme Court decision. But you would never find a Czar anywhere in the Soviet government.

Congress had the Constitutional authority to rein in this clear abuse of Executive power by simply not funding the offices of these "Czars." Unfortunately, Congress was not so disposed during the Obama years.

A major difference exists between the United States and the typical European Parliamentary system wherein the Chief Executive sets the agenda and compels the majority to fund and administer his policies. In the United States, the President can be and has been restrained by Congress. Nixon's conduct in Vietnam and Reagan's efforts to support the Contras in Nicaragua were most notable examples of Democrat-controlled Congresses doing exactly that.

In more recent years the actions of both Parties have shown a tendency of the majority to overreach if not properly checked. Our Constitution does not easily accommodate extremes, and we Republicans learned a tough lesson in the last six weeks of 1995. We had exercised our power to restrain expenditures effectively that year, and we had significantly cut back on the budget. We eliminated 300 programs and pared by roughly $50 Billion the Democrat Budget for fiscal year 1995, passed in the fall of 1994. But toward the end of the year, our efforts were strongly challenged by the Clinton administration. We decided that we could run over them by simply declaring that if they didn't do exactly what we wanted, the President's only option would be to close down the government. We might have succeeded had we pressed the issue before Thanksgiving, but we allowed ourselves to be bluffed into delaying the confrontation until just before Christmas. It was a major mistake. When the issues were joined and agreement couldn't be reached, we refused to pass a "Continuing Resolution" to keep the government going pending final negotiations. I personally was so convinced that we were right that I gave a speech on the House floor in which I attempted a poor imitation of Winston Churchill and hollered out to the world: "We will never, never, NEVER give in!"

It was only a couple of days before Christmas, so President Clinton shrugged and simply issued an executive order to close all the parks and lay off tens of thousands of federal employees. Well, all the families who had plans for Christmas in the nation's parks were outraged, as were all the affected federal employees who feared that they would be unemployed for the Christmas holidays. The media blamed Republicans for the impasse and the American people believed them. We read the polls, realized we'd lost that round and quickly folded our tent, my speech notwithstanding. A few days later, my mother called me and said she'd watched me on television. "You looked like a crazy person. You'd better 'never, never' do that again!" I didn't.

Ironically, the confrontation had a positive impact in that we saved a lot of money for the taxpayer that year. But that didn't tell the whole story. Since the Budget has two sides, discretionary and mandatory, our annual review of spending on government programs related only to the Discretionary budget.

Again, all of my fights as chairman of Appropriations were over items in the Discretionary side of the budget. I had no control or jurisdiction over the Mandatory programs. They were and are governed by the Ways and Means Committee, the Energy and Commerce Committee and other authorizing committees. And unlike annual Appropriations, those programs are not revisited by Congress for years or even decades after their creation.

Despite the furor about "earmarks" and other additions to "discretionary spending," the real threat to our fiscal stability has never been exclusively on the "discretionary" side. If America goes broke, and if action is not taken before long that is a distinct possibility, it will be largely because of runaway "entitlements" or items on the "mandatory" side of the budget.

In my last couple of years as chairman, I'd make a pitch about looming fiscal dangers to anyone who would listen. Those were the days before "Power-Points" and "I-Pads" and other modern technology, so I'd prepared two large colored pie charts printed on paper and mounted on two-foot by four-foot cardboard panels. They depicted the budgets in 1960 versus 1998. I'd take them with me everywhere I went to try and illustrate the depth of the threat facing the United States *back then*! To say that the threat has been magnified significantly since then would be an understatement.

Republicans controlled the House in Congress when George W. Bush (43) became President, and they intermittently traded control of the Senate with the Democrats. We were attacked on September 11, 2001, and the country launched the wars in Iraq and Afghanistan. Congress was overwhelmed with external threats to the nation, and serious thought about economics was wholly abandoned. Vice President

Dick Cheney, for whom I hold the highest respect and admiration, uttered one of the single most regretful comments of his political career in June, 2004, when he said: "Reagan proved deficits don't matter." That became the rule for the Republican Congress for the next few years, and President Bush (43) virtually rubber-stamped Republican spending bills.

But by 2006, the American people lost faith in Republicans to run the country in a fiscally prudent manner, and they brought the Democrats in to run both Houses.

Once in the majority, the Democrats didn't even pretend to care about fiscal solvency, and they raised the ante of unfunded liabilities in Mandatory programs. Republicans had achieved great success by 1999 through frugality in the discretionary budget, and for two fleeting years, we actually balanced the budget! But the memory of a balanced budget was forgotten by both sides. When President Trump relieved President Obama in 2017, he inherited an accumulated debt of $20 trillion, rising with no end in sight.

It's important to appreciate those numbers to understand what I was trying to convey in the latter '90s. Back then, we were still talking in terms of billions of dollars in deficits. Those were big numbers then, but today, it's trillions of dollars.

We are in a pickle, and it will take valiant forbearance and creative frugality to pare down the budget and insure that our children and grandchildren are not left with problems that exceed those of Venezuela or Argentina. Venezuela was an extremely rich country until Hugo Chavez took the reins. He imposed a corrupt and irredeemable brand of socialism on the country and utterly impoverished its people. Argentina was one of the richest countries in the world before WWII, but long after Juan Peron assumed the presidency and depleted their treasury with his program of populism, they now are only beginning to recover despite the abundance of natural resources and incredible beauty of their country.

America is not remotely comparable to those countries . . . yet. But we have over-extended ourselves for too many years, and the time to pay the piper could be coming sooner than we think. And our demise can be accelerated by misbegotten programs like the Community Reinvestment Act (CRA) of 1977, wherein Congress encouraged Fannie Mae and Freddie Mac to underwrite and securitize mortgages that couldn't possibly have been honored or paid off. As these mortgages were bundled into ever larger securities packages and sold off to the big banks and foreign countries, the underlying loans were never adequately appraised for the risk they bore. When the economy started to turn down in 2008, and the trickle of people who couldn't keep current on their mortgages turned into an avalanche of defaulters, it became inevitable that many of those bundled security packages would become worthless. Banks around the world had depended on appraisals of "AAA" placed by self-interested ratings services that intentionally inflated the value of worthless securities. As they collapsed in value, our financial system and many of those in countries around the world began to implode. Assets were devalued, residential real estate collapsed in value, shopping centers were emptied, and commercial real estate became worthless. Small businesses folded and people were thrown out of their jobs overnight. As the roles of unemployed expanded, masses of people began drawing on "mandatory" benefits in welfare and unemployment insurance for which Congress has made more and more people eligible, and Federal expenditures exploded!

In the past, an administration could just pass programs on to the next President and the next Congress with hopes that problems created by too much spending, both mandatory and discretionary, would solve themselves simply through economic growth. We have come to the point where that is no longer the case. Spending must be reined in *now*! We are fortunate that under President Trump, growth is indeed accelerating, but our aggregate debt is still surpassing our GDP at the highest rate in history. God forbid, if for whatever reason we find ourselves in a major recession and revenues to the treasury dry up, the rate of federal spending and increasing interest rates could drive us into serious trouble. And if unattended, the country would be seriously imperiled.

Social Security, Medicare, and Medicaid have all been going broke for years. Baby boomers are retiring, and demands on our Treasury are growing exponentially. We are in trouble. As long as interest rates remain low, we have managed to keep the wolves from the door. But if our bond ratings decline, interest rates could sky-rocket and at some point, there will no longer be lenders like the Chinese and Japanese willing to keep the system rolling. U.S. Treasury bills and notes will no longer attract purchasers seeking investment security. Inflation will set in, and we will either default altogether or pay our debts with worthless currency. There will be no way to raise taxes sufficiently to solve our problems and still keep the economy working. (After all, raising taxes failed to improve the U.S. economy under Obama and high taxes are already having a disastrous effect on New York, Connecticut, Illinois, and California. And high tax states have been dealt an even heavier burden by the recent tax bill passed by Congress. The deduction for high state and local taxes known as "SALT" has been capped so that those states can no longer rely on the rest of the country to subsidize their voracious spending habits.)

Hopefully, we can avoid the worst by correcting our policies. We must heed the lessons given us by Presidents Coolidge, Kennedy, Reagan and Bush (41). President Trump has begun putting us back on the correct path. After the anemic growth during the eight years of the Obama administration, Trump and Congress have begun to stimulate the economy with tax cuts. But that's not enough. Both federal and state governments need to scale back on spending commitments. For the sake of our children and grandchildren, we cannot afford to continue as we have over the past two generations.

1998

1998 was a difficult year. On the foreign front, the Chinese were consolidating their authoritarian regime and extending their power over dissenters in what had been a gradually opening China. The Russian economy had collapsed, the North Koreans fired a missile across Japan that was far more capable than anyone thought possible, and India and Pakistan put the lie to the non-proliferationists by exploding nuclear weapons. At home in America, we learned more than we ever wanted to know about Bill Clinton and Monica Lewinsky. As the year began, I was contemplating retirement from Congress.

Until the system was changed in the early '90s, if a member vacated his office for any reason, the next senior member could trade his own office for the vacant one if it offered more room, a better view, or was more accessible to his committees. This placed a major burden on the House Administration Committee and the staff to accommodate the logistical changes in the midst of the legislative calendar

Bill Nichols (D-AL) was revered throughout the House of Representatives by Republicans and Democrats alike. He was a true southern gentleman with an admirable record of service in WWII during which he lost a leg to a landmine in Europe. Bill had a practice of coming into his office at about 7:30 every morning. He'd sit at his desk, read his mail, and answer as many constituent letters as he could in the few quiet hours before his appointments began.

One morning in 1988, he had no sooner settled into his routine than he collapsed with a major heart attack and passed away. By noon, five members and their staff had come into the office to check the drapes, the furniture, the floor plan, and the view to determine if they wanted to claim his office.

That taught me an important lesson. When you are gone, you are gone. We can all easily be replaced, and the nation will survive just fine without us. I decided right then and there that I wanted to go out on my own terms and that I didn't want to be carried out of office like Bill Nichols.

I reasoned that with Newt at the helm for at least a couple more years, it was a good time for me to cash in my chips after twenty one years in Congress and a successful four years as chairman of the Appropriations Committee. I began going to lunch with lawyers and former congressmen to inquire about the prospects of life after Congress. I found that it was pretty good—not nearly the pressure, but certainly more money.

By January 1998, I'd been looking around for a couple of months, and I told my staff that I was going to hold a press conference in the beginning of March to announce my intent not to run for another term. Word got around that I was thinking of leaving, and increasingly, people would come up to me and tell me that I couldn't quit, that the Republicans needed me, and that the Congress needed me. At first I took it as a compliment, but in time I began to question it. "Of course I can quit," I said. "The country got along fine without me before I came, and it can do just great without me."

As I began to narrow my choices for what I wanted to do, my appointed press conference date was fast upon me. For some reason, I scheduled one last town meeting in Hammond, Louisiana, along with a few miscellaneous appointments throughout my Congressional District. The two wonderful people who ran my district office, Rick Legendre and Lisa LaGrange, hadn't been eager to see me hang it up, and they set up a series of appointments knowing that a few of them were going to work me over and try to persuade me to stay on.

I was fully determined to leave at the end of my term, and I was telling people as much when I arrived in New Orleans from Washington. Then I went to Hammond. Like most of my town meetings, the gathering brought in about seventy five people who wanted to talk about national issues. We got through two hours of discussion when I recognized one last person for a question. A slight, well-spoken man, Reggie Reed, stood up and made an eloquent case for why he thought I should reconsider my decision to leave my post. He explained that since I had finally landed a position of authority as chairman of the Appropriations Committee, I was in a very significant position to help the people of my district and the State of Louisiana. I was in my fourth year in my current office and I had another two years ahead of me under our self-imposed term limit for committee chairmen. He said that it was apparent that the Republicans were going to hold on to and even build on the majority, and that at the very least, I should hold my seat for at least another couple of years.

He was the first person who actually prompted me to rethink my position. I thanked him and ended the meeting, but on the way home, I thought about what he'd said. After riding down the highway a while with Rick and Paul Cambon, my top legislative aide in DC, I found myself thinking out loud.

"You know, this really is a very significant decision after these twenty one years. I guess it's the kind of thing you should talk over with a priest!" I'd never been deeply religious, although when Bonnie and I had gone through our toughest times, I'd begun going regularly with her to church on Sundays. It was a first since we'd been married—almost twenty five years too late—but better late than never. Anyway, I said it half in jest and figured that would be the end of it. After all, I was leaving, or so I thought.

The next day, I had some office appointments on my schedule, and I was to prepare for a press conference scheduled the following day to announce my decision to leave Congress at the end of the year. In fact, I'd already written my speech. I was ready to quit, and Bonnie and I were beginning to figure all the ways I could spend all that extra money. But a funny thing happened on the way to the press conference.

As I prepared for the eight businessmen I expected for the session in my office that morning, I walked into the reception area to greet them and the first person I laid eyes on was Archbishop Philip Hannan. I knew I was dead and that there would be no way I'd get through this meeting without agreeing to stay around for another couple of years.

Eighty-five years young, small, wiry Archbishop Hannan was as tough as nails. He'd been a priest for several years when he became a Military Chaplain in World War II. Shortly after D-Day, he joined the 82d Airborne Division in France and marched with them all the way into Germany. He enjoyed a full and varied career in the Church, and when serving as auxiliary bishop in the '60s in Washington, D.C., he personally counseled President and Mrs. Jack Kennedy. Following the President's assassination, Mrs. Kennedy invited him to deliver the homily at the President's funeral Mass. He later served for twenty three years as archbishop of the Catholic Diocese of New Orleans and was revered everywhere he went by Catholic and non-Catholic alike. He'd done Catholic media for twenty years, and he was still running a local Catholic TV station and producing videos in a work schedule that would tire a man half his age. When I spotted his collar, I could only think of my off-hand comment made the night before about seeing a priest.

With him were seven of the top businessmen in the city, most of them longtime friends of mine. They hit all the reasons why I shouldn't retire, and each was persuasive in his own way, but none of them hit as hard as the Archbishop. When I explained that I was fifty five years old and was running out of time to start another career, Hannan exclaimed, "Who are you kidding? You've got lots of time for that!" I had an answer for all the other arguments, but I realized I wasn't going to get around him.

Just when I was trying to bring the meeting to a close knowing I was on sinking ground, the phone rang, and Lisa told me that the Speaker of the House was on the phone. I took the call in front of my guests and found Newt on the other line. He was making one last pitch to keep me from announcing my retirement, and I wondered how much of a coincidence it was that he was calling now. I told him what had happened in the previous hour and then said, "Yes, I've changed my mind. I'll stay."

The next day at the press conference, I gave my speech. It was the same speech I'd written to quit Congress, but I changed the last few lines. I announced that I would run again for one more term. People who had come to say goodbye were flabbergasted. Some cheered; most applauded. It was a festive moment carried all over Louisiana on TV and radio. There were a number of questions and I fielded them all easily. Then I recognized a reporter for one last question.

"How long will you stay?" he asked. "Two years . . . unless I'm Speaker of the House!" I jokingly replied.

****

When I returned to Washington, I speculated with Allen about that comment, and we decided to call together a group of friends to talk about it. Newt had been interviewed in Atlanta as early as October 1997, and he'd indicated that if the stars aligned, he was interested in seeking the Presidency. I was personally convinced that he was inclined to make that race at some point and that he'd been thinking about it as far back as 1982 when he said as much to a reporter from the *Baltimore Sun*. I remember seeing the comment in the paper at the time and catching him on the House floor. I said, "You may be thinking of running, but you better not tell anyone again until you're ready or the Democrats and the media will destroy your chances."

He never said another word about it until his comment in Atlanta.

So we called a few friends together and I told them that I thought Newt was thinking of running for President. If he did, I said we'd need another Speaker and that I was interested. Hal Rogers (R-KY) spoke up at our gathering. "Let's form a committee and a leadership PAC!"

It was as easy as that. Our small group of people went out and recruited others for the next meeting, and so on. We met every other Wednesday at 6:00 p.m., and word got around that we were meeting. The reporters would camp out at the door, and after the first couple of meetings, I began to notice that votes were occurring just as we were to get together. I guessed that Dick Armey had heard about us as well. He was in charge of the floor schedule, and Dick made no secret of his desire to become Speaker.

The leadership PAC was filed and begun—without a lot of thought. I had never thought one was necessary and while I wasn't convinced that Newt would vacate his post as Speaker, I figured we might as well get ready. A leadership PAC is a Political Action Committee just like a personal campaign account, except that unlike the latter which then allowed a candidate to transfer up to $1,000 of his own campaign funds to other candidates, a leadership PAC permitted the owner-candidate to raise funds for Party building or leadership development and distribute up to $5,000 per recipient in any one election cycle. And if the candidate had a primary, another election cycle was triggered so he could receive an additional $5,000. Moreover, if the candidate had a debt from a previous campaign, even another $5,000 was in order. So a leadership PAC enabled a successful incumbent with strong ability to raise money and little reason to fear for his own election the latitude to hand out as much as $15,000 to a needy candidate. Now that's "leadership!"

In the months that followed I traveled to New York, California, and many places in between to campaign for both incumbents and challengers of sitting Democrats. Between my personal campaign account "Friends of Bob Livingston" and my leadership PAC, "Bob's PAC," we raised and distributed close to $2 million. My donation of $600,000 to the NRCC's "Operation Breakout," which raised money intended for Republicans in tight races made me the largest single donor to the Republican effort at the time. Too bad we didn't get more for my money.

While I was toiling in the campaign vineyards, I was also running the Appropriations Committee. In previous years, we had stayed fairly close to our deadlines of having all thirteen Appropriations bills completed by mid-summer so that the Senate could vote on them. That would enable us to conference the bills between both Houses and send them to the President for his signature on or around the end of the fiscal year on October first. But this year, the Budget Committee had delayed providing us with targeted budget numbers and I was becoming increasingly frustrated that we weren't able to get our bills out according to schedule. In fact, the schedule had gone to hell in a hand basket so that seeds were being sewn for a scheduling disaster in the fall.

Actually, I had been very concerned about the schedule for 1998 as early as November 1997, when Dick Armey distributed the calendar for the coming year. It was plain that we would be working three or fewer days a week and that we'd be taking two weeks off with every significant holiday as well as five or six weeks around August. I complained to both Armey and the Speaker that so much time off would delay our ability to keep on schedule, but to no avail. The schedule was published, and my complaints weren't heeded.

Nevertheless, by mid-summer we Republicans were all convinced that it was going to be an extremely good political year for our majority because of all we'd accomplished. Between welfare reform, some tax and regulatory reduction, and curtailment of excessive spending, we had a great story to tell. As late as September, I remember commenting that we could pick up anywhere from fifteen to thirty seats in the House. It didn't work out that way, and we should have seen it coming. But by the time we found out we were in trouble, it was too late.

In late 1997, Newt heard that President Clinton was faced with some very embarrassing revelations. He was convinced that all we Republicans had to do was lie low, let the President's problems take center stage, and that as long as we didn't unnecessarily stir the pot too much, we could rest on our laurels and reap the benefit at the polls, ... or so it seemed.

Clinton's problems came to light in January 1998, and he compounded them with his now famous line, "Now listen to me; I did not have sex with that woman, Monica Lewinsky!"

Newt's original strategy to let Clinton bury himself was the correct one, but by April, the Speaker had changed his mind and we changed course. That turned out to be a monumental mistake for House Republicans. First, we failed to provide time for the traditional agenda and the legislative initiatives we did undertake amounted to all the wrong stuff. Then we ran out of time to crow about the good things we *had* done. But worst of all, with Newt's change of mind, all the money that I'd raised as well as the millions of dollars that our other members threw in were spent on commercials attacking the President for the Lewinsky affair. In effect, the American people were never reminded about the tax cuts, regulatory relief, welfare reform, budget reduction or any of our other many achievements that we Republicans had piled up in the preceding few years.

Under intense pressure from Bud Shuster, chairman of the Transportation and Infrastructure Committee, with complete and unrelenting support from the Speaker, we spent a lot of time on and ultimately passed the largest and most expensive highway bill in modern times. It blew the hell out of the budget that we'd agreed on with the President only a few months before. Since Clinton had always pushed for far more spending than we Republicans had wanted, the increased highway funding was fine with him. For all of my tenure as Appropriations chairman, I had fought with his people at OMB (Office of Management and Budget) to restrain the budget over their objections. Clinton never wanted to spend less on anything unless it was on the defense of the nation. Even in his State of the Union speech of 1998, he promised roughly $150 billion more in spending programs and $120 billion more in taxes over a five year period than his own budget agreement had called for. This, despite his concession to the American People a couple of years earlier that "The era of big government is over."

On top of that the House Budget chairman, John Kasich, who was contemplating a run for the Presidency of his own, initiated a wholly unrealistic call for a trillion dollar tax cut over ten years. Now I've never been able to understand why we would ever try to confuse people about what we did by projecting as far out as three years, let alone five or even ten. The very best of projections about the economy rarely prove true beyond two years, and certainly not ten years, so in my opinion to do so is utterly foolish.

Worse yet, from day one of his unilateral announcement, Kasich never received concurrence in his plan from Senator Pete Domenici (R-NM), his Senate Budget Committee counterpart. Failing that, he offered no hope of implementing his plan yet he persevered well past April 15 when he was legally required to produce a viable budget. Time slipped by, past the end of May, June, and into July. John's intransigence denied us the opportunity to produce a timely budget for fiscal year '99. It kept us from producing timely Appropriations bills, and that opened us up to criticism from the Democrats and the press. Despite constant pleas to Newt to intervene and rein in Kasich, Newt just smiled and let John do his thing. I believe that Newt thought that John would self-destruct and eliminate himself from the Presidential race, but the consequences were far more onerous than that.

House Rules at the time called for the passage of a Budget Resolution prior to the passage of the Appropriations bills. Since there were at least thirteen of them, it took time for each of them to work through subcommittee, full committee, House floor action, similar Senate procedure, a House/Senate Conference, and final approval on the House and Senate floors. Because of the Budget Resolution delay and because we had no guidance on how much money to allocate to our Appropriations bills, we weren't able to really begin our process until mid-July, and then the August recess loomed in front of us. Meanwhile, the Senate ran into delays of their own making and it soon became obvious that we weren't going to finish our Appropriations bills by the end of the fiscal year on September 30. The lack of positive Appropriations news enabled the press to concentrate attention on the heavy cost of the Transportation bill we'd passed earlier on.

Actually, Kasich never did get a Budget agreement with Domenici, so we never passed a Joint Budget Resolution with the Senate. Tired of waiting, we finally "marked" our bills to the base line of spending in the previous year. But unfortunately, it wasn't in time to avoid delay that ultimately empowered the Clinton White House to demand more money for their pet programs. With the exception of the Labor, Health Education bill under Chairman John Porter, we still managed to pass all of our House bills prior to the August recess. But fully eight of the required thirteen bills never emerged from the Senate and were never conferenced between the House and the Senate, so all eight of them became hostage to final negotiations on a single Omnibus bill between the President and Congress.

Having been through the process several times since January 1995, I knew that we had to get the bills out on time to maintain maximum leverage over the White House. If not, the cost to the taxpayer would begin to creep upwards as legislators used pressure of the calendar deadline to "Christmas Tree" the bills by hanging a myriad of legislative riders, spending "add-ons" or "earmarks" on them at the last minute. We had made such a mess of the government closure in December, '95, that our members were petrified of another closure. But without the threat of government closure hanging over everyone's head like the Sword of Damocles, there was no leverage to close a deal with the President and keep spending down. I lamented that fact to the Speaker as we Appropriators did our best to complete our preliminary negotiations to settle the bills with the President's emissaries from OMB.

He blew up! "What do you mean we have no leverage?' he yelled. "Of course, we have leverage!" Whereupon he took me out of the negotiations over the final bills. He closed himself off with Senate Majority Leader Trent Lott and the President's Chief of Staff and together, they added close to $20 billion over and above what we'd agreed to when they took the negotiations away from us. That vastly exceeded any amount previously conceded to Clinton in my years as chairman.

All this was going on with a backdrop of the President's Grand Jury testimony, the referral to the Judiciary Committee of the Lewinsky scandal, and the public release of all of the infamous Grand Jury investigation records by Speaker Gingrich, Minority Leader Gephardt, and Special Counsel Ken Starr. By the time the election rolled around, Republicans no longer held the high ground with a credible claim to fiscal integrity; the American people forgot that we had balanced the budget for the first time in thirty years; they forgot that we'd provided the first tax cut in sixteen years (as well as a second one in seventeen years that passed the House but not the Senate); they forgot that we'd provided the first welfare reform ever; and they forgot that we'd overhauled the IRS for the first time in decades.

Instead, we went to the polls so obsessed by the President's scandal that we'd poured tens of millions of dollars into attack ads against Bill Clinton and his sexual peccadillos rather than provide extensive reminders of all the good we had accomplished in the preceding three years. And instead of gaining an expected minimum of fifteen seats, we lost five! Who would have thought it only six weeks earlier? Not I!

The American Dream Becomes a Nightmare!!!!

Was I thinking of running for Speaker if and when Newt announced for President? Yes. Should I have, in view of the warning I'd received during the summer that someone was investigating our backgrounds in South Louisiana? Probably not! When the story broke in the media in September about a thirty-year-old extramarital relationship involving Henry Hyde, chairman of the Judiciary Committee, I should have taken note. And when in October, Larry Flynt publicized his $1 million solicitation for any woman who would admit to an affair with a member of Congress, I should have been content to retain my role as a successful chairman of the Appropriations Committee.

As late as Election Day in November 1998, I had absolutely no intention of running against Newt for Speaker of the House. He had made me the chairman of one of America's most important legislative committees and for that I was then and will always be grateful. And on election morning, I was convinced that while our margin had narrowed since mid-September, we certainly still were going to pick up seats to add to our margin. Had we done so, no one would have challenged Newt, least of all, me.

That doesn't mean that everyone in the Republican camp was happy with him; far from it. Even in Georgia, people had come up to me at virtually every stop I'd made on the campaign trail to complain about some of his erratic decisions, and they would tell me that we had to replace him as Speaker. Newt had worn out his welcome, not just with the American people in general but among many Republicans around the country. In fact, during one stop in Detroit, an astute attorney listened patiently to my pitch on behalf of various Republican candidates and then offered this warning. "I hear your optimism about the elections," he said, "but I'm worried. If you guys DON'T add to your majority like you think, then YOU ought to replace him as Speaker as soon as possible, or you will certainly lose the majority next time!" I tossed it off, and didn't think of it again . . . until the day after the election.

Again, despite our failure to crow about our accomplishments, I thought we'd pick up seats that year. The first time I really started to worry about the elections was at about 6:00 p.m. Tuesday, Election Day evening, when I received a call from Cokie Roberts of ABC. Cokie's mother, Lindy, and I had served together from the time I arrived in Congress in 1977 until her retirement in 1991. She was a wonderfully gracious lady, and we became good friends over the years, notwithstanding our political differences. She later served the country with great distinction as our Ambassador to the Vatican in Rome, and Bonnie and I had had the honor of visiting her in the previous year. So it wasn't unusual for Cokie or her husband, Steve, to call me from time to time to share and gather political insights.

Cokie called to take my political temperature before the results started coming in, and then dropped the bombshell that ABC's exit polls were showing that we Republicans were in great danger of losing control of the House of Representatives. "Oh nooooo," I exclaimed. "Exit polls are notoriously inaccurate, and things are looking fine," I said. Well, I acquired a new respect for exit polls.

The returns came in; Republicans retained the majority but we lost five seats in the House. My old friend and former Congressional colleague, Dan Lungren, lost the California governor's race. Matt Fong was defeated by incumbent California Senator Barbara Boxer in a "can't lose" race to replace her. Senator Al D'Amato was replaced by the loquacious House member, Charles Schumer. And we didn't pick up a single seat in Michigan, even though Jack Kevorkian's lawyer was trounced by Republican incumbent Governor John Engler.

On the brighter side for Republicans, Carol Moseley Braun was defeated in her bid for reelection to the U.S. Senate and the Bush brothers romped to easy victories in the gubernatorial races in Texas and Florida. We still held thirty-one of the fifty governors seats and roughly half of the State legislative houses. But without a gain in the U.S. Senate, it certainly was not a banner year for Republicans.

On the morning of Wednesday, November 4, 1998, the day after the elections, the world had changed. The Speaker was in denial, and he rapidly went public to explain how we Republicans were still in great shape because it was the first time since 1928 that a Republican majority had been elected for a third consecutive term to run the House of Representatives.

But it wasn't washing. He and the elected leadership held a telephone conference call with the rest of us more senior members. Once I'd heard enough, I raised some concerns I'd been hearing from Republicans all over the country in the preceding few hours. After the call, people continued to grouse both in public and privately to me. House members, elected leaders like governors and state legislators, finance people, Republican businessmen, and concerned citizens began to deluge me and my office with calls of concern, outrage, regret, and pleas to consider running against Newt.

When I awoke that day, it was the furthest thing from my mind. That's the way it should have stayed. But by the end of the day, I was considering it so strongly that I called Newt and expressed my concern that his strategy to rest on our laurels and just attack Clinton rather than engage in a legislative offensive to crow about our achievements wasn't just flawed; it had been a disaster. He took the criticism in relative good humor and reminded me that as chairman of the Appropriations Committee, I shared the blame for not getting our bills done on time and for spending more than the 1997 budget agreement with the President had called for. I agreed, but pointed out that had we not passed the expensive highway bill at his insistence; had we not wasted four months on a fruitless budget bill with his consent; and had we not given away all our workdays so that members could stay home and "campaign," we could have finished our business on time and would not have muddled our message.

I might have added that had we not spent our millions of political dollars, much of which I had personally raised in "Operation Breakout," on useless Clinton scandal attack ads, but rather had we used paid reinforcement ads to brag about our positive legislative achievements, the results might have been different. Furthermore, had the Speaker together with Gephardt and Starr not put all the salacious details of Clinton's problems on the internet, the American people might have paid more attention to our leadership in Congress than they apparently had. But any positive message we had to sell was lost in the noise of scandal, and Republicans were blamed instead of the White House that was responsible for the mess!

At the end of the conversation, I suggested that I thought we had blown a very good shot to substantially increase our majority and that as loyal as I had always felt toward him, I was entertaining the idea of running against him for Speaker. Again, he was gracious but cool and said that we all had to do what we had to do.

For the rest of Wednesday and Thursday, I continued to speak with people all over the country and with my colleagues in the House. As self-serving as it sounds in hindsight, I did not want to run against my friend, Newt Gingrich. But certain Republican House members like Matt Salmon and Chris Shays began to say publicly that they couldn't support Newt's reelection as Speaker under any circumstances. With only a five-vote margin for our majority in the new Congress, we couldn't afford to lose more than five votes on any issue or the Democrats would out-vote us. Worse yet, they were poised to retake the House majority in a subsequent election.

Thursday night, I met quietly with Congressman Steve Largent, the former All-American and Hall of Fame football player from Oklahoma. He told me that if I didn't run against Newt, he would. And I later found out from Chris Cox of California that had I not announced for Speaker, he would have. Looking back on it, I obviously should have wished them each the best of luck.

I was not thinking about myself or for that matter, my family. That was a major mistake. Instead, I went to bed thinking about the Republican majority and the future of the party. I thought of all the people who told me that I was the only person who had the experience and the political judgment to run the House in Newt's absence. As much as I have always told myself I would never again make the same mistake I made when I ran for Governor of Louisiana, I began to intellectually decide that Newt had to go and that I was the only person who could serve in his wake. No one I knew was as bright and as capable of seeing the big picture as was Newt, but he had failed to run the nuts and bolts of the House, and I could run the House . . . or so I thought.

By the next morning, Friday morning, things had changed. When I woke up at 4:00 a.m., I was convinced that I could not run against my friend, Newt Gingrich. We had come too far together. As much as I was convinced that his mistakes had brought us to the sorry state in these last elections, perhaps he could overcome the problems and keep us on track if he would change his operational style and leave me free to run my committee and get my bills out on time without his constant interference. So I got up, scribbled out my ideas of a manifesto demanding autonomy for the Appropriations Committee, and then called my assistant, Rayne Simpson, to ask her to come in early. I took a quick shower, got dressed, and drove into work.

I smoothed out my draft on a dictating machine and waited for Rayne to type it up. I called Newt to tell him that I didn't want to run against him and that if he would agree to my list of demands to improve the administration of the House, I would go back to business on my committee. It was a fact that I didn't want to run against him. Certainly if I had, I would have no guarantee of winning but that wasn't my concern. Newt and I had been friends since he arrived in Congress in 1978. We had a lot in common. I'm three months older than he. We both received our advanced degrees from Tulane University in the same month of the same year: he, a Masters in History and I a J.D. in Law, in May 1968. He subsequently earned a Ph.D. in history at Tulane in 1971. He progressed as a backbench revolutionary; I advanced as a committed member of the Appropriations Committee. We worked together on innumerable Republican projects, most notably, the Contract with America. I headed and wrote the Defense plank and contributed to much of the Foreign Policy section.

Speaker Gingrich had reached over four sitting members and appointed me the chairman of the Appropriations Committee, and I was devoted to making him a successful Speaker. Though in recent years, I was no longer a member of the Committee on Standards of Official Conduct (the Ethics Committee), I counseled him and helped lead his defense when he was under fire for ethics charges for misstatements on two of the 5,000 documents he filed with the committee.

In June 1997, Tom DeLay, Dick Armey, Bill Paxon (R-NY) and mavericks in the Class of '94 decided that we needed a new Speaker. They weren't happy with Newt's leadership, and they had long since lost their gratitude for his guiding us into the majority. I didn't share their feelings, so with Rules Committee Chairman Jerry Solomon (R-NY), we defended him by rallying most of our fellow committee chairmen to contact their members to suck the steam from the revolt. We won the day and the coup was defeated before it was really begun.

Finally, Bonnie and I had traveled with Newt and his then wife, Marianne, at his invitation on two occasions, once to seven countries in Asia where he was absolutely brilliant in remarkable contrast to a contemporaneous trip by Vice President Al Gore, who'd received miserable reviews for his own performance. Newt's performance during a second trip to Israel drew less acclaim, but we had a great time together.

In short, I was a Newt loyalist to the core and yet I knew that a change was imperative. If Newt could hold on and implement the change, I was prepared to help it work. But, clearly, we needed change. After four years as Speaker, he was becoming more of a liability than a spokesman for our success. He said in February that Clinton would never get to the left of him on an issue of penalizing the tobacco companies, yet a few months later he was (rightly) leading the fight against punitive taxes envisioned by the Democrats for more and bigger and ever more costly government.

He told us privately at the end of 1997 that Clinton was going to self-destruct because of his problems. He shaped the schedule and Republican policy around the expected scandal. Initially, he said he wouldn't ever comment on Clinton's problems, but later in the spring of 1998, he vowed to condemn Clinton in every speech he would ever make from then on for providing "the most systematic deliberate obstruction of justice . . . we have ever seen in American history." Later, when Clinton's poll numbers stayed high while Gingrich's began to plummet, he changed course again and stopped the vitriol. But he made the call for the Judiciary Committee to put the Clinton evidence on the internet, and he was the one who directed John Linder, chairman of the National Republican Congressional Committee (NRCC), to put their millions of dollars on scandal ads rather than on Republican puff stuff.

In short, Newt had played out his mystique. I have always said I thought he was the brightest man in American contemporary politics — including Clinton. But after the elections, even I had begun to question his judgment—and I was one of the last to do so.

So, there I was on the Friday after the ill-fated election going through a gut-wrenching internal dispute with myself. One side of me said that Newt couldn't survive, even if no one ran against him. Some Republicans had announced publicly that they wouldn't support him under any circumstances even if it meant that we could lose control of the majority. That was a real problem, since if a few Republicans joined with all of the Democrats to deny Newt the Speakership, the majority of all the committees and chairmanships could have been claimed by the Democrats. That side of me said I was the only one who could challenge him and win and still run the House.

With my years on the Intelligence Committee and the Defense and the Foreign Operations subcommittees of Appropriations, I had established a strong background in those issues. As Appropriations chairman, I'd been able to push through more significant legislation in each of those four years that Republicans controlled the House than virtually any other member. As the co-chairman of the only truly bipartisan task force to successfully work with Democrats led by Ben Cardin of Maryland, I'd reported out and passed a very significant bipartisan-nonpartisan revision of Ethics Procedures in the House. Thus, I felt I was uniquely capable of not just becoming Speaker, but of overcoming the hostility between members of both parties and restoring a sense of comity and pride among all members in what we were elected to do,

But on the other side, I still cherished my friendship with Newt, and I still revered what he had accomplished in creating and nourishing the first Republican majority in the House in forty years. So at approximately 8:00 a.m. when I spoke with him on the phone, I told him that I didn't want to run against him. I said if he would sign and acknowledge my demands that I was faxing to his home in Atlanta and fax it back to me, I would not run. We finished the document, marked it "Personal and Confidential" on each page, signed it, faxed it to him shortly before 9:00 a.m., and waited.

I didn't hear from him for another two and a half hours. In that time, the calls continued to come in urging me to consider running. I called Archbishop Hannan, with whom I'd spoken when I decided to stay in Congress, and I consulted with him. Then I called my staff together and put the question to them. Not just my Washington staff; my New Orleans staff was on the speaker-phone as well.

I explained the situation as I saw it, both pro and con. I told them that I was suffering with the decision because of my friendship with Newt, but that I was convinced that either he could not win reelection to the Speakership in any event, or that worse, that we could get to the opening day of Congress and lose the majority altogether. I didn't have to tell them what that meant; loss of the Speakership, all the chairmanships, and advancement of the Democrat rather than the Republican agenda. Only a few of my staff knew of my past history of marital problems, but of those who did know, only one appeared concerned.

I put the question to a vote and gave each staff member a chance to speak on whether he or she thought I should run. One by one, each explained that in his or her opinion, I should go for it. Only Paul Cambon, who had been with me from the beginning of my first winning campaign and who had become one of the best legislative assistants on Capitol Hill, had a concerned look on his face and voiced his dissent. I read his face and ignored his warning. It was a terrible mistake. Paul was right.

I decided then and there to go ahead and run. When I'd left home that morning, I'd told Bonnie that I was going to try and get Newt to buy into my changes, but he hadn't gotten back to me and I was ready to revoke my offer. I tried reaching him, but no one answered at the number where I'd reached him three hours earlier. So at about 11:00 a.m., I faxed him a scribbled note saying that since I'd not heard from him, I was revoking the offer.

And then Newt called. It was 11:30 a.m.

He told me that he'd had great difficulty getting through to me because of our clogged phone lines, and that he and his people were still looking over my proposal. "Didn't you get my fax?" I asked. "No, what fax?" "The one I sent a half hour ago to the same number where I sent the original package earlier this morning." "No," he said, "I'm at my Congressional Office now. You sent the original to my home." "Oh," I replied, "Well, I sent you a revocation a half hour ago. I've decided to go ahead and run against you." "OK," he said. "Don't forget that as an Appropriator, you'll share the blame for the failure of the budget process." "I know, Newt. I'm sorry!" "That's OK. Let's just see what happens . . . I'll see you." "Bye"

My list of demands had by then found its way into the press in its entirety. It had been released at about 9:30 a.m. that morning, and it didn't come from my office.

At 2:00 p.m., I held a news conference in the front of the Capitol. I girded for a very tough fight but told the press that I had every confidence that when the dust settled, I expected to be the Speaker of the

House. As I look back on that moment, I still feel a mixture of sadness and daring and commitment. I had no sense of foreboding, though maybe that would have been more appropriate.

At 5:00 p.m., the first Republican Speaker of the House in forty years, Newt Gingrich, held a press conference and took himself out of the race by announcing that he would be leaving the Speakership and his seat in Congress by the end of the year.

*****

After my press conference, I returned to my office and began to call every Republican colleague I could find. I called them in Washington, but since it was still election time, many weren't there. I called them in their districts; I called them at their homes; I tracked them down on the golf course; I caught them at their campaign headquarters; and I caught them in their travels around the world. I spoke with three in Argentina and one in Australia. One was in London, and one called me on his way back from Russia. All in all, I spoke with almost every one of the 223 new and reelected members, not just to say "Hello," but to ask each and every one for his or her vote for me for Speaker.

I could not rely on staff to staff communication, nor could I take it from a family member. I had to hear it from the individual members' mouths that they were going to vote for *me* and no one else. I couldn't take it for granted even if they had been encouraging when I'd spoken to them *before* I made my mind up to run that they would vote for me. I had to hear them say they would now. Tracking them all down took me roughly five days of non-stop telephone campaigning. In the meantime, I was not without potential opposition.

Chris Cox of California announced for Speaker on the Larry King Show that Friday night, a few hours after Newt dropped out. Steve Largent had already held a press conference that morning to say that he expected someone to be running against Newt. I'm not sure if he meant me or Chris, but then he announced that he'd be running against Dick Armey for Majority Leader. Ways and Means Chairman Bill Archer announced that evening that he would have a conference about his own intentions on Saturday morning. He did, but only to say that while he had been encouraged to run, he would not do so.

Jim Talent of Missouri, chairman of the Small Business Committee, let it be known that he was interested, but by Sunday night he and I had met, and on Monday, he took himself out of the race. Likewise, I heard that Chris wanted to meet, so we got together on Sunday as well. He claimed to have about ninety votes, but he hadn't been on the telephone like I had, and he had no idea how difficult it was to round up votes by telephone from all around the globe. Besides, I was pretty confident that by that time, I had it wrapped up. I didn't tell him that and I was very gracious when he told me that he was inclined to drop out and endorse me.

The next month was a blur of nonstop activity. From the moment that Newt announced his departure, my staff and I hit the road running and we didn't look back. Allen Martin, my Administrative Assistant, took over the operation like a field general. All my staff checked in from seven in the morning until nine in the evening, sometimes later, often working past midnight. Then they'd get up the next day and start all over again. And they weren't alone. Congressmen Ron Packard and Buck McKeon of California, both of whom had been of so much help since I first evinced an interest in March, turned their staffs out to work themselves to the bone to create an effective transition. Congressman Mike Forbes and his staff were invaluable in helping us prepare in innumerable ways. Through Mike, I located speech writer Peggy Noonan, who had been so helpful to President Reagan. She came down from New York to help me on my first speech to the new Republican Conference.

I appointed Mike Forbes, Buck McKeon, Sonny Callahan of Alabama, and Anne Northup of Kentucky as "Assistants to the Speaker" because I felt I could rely on them to keep their ears to the ground and let me know when I ran into trouble. Hal Rogers was a little upset with me about this because he had been with me from the beginning, but I felt I needed more diversity in age and time in service and opted for Anne. Ron Packard and his staff had been so helpful that when I heard he was also upset, I named him to be one of my Transition Captains along with Marge Roukema, who with Lindsey Graham and John Dolittle, gave a nominating speech for me when the elections rolled around. Had I had the chance, I would have had something for my friend Hal Rogers as well, but time ran out.

People all over the country were excited and were calling to be of help. Hundreds of resumes started rolling in by mail, fax, or hand delivery. Priscilla Allen, who had worked as a staff assistant eighteen years earlier, came in and never left. She just started pitching in and helping with the overwhelming workload—as did people from other staffs and folks we'd known along the way. It was a madhouse, but we worked as hard and as fast as we could and the mess gradually started taking shape. By the end of November, I began to liken the exercise to watching a seemingly impossible magic trick. Once you get into it and understand it, you begin to realize, "I can do this!"

Our formal Congressional reorganization meetings had been scheduled previously by the Speaker to take place two weeks after the elections We immersed ourselves in the takeover for the full two weeks, and considering how little time we had to get started, things went surprisingly well. Much credit is due to Newt, with whom I finally spoke on Sunday night, two days after he had dropped out. He couldn't have been more gracious, and he invited me to join him and his wife and family the next evening at the GOPAC dinner in his honor at the Willard Hotel. Always the master politician, he was aware how this could heal the wounds felt by many of his fondest supporters, many of whom would be there that night. Plus it offered an incredible opportunity for a demonstration of unity in the Republican Party with a visual photographic display that money couldn't buy. Bonnie and I took him up on it, and it was everything I might have imagined and more. Front page stuff!

Newt and his staff met with Allen and me the next day to give me an idea of what we were up against. Indeed, we were faced with an awesome task ahead and clearly, Newt reveled in describing it in detail. He was extraordinarily frank and gracious, both with his time and his offer of backup from his staff. None of the Gingrich staff, save the top people, were eager to go out and hunt for jobs and it was obvious that we could not, nor would we want to, replace all Newt's people. So it was easy for us to do as I had done when I took over the Appropriations Committee to keep as many of the people as was prudent on the job to allow for an easy transition. In fact, we agreed to keep everyone on through the end of January while we interviewed the people who might or might not be replaced together with prospective applicants for their jobs.

I began to give thought to how I would change the structure of the Republican Conference to improve the process of House business. First came the committee structure and the chairmanships. I held an early meeting with the committee chairmen to both encourage them to greater productivity than in the past and put their minds at ease about my intent not to circumvent them in their jurisdictions. Newt had never been a committee chairman, and he didn't trust the committee system. He had spent much of his time creating cumbersome taskforces and reinventing a system that had evolved over two hundred years. He often created chaos and frustration leading primarily to lack of action and inertia. I believe that was the way he liked it, since little would happen without his approval or instigation.

*****

My intent was to cut task-forces to the bare minimum, leaving only the functions of agenda planning, issue development, and communication as the primary jurisdiction of the Conference chairman. I believed the committee chairmen were my allies, but I would have to inspire them to act and to resolve their disputes with each other.

I felt very strongly that with a narrow margin of 223 Republicans to 212 Democrats in the House, I could only lose five of my own members on any single vote without risk of losing an issue at hand. Every time a bill is brought to the floor, it must first be assigned to the Rules Committee for direction on how a particular debate is to be handled. With a comfortable margin of members, the Rules Committee might either allow for freewheeling debate under an "Open Rule" or it might restrict debate under a "Modified" or "Closed Rule."

Since a rule must be approved by a majority of members voting before legislation is even considered by the House, a tight margin between the Parties meant that we weren't going to be able to rely on rules to avoid embarrassing amendments on legislation like we often had tried to do so in the past. Had we done so, we would have lost the rule and hence control of the bill on the floor.

I knew that meant more "Open Rules," more amendments, and more "bipartisan" legislative product. We could still control against passage of egregious legislation that really strayed from the Republican agenda of lesser intrusive, lesser government with lower taxes through our Republican majority in the Senate. It was to be a daunting task, but it was all the more reason to have a good working relationship with the committee chairmen so that the legislative product could be better crafted before it hit the floor.

In fact, we had to produce legislation. The last year had been a disaster in terms of productivity with our focus on Clinton's salacious activity rather than our own significant and timely legislative accomplishments. Too many times, committee chairmen engaged in turf battles by objecting to movement of legislation in a companion committee, demanding concurrent jurisdiction and stifling consideration of important issues. The Speaker, himself, was not above spiking legitimate legislation. He killed an attempt by Bill Archer to remove a mandate for the costly ethanol program in order to avoid upsetting farm state representatives. Moreover, although the plan had been on the books for years, he refused to allow the scheduling of legislation to store the nation's nuclear waste in Yucca Mountain, Nevada, because he felt that to do so would hurt our chances for victory in the Nevada Senate race.

He was probably politically right in both cases, but the nation's interest took a back seat to politics, and had we trusted the process or our colleagues by bringing the issues to the floor for full debate, the election might have turned out differently. I believed then and even more so now that our base of Republicans around the country was tired of "political" decisions. As naive as it sounds, my twenty two years in Congress and many years after have not deterred me from the belief that best policy is the always best politics. Thus, I would have brought both issues to the floor for action and let consensus take its course. To effect change, I advised committee chairmen that if legislation came up in one committee that was objected to by another committee, I would give the objecting committee thirty days to shape the proposed bill in its own image or else the bill would be brought to the floor for debate and amendment. No longer would issues just be stifled by objecting members. This change would encourage open debate, resolution of disputes, and production of legislation from the House.

The Senate is another problem, altogether. Gone are the days when people like Huey Long, the famous Senator from Louisiana, would take to the floor with fiery oratory for days on end in an authentic filibuster. With few exceptions, a Senator, Republican or Democrat, need only proffer a "hold" on virtually any piece of legislation, and unless the majority can muster evidence of sixty votes to invoke "cloture," the issue is effectively spiked or held indefinitely. To allow one unnamed and anonymous Senator to hold up legislation in the nation's interest without at least making his name public and known is unconscionable. Change doesn't happen quickly in the Senate. But a modest and very important change in the Senate would require that any Senator wishing to hold up legislation must either actively launch a filibuster or at the very least, make his name known to the world, so that proponents and opponents alike learn who had held it up.

Back in the House, we had to prepare for the reorganization of the Republican Conference scheduled two weeks after the election. We needed Rules changes for the next Congress so I planned to meet with the Minority Leader Dick Gephardt. We had to work out committee ratios of Republicans to Democrats on committees adjusted for the tighter margin in the full House. We considered renaming committees to avoid the constant confusion. We had to activate the Republican Steering Committee to assign people to committees. Every member's political livelihood depends on his committee assignment so it's a highly intense process that in past years has taken as long as three days to complete. In my spare time, I had to do the minimal TV appearances to show that the transition was progressing easily. With Peggy Noonan, I was closing in on my initial acceptance speech to the Republican Conference. None of these were easy.

In previous years, dinners, theater and sporting event tickets, and miscellaneous gifts to members of Congress had become far too much temptation for members with even the best of intentions. In seeking a justifiable correction, Newt and Dick Armey supported and passed a "zero tolerance" rule, meaning that members were prevented from even accepting a free sandwich or a pen with a logo while discussing district business. In my opinion, that was just nuts! I'd indicated on one TV appearance that I favored conforming House Rules from zero tolerance to the Senate's minimal gift rule because I was convinced that under the House Rule, one or more of our number was going to be embarrassed when caught in an inconsequential breach. But I needed

Gephardt's cooperation to do that because it required bipartisan support to happen. Since the change benefited members of both parties, I thought we could work together on that. But with differences on committee ratios and on other Rules changes, any agreement was elusive.

Creating extra subcommittees for oversight was easy enough provided committees were prepared to staff them with existing resources, but taking away jurisdiction or eliminating subcommittees was another challenge altogether. No chairman likes to lose jurisdiction even if he had just recently acquired it. That was the problem I ran into when I tried moving the Subcommittee on Census away from the Committee on Government Reform and Oversight, which I proposed changing back to "Government Reform." Dan Burton (R-IN), the chairman objected to my moving the Census to Chairman Bill Thomas's (R-CA) Committee on House Administration, which I proposed to rename the "House Oversight Committee."

But Burton's committee had eight subcommittees, and I thought since all the Committees other than Appropriations had no more than six subcommittees, it wasn't too much to ask that the Census be transferred. Census is the single most important issue governing House reapportionment, and rather than subjecting it to a fifty one member committee with a four vote margin between majority and minority, it was better served under the House Administration Committee chaired by Bill Thomas, a committee with nine members and a two-to-one ratio of Republicans to Democrats. But it wasn't easy to do. Dan Miller (R-FL) had chaired the Census effort under Burton, and while he was also a member of the Appropriations Committee which demands full time attention by itself, Census gave him a subcommittee chairmanship that he was reluctant to forgo by moving the issue to Thomas's committee, which had no subcommittees.

Other "must do" items were on our agenda, as well. John Kasich had run wild in the previous year with his Budget Committee. I was determined not to let that happen again, and when I learned that he could not serve as chairman of the committee without a "waiver" under our Rules, I set about the process of trying to insure that the waiver meant that he served "at the discretion of the Speaker." I wanted to avoid getting embroiled once again in a futile battle with the Senate over the budget. If he couldn't be realistic in his goals and report out his budget bill on time on April 15 as prescribed by law, then I would have the right to make other arrangements. To his credit, John was aware of my concerns and went out of his way to assure me that he would meet our goal so that the Appropriations process would begin on time.

Just in case, I decided to move David Hobson (R-OH), who was to become a new chairman of a subcommittee on Appropriations, off the Budget Committee altogether. I had become concerned that David, as the number two man on budget, was simply unable to rein in the dynamic Chairman Kasich. Hobson, a very nice man, had been Newt's choice to do exactly that. But when John dragged out the process so unnecessarily the year before, Hobson, who like John was from Ohio, became more of an amplifier than a restraint on Kasich. This I could not have, so I replaced him with Saxby Chambliss of Georgia, a savvy and physically imposing high school and college athlete, whom I believed to be extremely capable of anchoring the Budget Committee chairman in place. I must note that Dave Hobson subsequently became chairman of both the Military Construction and the Energy and Water Subcommittees, and few if any of his co-chairmen had the grasp or knowledge of the work in his own subcommittee that David did. David worked hard and performed invaluably in the succeeding years until he retired in 2008.

Other matters to occupy my time included meeting some of the Republican governors to search out common ground for the next two years. They were concerned that we had muddled our very good message of performance over the previous year, and they wanted to be darn sure that we didn't do it again. In several different meetings over a month's time, I personally met with at least twelve or fourteen of the thirty-one Republican governors around the country, and I spoke with several others on the telephone.

They were insistent that we simplify our message to three or four key issues and that we all would sing from the same sheet of music. They had had great success in welfare and education reform, in tax reduction and providing efficiency in government, and in sustaining a healthy and vibrant economy in their respective states. They wanted to be sure that we complimented rather than detracted from their successes. And they wanted Congress to leave them the flexibility to do their jobs. That meant that with issues like the new tobacco settlement, they wanted control over the revenues without having to send the money to Washington, D.C. or President Clinton. They were right.

Tip O'Neill called it "holding confessions" in his book, "All Politics is Local." It is making oneself available to any member who wants to come by to offer suggestions, complain, or just shoot the bull. I did a lot of that while everything else was going on. Lots of people had suggestions and many were very constructive. My toughest job was to read their memos as fast as I could so that I could separate the wheat from the chaff and use the good stuff to organize our outfit. Doing all this within our time constraints took superhuman effort.

The hardest sell I had was to convince members that we needed to work longer than two-and-a-half days a week. Lots of members had leaned increasingly toward leaving their families in their Congressional Districts, and they liked working two or three days a week in DC, then returning to their families. The problem is that serving in Congress is a full time job, and we were paid well for being in town and for casting our votes in DC. The previous year might have been great for family life in the Congressional District, but it was hell on the Republican work product. We just couldn't get our work done on time by coming to town on Tuesday afternoon, working Tuesday night through Thursday afternoon and then going home. Add in two week vacations at every major holiday and five weeks off in August, and I felt that 1998 had been one of the least productive in memory.

So I proposed to change the work week to allowing votes after 5:00 p.m. on Monday through noon on Friday with twenty five to forty more legislative work days between January and October 30. This was not popular. Many Americans believe that whenever Congress is in session, it poses a threat to the nation. They would be happy if we never met. One member tried to make the case that we could do a lot better for our constituents if we were back home. I thought maybe he should consider running for City Council or the State Legislature, but I checked myself from telling him so. I firmly believed then and I believe now that America is a full time nation and she deserves a full time Congress. Without coming in every day to attend to committee and other Congressional business, oversight becomes impossible. Members lose control over their bills, unelected staff becomes empowered to do all the work, and no one really understands the process sufficiently to rein in the natural growth of government.

In short, the failures of the past two administrations since I left Congress can be laid at the doorstep of one proposition: most members of Congress aren't in DC enough to understand or perform their Constitutional responsibilities. The furor over "earmarks" can be blamed on precisely this problem. If members aren't in DC, they aren't providing adequate oversight. Without oversight, they have no idea if earmark requests have merit. Inevitably, decisions on earmarks were turned over to unelected staff who were reluctant to tell requesting members, "NO!" So, after 2000 but before the new Republican majority invoked the ban on earmarks in 2010, thousands of earmarks were adopted, meritorious and otherwise. It was the abuse that led to the ban.

Despite all that was on our plate, we survived the initial reorganization of our Conference without mishap. I was elected by acclamation and no one rose to oppose me. I gave my acceptance speech to the Republican Conference with Bonnie and my daughter, Susie, at my side. My speech won notable praise for my replacement of the "Big Tent" with the "Big Ship," on which everyone scurries around on the flight deck of an aircraft carrier. Each is doing his or her job but running in different directions, while the ship continues steadily on course, guided by the brightest star in the heavens, the U.S. Constitution. Truthfully, the "ship" concept came from Steve Largent in a conversation I had with him about his condemnation of "the Big Tent." Unlike Steve, I was concerned that with our small majority, we couldn't afford to exclude any well intentioned Republican who voted with us 65 percent to 70 percent of the time, rather than 100 percent of the time. Still, I gave Steve oblique rather than direct credit in my speech since he was still running against Dick Armey for Majority Leader. As a former Navy enlisted man, the "Big Ship" analogy worked wonderfully for me, and many Navy friends wrote to say how much they appreciated it.

As it turned out, Dick Armey defeated Steve Largent, Jennifer Dunn, and late entry Denny Hastert, on the third ballot with a narrow margin. Tom DeLay was reelected without opposition as Whip and John Boehner was defeated by J.C. Watts for Conference chairman. That was somewhat surprising, for the early money would have predicted that Armey would have lost and Boehner would have held on.

But when Armey won his race, Boehner's loss was the token sacrifice for the dismal election returns. Likewise, John Linder was ousted by Tom Davis as chairman of the NRCC. Deborah Pryce and Tillie Fowler won the posts of secretary and vice-chairman respectfully, the first without opposition and the latter in a fairly stiff contest.

The really interesting result was the fact that Tom DeLay was unopposed. Tom had been integral to an attempted coup against Newt a year and a half earlier, but he had never dissembled, never denied his role, and he always told everyone who was interested exactly why he had done what he did. The net result was that whether or not members agreed with the coup, everyone respected him for his forthright and unwavering admission. He was a good Whip. He knew his job and was well organized. Plus, when Congress worked late into the evening, he would often host barbecue or buy pizza so that members and staff could get something to eat. He was tough, he was very conservative, and he made no excuses for himself. Thus, despite the unhappiness over our previous year, Tom simply could not have lost.

When I got into the race for Speaker, Tom was one of the early people to sign on with support. That meant a great deal, since his very politically savvy and well organized staff came with him—Ed Buckham, Tom's former Chief of Staff who still helped as a consultant, had also been a friend of Allen's and mine for years. Susan Hirschmann was Ed's replacement, and she was invaluable to us in those very hectic weeks.

So, with the elections over and the proposed rules changes adopted, we moved the Steering Committee into operation to assign members to committee slots. Since I was to be Speaker, I had to vacate my chairmanship of Appropriations as well as my seat on the committee. Bill Young of Florida moved in behind me and became the full committee chairman; Jerry Lewis of California took his place as chairman of the National Security Subcommittee and so on. Musical chairs prevailed in its highest form.

Likewise, vacancies left by departing members on the other committees were to be filled, and we had to find decent places for the incoming members to land. I'd had the notion that the committees had gotten too big and unwieldy. But in order for us to reach an accommodation with the Democrats who had added numbers to their minority and wanted more seats for their members, we ended up growing rather than shrinking some of the committees. That was a big disappointment for me because I was convinced that the larger the committee, the more difficult it was for both the chairman and the leadership to manage.

We succeeded in assigning all our members in little more than one day, then went back to the administration of the House. It was relentless. Just keeping up with the mail became a full time job for many of us, especially me, but we persevered, taking a couple of days off for Thanksgiving. Planning for leadership meetings in the first week in December took us at least a day. We also managed to cover the White House scheduled conferences on Social Security, meetings with my friend and now the Senate Majority Leader, Trent Lott (R-MS), Jim Nicholson, chairman of the Republican National Committee, and several Republican governors.

The leadership meetings went smoothly, but not without a lot of give and take. Feedback from our colleagues let us know they appreciated that we were well organized and that it was refreshing for members and staff to feel that they were being listened to and not just lectured at as had been the case in much of the past. There was some concern among the elected leaders that I had invited my four "Assistants to the Speaker" to the meetings and had encouraged their participation, but the grousing was nominal.

******

We Republicans have consistently argued that the American people were overtaxed. In 1997, for the first time in sixteen years, Congress passed a moderate middle class tax reduction package, and we promised more cuts in 1998. Although the House actually sent the Senate a nominal cut of $80 billion in taxes over five years in 1998, the bill did not pass. Our constituents had hoped for more and were disappointed when we fell short.

Even with our cuts, by 1999 the net Federal, State, and Local tax burden on the American family was higher than at any time since World War II. Subsequently, George W Bush (43) improved the picture with more significant tax reductions once he came into office in 2001, but because of Senate Rules, his tax cuts were scheduled to "sunset" and legally expired at the end of 2010. Those tax cuts did pull us out of the early 2000s recession by stimulating the economy, but by 2008, the market began to weaken, reflecting concern that the reductions would not be renewed. The anticipated loss of those tax cuts contributed to the second greatest market collapse since the Great Depression, a recession exacerbated by Obama's doubling down on useless, misguided spending, and higher taxes on every aspect of life.

*****

We'd been very concerned that President Clinton's planned "Social Security Conference" would be used by the White House as a publicity stunt against us. The President's constant mantra to "Save Social Security First" was trumpeted each time we mentioned the need for tax cuts. It was a phony slogan. Under the Republicans, we balanced the Discretionary Budget for the first time in thirty years meaning there was less pressure. Let's not forget that the problem started with Lyndon Johnson who put Social Security revenues "on budget" to mask the cost of the Vietnam War. Not a single Democrat-controlled Congress was willing to reverse that practice. Since 1983 when we did address the fiscal shortfall in Social Security by raising payroll taxes, nothing has happened to significantly improve the situation.

As for saving Social Security in the short term, I believed it important that we ultimately change the Rules so that *none* of the trust fund revenues could be used for any purpose other than to support the Social Security program. Put another way, all of the Social Security revenues would once again be "off budget" and separated from the general obligations of the U.S. Government, just like they had been before President Johnson. As an indication of just how important this restructuring was, one of my first initiatives was HR2, a bill to restore the firewall protecting Social Security revenue. HR1 also addressed Social Security reform, but the bill was more rhetorical than relevant.

With this plan in mind in the waning days of 1998 I appointed twelve members to the President's "Social Security Conference" and held my breath anticipating that the Conference could result in a political diatribe thrown at us for trying to "privatize" Social Security! As it turned out, the members who attended said the conference was a very thoughtful affair. Although the Unions and Reverend Jesse Jackson did attack "privatization," their comments were for the most part drowned out by other news that had nothing to do with the Conference.

******

While the White House was discussing the future of Social Security in relatively bipartisan fashion and we in the Republican leadership were making plans for the next year, the Judiciary Committee was completing its action on the President's relationship with Monica Lewinsky in anything but a bipartisan atmosphere. Others have written volumes on this subject over the years, but I must make this point. Democrats often decry the lack of bipartisanship and point to the bipartisan atmosphere during the hearings on President Nixon. But back then, some members of the Republican minority working under the leadership of Senator Howard Baker collaborated with the majority Democrats to foster such bipartisanship. In this instance, the wholesale refusal of any Democrats to even consider any sanctioning of President Clinton for his ethical scandals and foibles and violation of established law on perjury compromised the undertaking.

Granted, Republicans often have been overly partisan and in 2006 their overbearing arrogance prompted a loss of the majority to the Democrats.

But in the late '90s, it was not Republican high-handedness that brought about the hardening of partisanship. It was the refusal of any single member of the Democrat minority to acknowledge or confront the corruption and failings of the Clinton administration. Despite clear evidence of his flagrant perjury under oath, not a single Democrat on the Judiciary Committee expressed the slightest sense of concern about the President's betrayal of the people's trust. That was terribly sad commentary, not about scarcity of bipartisanship, but about the Democrat Party's blind political ambition.

It became clear in the fall of 1998 that the Republican-controlled Judiciary Committee was preparing Articles of Impeachment against the first President since Richard Nixon. The charges covered perjury, obstruction of justice, and subornation of perjury. If affirmatively voted on by the House, the articles would have been the first of their kind to be officially lodged against a President in 131 years.

With 70 percent of the public opposing impeachment, the polls were clearly against us. But neither I nor any of my colleagues felt that we were elected to vote solely according to polls. America is and will be a representative democracy as described by Benjamin Franklin at the close of the Constitutional Convention of 1787 when he was asked, "Well, Doctor, what have we got—a Republic or a Monarchy?" "A Republic . . . if you can keep it."

What we were soon to do was not popular, but the evidence of Clinton's perjury was undeniable. U.S. citizens, both civilian and military, were in prison following charges virtually identical to the ones against the President. We each had sworn to abide by the Constitution to fulfill our duty as Representatives of the Republic. By moving forward with impeachment, we demonstrated that we were prepared to abide the challenge handed down by Franklin. We would invoke the law as we saw it, albeit at great cost to some of us.

I felt that the Clinton administration had made it clear that there was no price too high for someone else to pay so long as this man could stay in power. When "Whitewater" became a threat, the McDougals, Webb Hubbell, former Arkansas Governor Jim Guy Tucker, and Vince Foster paid the price. In "Travelgate," career bureaucrat Billy Dale was thrown to the wolves, indicted but acquitted on trumped up charges. "Filegate" arose from a mysterious White House collection of 1100+ FBI files on innocent Americans obtained for political intrigue when Craig Livingstone (no relation of mine), the onetime bouncer-turned top White House security agent whom nobody hired, became a sacrificial lamb.

When Paula Jones, the Arkansas state employee accosted by then Governor Clinton, and Juanita Broaddrick, who maintains she was raped, took their stories public they were attacked and humiliated in an unsympathetic press under the guise of "bimbo eruptions." And so it was for six years through "Monica-Gate." Linda Tripp, who reported on her conversations with Monica, paid a heavy price at the hands of the Clinton attack dogs. But for the positive finding of evidence of her relationship with the President on her famous dress, Monica, herself, would have been torn asunder by the malicious charges from the President's sycophant, Sidney Blumenthal, that she was a "stalker" who took advantage of the poor President. The DNA finding squelched that attack, so the President was reduced to quibbling about what the meaning of "is" is. But that didn't stop attacks on other fronts.

Earlier that year, when Congressman Dan Burton proved too much of an irritant to the President, his history of an out of wedlock child was "revealed" in a left wing periodical. Congresswoman Helen Chenoweth was hit with a revelation of infidelity in her Congressional campaign, and revered Judiciary Committee Chairman Henry Hyde was pounded with evidence of a past affair when he wouldn't retreat from his hearings on Clinton's conduct. And there was no mystery where the attacks came from. James Carville, the President's former political advisor and good friend, declared "war" on Independent Counsel Ken Starr and Speaker Newt Gingrich, and he didn't relent when the nastier aspects of his "war" were publicly revealed. Moreover, despite his crocodile tears of condemnation of "the politics of personal destruction," the President "never once, not a single time" (to use his words about Monica) asked any of his pit bulls to stop the personal attacks.

So I should not have been surprised when an implied threat came in from an acquaintance to Allen Martin. The caller, who wanted us to back away from the impeachment or at least reduce the process to a simple "censure" said in effect, "Surely the Speaker-designate will want to allow for a censure in the House . . . . By the way, can he stand scrutiny?" Allen mentioned the call to me after it was over, and we just filed it away. Even if we had taken it more seriously then, I'm convinced that it wouldn't have made a bit of difference in the final outcome.

The caller, a retired Democrat Congressman, had become a consultant to the President to work through his impeachment problem. In conversations with him years later, he denied having made this call so I have not named him here. But Allen's recollection stands to this day. I just did not heed the warning.

At approximately the same time Allen received that call, I got a call from an old Republican friend and former colleague who was then working for a predominantly Democrat lobbying firm. "People in the White House have contacted folks around here, and they want to know who they have to deal with to resolve this problem. Do they go to you?

Do they go to Newt? Who is going to be the broker?"

By this time, Newt understandably didn't want this issue to mark the end of his Speakership so he had virtually withdrawn to Georgia, though he was available to me for consultation. Unless asked, he was not injecting himself in the decisions for the balance of the year or for the 106th Congress. Besides, Newt had taken a lot of heat from the Democrats and the press in September for taking too strong a role in the release of the Grand Jury material to the Internet in September.

Knowing I could have little influence over the Judiciary Committee findings in any event, I assiduously avoided interfering with Henry Hyde's steering of his committee through the deliberative process. I had no reason to do otherwise. I told the caller, "The Judiciary Committee still has the matter under consideration, so Henry Hyde is the man they must deal with. That's where the decision on censure will be made."

"Well, OK. That's good to know! That's what they need to know!" He thanked me, and that was the last I heard from him.

In fact, there was a vote in Henry's committee on a Democratic motion to allow censure as an option, but it failed mostly along partisan lines.

When it appeared that the White House had lost the battle in committee, we started getting calls from the President's friends inquiring about a deal to censure but not impeach the President. Sitting Democrats in the Senate, former Republican and Democrat Senators and House members, friends in the business community, and even contacts inside the White House all called to inquire about how and with whom to cut a censure deal.

Tom DeLay had assumed the role of point man, and he publicly staked out a position for Republicans against censure in favor of an up or down vote on impeachment in the House. I was the Speaker-Designate of the House, and therefore the prospective leader of the whole House. I felt it my duty to concentrate on preparation for my new role, but if needed, I was prepared to facilitate the impeachment process and then move on.

I was aware that if we handled this issue badly and alienated our base, we would lose a foundation on which to campaign in the future. But I was personally convinced that "censure" was not an option for the House to consider. As a former prosecutor, I felt strongly that the House's specific role was to charge or not to charge, to impeach or not to impeach. Whatever punishment, including censure, might be levied upon the President could only be considered by the Senate, and then only if the House had found that he indeed should be impeached. Our Republican base expected us to adhere to the Constitution and as far as I was (and am) concerned, the Constitution did not envision the House levying punishment of any sort on a President. Censure was an option for Senate consideration, but it had nothing to do with the question of whether or not to impeach.

We convened an organizational meeting of our leadership, and as it drew to a close, Tom brought the matter up. We discussed it and not a single one of our elected leadership dissented from my view. We decided that pending a vote of the majority of the Judiciary Committee to proceed, we would put the question to the full House to vote to impeach the President of the United States without the possibility of a censure option. To every inquiry, our answer was, "If Henry Hyde and the Judiciary Committee provide for censure, that's fine; otherwise there will be no deal." Tom then initiated an effort to focus public attention specifically on the key issue of impeachment.

On December 12, 1998, the Judiciary Committee reported to the House floor four separate Articles of Impeachment of President William Jefferson Clinton.

I asked Newt, still officially Speaker, to call a lame-duck session to present the question of impeachment to the House. The Speaker sent out a notice for all members of the 105th Congress to return to Washington for a "lame-duck" session to consider the impeachment of the President by Wednesday, December 16, 1998. The future of my Speakership was cast in stone.

Meanwhile, there were a few other things on our plate. We continued planning for the coming year: I prepared for my speech to accept the gavel on the House floor on opening day, Wednesday, January 6, 1999. I'd met with Reverend Jesse Jackson and agreed to make an appearance with him on Wall Street to encourage private investment in Appalachia and the Mississippi Delta. I committed to fly to Florida at the end of the month to help the RNC and NRCC raise campaign money. And all the dates in January and February were filling up rapidly with appointments with people, foreign and domestic, who wanted to meet with the new Speaker.

*****

A few weeks earlier, I'd been advised by Secretary of Defense William Cohen that the U.S. was likely to take military action against Saddam Hussein of Iraq for failure to adhere to the requirements imposed upon him by the United Nations as an outgrowth of the Desert Storm exercise in 1991. The President had threatened action as early as February, 1998, but he'd taken none, and UN Secretary-General Kofi Annan had traveled to Iraq to tell Hussein that he'd better watch his step or else. Hussein ignored the conditions imposed on him; he denied the UN access to inspect weapons sites and thumbed his nose at the international community. In November, the U.S. Defense establishment lost patience and geared up for a large strike against Iraq. Hussein tried to defer U.S. action and sent a letter promising to do better. It should have been too late since the planes were already in the air, but it wasn't. The President hesitated, as he often did on national security matters. He canceled the strike, and the planes turned around.

Imagine my surprise on Monday, December 14. As we were scrambling to prepare for the new Congress, implement the impeachment session, and hold the last Republican Conference in two days, I got a call on a secure line from Defense Secretary Cohen to tell me that they were considering another strike against Iraq.

"You've got to be kidding!" I exclaimed.

"No," he said, "everything is set. The UNSCOM report will be coming in tomorrow and it won't be good. Hussein still isn't cooperating. If we're going to hit him, we have to do it before Ramadan, the Muslim holy days, which begin on Saturday night at midnight. We have everything in place and Britain will be helping us."

I had to ask him if he was aware of what was happening on the Hill.

"Yes, but please believe me. We have to do this. Sandy Berger (the President's National Security Advisor) and the Joint Chiefs are all convinced that this is the best time, and if we wait until after Ramadan, we won't be able to put the political pieces in place again. I'm sorry about the timing, but you must know that the fact that this is happening while you are engaged as you are, is totally coincidental." He told me about some of the plans, but I could not characterize what he had to say as "consultation." He was very simply advising me of what was coming and imposing a condition on me that I protect the integrity of the operation by maintaining absolute secrecy about their plans.

Needless to say, I was skeptical about the coincidence, so I called General Hugh Shelton, the Chairman of the Joint Chiefs.

"Did we have to do this? Must it be done now? Is the timing really a coincidence?" "Yes," to all my questions. Similarly, I called George Tenet, Director of the CIA. Same answers. Well, it was going to be an interesting week. I just didn't know how interesting!

*****

Tuesday, December 14, 1998, began the worst episode of my life only to be eclipsed by the day seven and a half years later when my wonderful son, Richard, was accidentally killed in New Orleans. In anticipation of my becoming the next Speaker of the House, we were still working like mad to handle the mail, interview job applicants, prepare for the impeachment process on the floor, and keep things going for an orderly beginning of the 106th Congress. But that morning, I received separate calls from the Secretary of Defense and the President to tell me that they meant business this time and that a four day military operation would begin within the next day or so in order to set back Hussein's war making machine. I told them both that while I was uncertain about the plans of the previous February, I had been supportive of their efforts in November, and that I had thought they'd missed their opportunity by not proceeding at that time. I said I would have no choice but to support this effort, but that I had strong questions about the timing. I then told the President that I expected that we could possibly hold off floor proceedings on the impeachment pending military action, but that I fully expected the impeachment proceedings to go forward in this Congress. He said, "Yeah, I thought so," and we said "Goodbye."

As soon as I hung up, I began to realize that the military conflict could drag out indefinitely for any reason and that we could never tolerate an indefinite postponement of Impeachment proceedings. So within two hours, I called the President back and told him that while I'd put it off as long as I could so as not to interfere with the success of the mission, we would at some point have to proceed even if the mission was not complete.

Shortly after that call, I learned that thirty-eight-year-old Navy Commander Eric Massa, a former New Orleanian with a wife and two children whom I'd known since his appointment to the U.S. Naval Academy in 1977, had just discovered that he had lung cancer. And an hour or so after that, I learned that Beverly, wife of Congressman Bill Young, my next door neighbor in the Rayburn Building and soon to become the new chairman of the Appropriations Committee, suspected that she might have breast cancer. I left the office at about 9:30 p.m., and when I got home, flopped into bed and went right to sleep.

Just before midnight, my District Representative Rick Legendre called and woke me up.

"Bad News!" he said. "The media are camped out at (that lady's) house. She's got papers from Larry Flynt along with a half million dollar offer and she wants to talk to you!" Well, since a taped conversation in the middle of the night was the last thing I wanted, I told him to tell the person who called him that I wasn't going to call, but that I'd deal with it in the morning. Then I took an Excedrin PM and went back to sleep for as long as I could.

Wednesday, December 16, 1998

The next morning, I rode to work with my temporarily appointed security detail thinking that the world had gone to hell and stayed there. We were heading into the first vote on impeachment of a President in nearly 131 years; we were going back to war with Saddam Hussein; friends of mine were fighting cancer; and now Larry Flynt had decided to make me the poster child of *Hustler Magazine* just as I was to assume the reins as the third ranking elected official in the land. For the second Republican Speaker in almost fifty years, the day was not starting well.

On Saturday morning just three days earlier, I had returned to Hammond, Louisiana, to speak to the graduating class of roughly 960 people at Southeastern Louisiana University and given my best commencement speech ever. I provided some insight on lessons I'd learned over the years, and wrapped it up by saying, "Ladies and Gentlemen, I am living the American Dream, and I hope that each and every one of you will, too!" Well, hopefully not entirely like me.

How the world had changed in just the few intervening hours! As soon as I arrived at the office, I called my friend, Dick Leon, who had served as my chief counsel on our task force to rewrite the Ethics Rules. Dick is a very nice guy who worked mainly as a criminal defense attorney (later to become a Judge on the Federal District and Appellate Bench), but his credentials as a knowledgeable and respected advisor on the Hill were extensive, having served as Counsel to the Iran Contra Hearings and other complex public problems. Dick came to the office and spoke with Allen and me, and he then called Rick. When he was fully up to date on the facts, he made contact with the person who had called Rick in the first place. He handled all the discussions, and I was free to prepare for a 6:00 p.m. bipartisan briefing of the House by Secretary Cohen and General Shelton as well as plan for our major Republican Conference on impeachment immediately following the defense briefing. In the meantime, both Republicans and Democrats were calling throughout the day to register their concern about impeachment.

Secretary Cohen and General Shelton did a credible job of addressing the House in the face of intense Republican skepticism about the timing of the proposed action. The Democrats, on the other hand, tried to establish a case to stop proceeding with impeachment of the Commander in Chief while troops were preparing to go in harm's way. Neither Cohen nor Shelton bolstered their case, although they were reluctant to say on the record whether proceeding with impeachment would disrupt the mission.

Various other military experts were appearing on television to take one side or the other on the question, but when I saw General Schwarzkopf, the commander of Desert Storm in 1991, tell Brian Williams on MSNBC that the troops would not be affected in the slightest by simultaneous impeachment proceedings, that convinced me that this was a bogus issue raised by the Democrats.

The bombing began just about the same time as the Defense briefing; and the impeachment debate was scheduled to begin at 10:00 a.m. the next day. In this environment, the Republicans of the waning 105th Congress convened in Conference for the first time since the ill-fated elections. Several of our number had been defeated, but they were back in DC and they couldn't have been too pleased about it. But here they were greeting their re-elected colleagues to undertake an effort second in importance only to a Congressional Declaration of War. And just minutes earlier, President Clinton had preempted them by using that very issue.

J.C. Watts opened the Conference and turned the floor over to me. I knew that Cohen only planned a four day action that was to end by the beginning of Ramadan, but I couldn't say as much. That was classified information, and to divulge it could have jeopardized the mission. I also knew the Democrats were going to launch a full scale attack on us for proceeding while the troops were in the field, and I felt that we should make some accommodation. Many in our Conference wanted to start right away, but I felt strongly that to do so could have been a mistake. The Democrats had no qualms in pursuing President Nixon while troops were actively engaged in Vietnam, and several of the loudest objectors to President George H.W. Bush's efforts in Desert Storm had never been quieted for any reason. Still, I felt that simultaneously moving forward with impeachment and with military action was an unnecessary distraction.

I began the discussion with a proposal that we put off debate on impeachment for a few days. This prompted over two hours' worth of heated discussion. When the dust settled, we agreed that we would dedicate the next day, Thursday, to a debate on a Resolution in support of the troops in the field. But as circumstances developed, I as Speaker-designate would have the latitude to determine when we would reconvene the debate on impeachment. Under no circumstances would we defer impeachment later than the following Monday. When we adjourned the Conference, I spoke with lots of Republicans and Democrats and was convinced that with Christmas approaching the following week, almost all our members were hoping to get the thing over with as soon as possible. Furthermore, despite public posturing on the Democrat side of the aisle, there was very little sympathy for carrying the matter into the beginning of the next Congress in January.

When I got back to the office, Dick Leon was gone, and there wasn't much that could be left to do. It was clear that Flynt had determined to make the beginning of the next Congress a miserable event for me and nine or ten other Republicans. I called Dick at home, and he summarized the situation. Needless to say, none of what he had made me feel any better. But he said he was working on an idea and would share it with me in the morning. Another Excedrin PM and back to work the next day.

Thursday, December 17, 1998

At this point, I must say a word about my extraordinary and wonderful wife, Bonnie. We'd been through some tough times some years earlier and they had been entirely my fault. I had strayed, but we'd managed to keep our marriage intact. We went to counseling, and we have remained together. I am a very lucky guy that she chose to stay with me for I'd treated her quite poorly. Nonetheless, she was tough, resilient, and wonderful. She is a great wife, mother, and partner, and I was a self-centered, stupid man. When I got into the Speaker's race, she and my kids questioned whether I should be going into it knowing that under the worst of circumstances, we all could be embarrassed. To their credit and my stupidity, I dismissed their concern and said that nothing embarrassing would happen. Well, they were right to be worried. Once the worst did happen, my family was absolutely wonderful. It was a terrible time in our lives, but we survived the trauma. We have been married for fifty-two years, and I love her very much. She frequently reminds me that I make the living, but she makes the living worthwhile.

I arrived at the office Thursday morning, and Dick came in shortly afterwards. He had fleshed out an idea to preempt Flynt. He suggested that I admit to my indiscretions by pointing out that they had not involved women working for me, that Bonnie and I had dealt with them years earlier, that we had sought counseling, that I hadn't been called to testify, and I hadn't perjured myself on this or any other issue. I thought about Dick's proposal all day long; I changed it and smoothed it out and worked on a hundred other problems, not the least of which was monitoring the floor debate on the Resolution supporting the troops. By the end of that day, Thursday, I'd decided to 'fess up and put my problem before my Conference that evening in order to reconvene the impeachment debate the next morning.

I thought that if I was lucky, impeachment and the war in Iraq would make my difficulties a two-day story. If not, well, at least I wouldn't be surprising my colleagues with a *Hustler Magazine* story on the opening day of the 106th Congress. It was better to get it out now. Great plan—I called Bonnie and read the statement to her and told her of my intent to read it at the end of my conference. Then I said I'd have Mark Corallo, my press guy, hand out the statement to the media. Bonnie understood the situation, and while she was grieving especially for me, she supported what I intended to do.

Newt was back in town for the impeachment debate and the vote, and when I found him in the Chair during debate on the Troop Support Resolution, I approached the dais and whispered to him that I had a problem. He nodded and said, "Yes, I heard a couple of weeks ago that they were going after you and . . . ." He named another colleague of mine with his own problem, and he said he was sorry. He asked what I'd planned. I told him that I intended to let the Conference know that evening. Ever the strategist, he agreed with the timing and wished me well.

As I was leaving the Chamber, I spotted the member mentioned by Newt, and I stopped and told him what I knew and wished him well. I then called a meeting of my elected leadership and Assistants to the Speaker. After some preliminaries about procedure I dismissed the staff and told the members I had some bad news. I read them the statement intended for the conference and asked them not to say anything about it until I could release it on my own terms. They were crestfallen. Everything had gone so well until now. All the plans for the new Congress were taking shape, we were almost through this impeachment battle, and Christmas was almost on us. How in the world could something like this happen? There was anger at Clinton, at Carville, and certainly at Flynt, but not at me; just sorrow for me, for my family, and for the Conference. Virtually everyone there made supportive comments and agreed not to say anything to the press, which was waiting en-masse just outside. They would await my announcement.

We called together the Conference and while the members were assembling, Tom DeLay, Sonny Callahan, and I went over to Tom's Whip Office in the Capitol to kill time before the meeting. We got wind that someone had begun to leak the story, but there wasn't much we could do. At 6:00 p.m., we walked to the conference room and began the meeting as if nothing out of the ordinary had happened. I told the members that I'd decided to start the impeachment the next day and cautioned them to provide the debate with the dignity and decorum that would be demanded of us, and then I turned the conference over to Jerry Solomon for a discussion on the Rules that would guide the debate. The issue of "censure or none" was explored beyond the discussion we'd had the day before, and we made a plea for everyone to abide the rulings of the Chair, which was to be occupied so very ably by Ray LaHood of Illinois. We had always said that members were free to vote their conscience on whether or not to report out Articles of Impeachment, but it was critical for the control of the majority that we not lose any of our members on procedural motions or contests of the Chair's rulings. As it turned out, we lost not a soul on votes of this sort.

I'd had my eye on the clock during this conference because the press was outside and word had started leaking out that something was up. I'd only told a very few members about what I intended to do, but as the saying goes, "The only way that two people can keep a secret is if one of them is dead." Rumors started coming in about the press posing questions so I figured I'd better get to it. Even though there were still some members inquiring about the procedure for impeachment, I sought and received recognition from Chairman Watts.

"Ladies and Gentlemen," I began, "I very much regret having to tell you that I've been Flynted!" A buzz went around the room, which was filled with members and staff. At least I had their attention. I said that I was going to read my statement and that while I wouldn't be making a press appearance, I would hand it out to the press as soon as I had finished. I told them that the statement was self-explanatory and proceeded to read it.

They sat in shock. Then slowly, some of my friends rose to decry the White House for first declaring war and then personally attacking us as members, all in defense of this perjuring President. One member said he'd heard we'd been blackmailed with the Flynt information, but we quickly disabused him of that notion. It wasn't true . . . at least not in such explicit terms. There were a number of supportive comments, and then someone made a comment about how brave I was to face this issue like this (a sentiment I really didn't share) and they gave me a standing ovation. As I prepared to leave, several of the women gathered around to walk out with me to show support to the press, and we walked right past the massive press stakeout. Marge Roukema of New Jersey stopped for an interview and gave an eloquent statement on my behalf, but I didn't stay around to hear her. I was making my way out of the Capitol to the security-driven Suburban that was warmed up and ready to go as soon as I got in.

The world had stopped, but I hadn't gotten off. That was to come later.

Friday, December 18, 1998

When I arrived at my office on Friday, I was in a state of shock, horror, disbelief, denial, fear, anger, numbness, and a plethora of other conflicting emotions. Words fail me to express how I felt. I had reached the top of the world, and the bottom had been pulled from beneath me. And today I was to shepherd the first impeachment of a President in 131 years . . . while our country was at war. My schedule called for me to see former Secretary of Defense Bill Perry, who had taken on the North Korean issue in an effort to pull the administration back from the disaster created by their appeasement of that rogue nation. Well, I couldn't do everything, so I arranged for Bill Ingle, clerk of the Foreign Operations Subcommittee, to take that issue off my plate.

The morning began with an impromptu visit by Dr. Greg Ganske (R-IA). A gentle soul and somewhat of a maverick in the Conference, Greg asked for five minutes with me alone in my office. I welcomed him in and he explained that he'd missed the Conference to go to a performance of "The Messiah." He said that he'd seen the news when he'd returned home and that he'd wrestled with it all night. When he arose that morning, he felt that he needed to come see me and offer a suggestion that I consider standing down from the race for Speaker. I didn't need an explanation. The thought had crossed my mind, but I'd been hopeful that the issue would blow over and be forgotten in a couple of days. Anyway, I thanked him for coming and told him that I would consider it . . . but, I thought at the time, not too seriously.

The debate on impeachment began at 9:00 a.m. that Friday morning. It was well organized by Henry Hyde and the Judiciary Committee and there were no surprises. Members conducted themselves with dignity, and Ray LaHood did an outstanding job in the Chair. We won all the procedural votes and handily met and defeated the arguments that we couldn't proceed with troops in the field and that the charges didn't constitute an impeachable offense. The debate stretched until roughly 8:00 that evening, and we broke until 9:30 the next morning.

As chairman of the Appropriations Committee for the preceding four years, I'd enjoyed my alternate office across the hall from the House Chamber. It is one of the most beautiful rooms in the U.S.

Capitol. Tom DeLay had told me that I should visit with a few of the members who were concerned about my revelations and of course I assured him I would. The problem was I couldn't think of much to say to them, and frankly, I couldn't see myself pleading my case to them under any circumstances. But several of them came to that office, and I spent the better part of the morning there just hearing them out.

I'd not intended to speak on impeachment on Friday. I decided that I had the choice of remaining mute altogether or I could speak on the subject on Saturday. We'd agreed with Minority Leader Dick Gephardt and the Democrats that final debate would include a few wrap-up comments on Saturday, followed by some quick procedural debate and votes, finishing with the votes on impeachment. If passed, a vote would be had on the appointment of managers for the trial in the Senate. I felt that if I were to speak, it would be inappropriate to do so near the end of debate since the senior people on the Judiciary Committee wanted the privilege to wrap things up. So I agreed that if I spoke, I'd appear on the floor as one of the first speakers on Saturday morning. This was not a wise move as it turned out.

Holing myself up in the Appropriations Committee Office in the Capitol for the better part of Friday afternoon, I wrote a speech for the next day. When I went over it with Allen and Paul, I realized it wasn't what I wanted or needed, so I scrapped that one and rewrote an entirely new one that I finished about 7:00 that evening. My assistant Rayne Simpson came over from the Congressional office in the Rayburn Building and took what I had written back to her desk to type it up. When the impeachment debate concluded for the night, I returned to my Rayburn office, read the typed speech, and commented that while it was a good speech, it needed a punch line. At 2:00 a.m. that Saturday Morning, I woke up at home, wrote the punch line, then got a glass of milk and went back to bed.

Saturday, December 19, 1998

When I arrived at the office Saturday morning, I began to tell my staff about the end of my speech. I told Paul first, then Allen who blurted out, "You can't! What about the Party?" I pounded on the desk and yelled, "I've been looking after the Party for the last twenty-two years; I considered the Party when you guys talked me into staying last year! You knew I had this problem, and the only person to warn me that I'd better not do this was Paul! This has gone too far and I can't run a Conference with a margin of five votes when more than that are condemning me for what I've done! I can't undo the facts, but it's time I faced up to it. This is nuts and I know what I've got to do." We were all in tears. Allen, all our staff and all our volunteers from on and off the Hill had been working nonstop for fifteen to eighteen hours a day for the last seven weeks. It was all coming apart.

I, on the other hand, was in the process of seeing everything I'd worked so very hard for washed down the drain. I was fifty-five years old and until this week, my reputation had been virtually unblemished. Now that was no longer so. I'd gotten used to the high praise, the admiration, and the increasingly heard and genuinely felt comments from people who thought I should run for President; all that was gone, evaporated, and it was my own damn fault. I'd let down my wife, my family, all my many friends, the thousands of people who over the years had volunteered in my campaigns, and the hundreds of thousands of people who had voted for me. Now I was letting down my colleagues and yes, the Republican Party, but I could see no way out. It was either, "Do this now, while I can hold my head up and go out with dignity or let Larry Flynt do it for me later on his terms."

I called the Whip Office and asked them to tell Tom DeLay that I was on my way over to the Appropriations Office. He met me just before I was to go on the floor. When I told him what I was about to do, he protested in tears. "You're going to kill us! You can't do it!" He pled. I was as determined as I've ever been in my life. "No, Tom. I've got to do it. Don't you see that if I don't, Flynt will destroy me on opening day? And what will that do for the Conference? Besides, you know I can't lead those guys who claim they have never done anything wrong in their lives. It's hard enough leading them when I've got full moral authority to do so when my heart's completely in it. Neither is true now. You know as well as I do, that many of them won't follow me!"

"You're right!" he said as he wiped his eyes. "When are you going to do it?" "Right now," I said. And with that I got up and walked with speech in hand to the House floor.

Before I was able to get recognized to speak, I spoke with at least three people. The first was Henry Hyde who was managing the bill from the Republican Table. As soon as he saw me, he brightened. Not knowing what I was about to do, he said, "Bob, don't let that problem get to you. They did it to me and it lasted two days. It's over, and you'll find the same thing!" I smiled weakly and thanked him. As I turned away, I came face to face with Zach Wamp of Tennessee.

"Can I give you a realistic damage assessment, friend to friend?" he asked. "I figure you've got eighteen folks who have some serious concerns, and you need to speak with them!"

"They're troubled by my situation?" I asked.

"Yes, but you can talk to them."

"Yeah, I think they'll be satisfied," I responded.

I sank into a seat next to my friend and chairman of the Rules Committee, Jerry Solomon, waiting for my turn at the podium. "You gonna speak?" he inquired. "Yeah, as soon as they call on me." "What are you going to say?" I just looked at him and he knew. "I wish you wouldn't," said my friend. Henry Hyde then introduced the Speaker-Designate of the House of Representatives.

*****

I would never want to relive those moments but if I could, I would change the speaking order. After my speech in which I called for the President to resign in order to heal the damage he had done to this country, and after I had quieted the catcalls from the Democrat side of the aisle, I announced my own decision not to stand for Speaker of the House and to resign from Congress. Dick Gephardt is said to have flown into a panic. He allegedly called the White House to tell them what I'd done, and together he and the President's people worked out a strategy to "Praise Caesar, not to bury him!"

He threw his speech away and hastily wrote another which set the tone for the President to join him in deploring "the politics of personal destruction!" At his encouragement, the entire House gave me at least two standing ovations, and Gephardt got great plaudits from the media for his generous speech. I should be thankful, but as the events unfolded that day and thereafter, my gratitude ebbed.

With the procedural motions defeated, the House finally voted on four separate Articles of Impeachment of William Jefferson Clinton. The First Article charged him with perjury to a grand jury and passed the House of Representatives by a vote of 228 to 206. The second article charging obstruction of justice passed by 221 to 212. The remaining two articles, a second perjury charge and an abuse of power charge, failed 205 to 229 and 148 to 285 respectfully.

Before we voted on appointing managers to handle the proceedings in the Senate, three-fourths of the Democrats marched out of the House and reconvened in a party atmosphere in the White House Rose Garden. Michael Kelly, the editor of *National Journal*, described the surreal atmosphere in an editorial:

> So, there was the first impeached elected president in the history of the United States, standing on the South Lawn. There, with the stain of disgrace still fresh as paint upon him. And the man seemed to believe he was speaking from the moral high ground.
>
> The president listened appreciatively as Dick Gephardt labeled the impeachment vote "a disgrace to our country" and as Al Gore called him "one of our greatest presidents." He nodded; so true, so true. He thanked the nearly lock-step House Democrats and a "few brave Republicans," for defending "plain meaning of the Constitution." And then he piously intoned: "We must get rid of the poisonous venom of excessive partisanship, obsessive animosity and uncontrolled anger."
>
> "Excessive partisanship?" Certainly the President was not referring to House Democrats, who voted to not impeach a man they themselves had described as having "violated the trust of the American people, lessened their esteem for the

office of the president and dishonored the office which they have entrusted to him."

"Poisonous venom?" Certainly this was not aimed at California Democrat Tom Lantos, who, on the floor likened the House to "Hitler's parliament" and "Stalin's parliament." Nor at Illinois Democrat Jesse Jackson Jr., who compared the vote to the racist overthrow of Reconstruction. Nor at House Democratic Caucus Chairman Martin Frost, who said Republicans could have "blood on their hands," for debating while American pilots bombed defenseless Iraq. In deploring "uncontrolled anger," the president was assuredly not referring to actor Alec Baldwin, a prominent Clinton defender, who recently ranted to Conan O'Brien:

"I am thinking to myself in other countries they are laughing at us twenty four hours a day, and I'm thinking to myself if we were in other countries, we would right now, all of us together, all of us together would go down to Washington and we would stone Henry Hyde to death. We would stone him to death! . . . We would stone Henry Hyde to death and we would go to their homes and we'd kill their wives and their children! We would kill their families!"

In inveighing against "obsessive animosity" the president meant no disrespect to James Carville, who appeared on *Meet the Press* the day after the president and frothed thusly: "These people are going to pay for what they did. This was a cowardly and dastardly thing that they did, and there's going to be retribution, and the retribution is going to be at the polling place . . . . They tried to destroy this president. They tried to destroy his friends. And they tried to destroy this country and this Constitution, and there must be a price."

Nor, I am sure, was the president sniping at *Salon* magazine editor David Talbot, who brutally outed House Judiciary Committee Chairman Henry Hyde for a thirty-year-old extramarital affair having nothing to do with violations of civil and criminal law, such as obtained in the president's

> case ("Ugly times call for ugly tactics," said *Salon* in an editorial). And, rest assured, the president meant no censure of Talbot's soul mate, the pornographer Larry Flynt, who orchestrated the impeachment-eve exposé of Republican Speaker-designate Bob Livingston. "Desperate times deserve desperate action," said Flynt . . . .
>
> The vast wreckage about us is one man's work. And this work will continue with that man's blessing. The president's press spokesman, Joe Lockhart, was asked on Monday if the president, in his desire to end the politics of personal destruction, would ask James Carville to stop threatening Republicans with retribution. "Nah," said Lockhart.
>
> Bill Clinton and his morally bankrupt defenders intend to do whatever it takes to discredit his impeachment, to savage the reputations of those who supported it and to establish Clinton as a sort of hero, the president who bravely defended the Constitution against a small band of hate-blinded fanatics. The critical step in this campaign is to avoid conviction in the Senate. The 100 jurors who must now weigh the welfare of one endlessly selfish man against the welfare of the republic should consider this.

Was Clinton aware of Flynt's action? On the day of my first announcement to my Conference, Cokie Roberts told a story on television of how a person close to the President began to relate information they had dug up on me at the White House Christmas party. She said she was appalled.

The day after his impeachment, the *Los Angeles Times* reported that Clinton held a party for old friends and joked with them about the fact that Larry Flynt had become the latest influence in the Washington political debate. The article said that Clinton "regaled his listeners with a description of a letter Flynt wrote to independent counsel Kenneth W. Starr congratulating Starr for aiding the cause of pornography."

How did Clinton know of the letter? Surely Starr didn't tell him. Just how close were Clinton, Carville, and Flynt? Somehow his protestations of the "politics of personal destruction" run a little dry and hollow. And I never did hear Dick Gephardt specifically condemn the actions and words of Flynt or Carville.

When I finished my speech, I returned to the Appropriations office, and greeted friends who streamed in to see me, many openly weeping and asking me to reconsider. The decision was made, but the controversy wasn't over. Some friends tried to get a "Draft Livingston" movement together. When DeLay heard about it, he counseled me not to encourage it. "You were right, and if you change your mind, they'll destroy you!"

He was right. Someone else asked me, "Who can do what needs to be done in your absence?" "Denny Hastert is well liked and can bring the House together," I responded. Four hours later, with Tom's help, Denny had it wrapped up. Now as I look back on the events of the last many years, if there was any single comment of mine I could retract or withdraw, that was it. But more on that later.

For roughly thirty years of public service, including a full twenty-three years in or campaigning for Congress, I had worked hard to make my family, my constituents, and my nation proud. I had rendered service with honor and integrity, and apart from the actions for which I paid dearly, I never betrayed that commitment to the people and the nation I served and do still revere. I regret none of it and would change none save my personal failings within my own family, which while unrelated to my performance in office, I do so deeply regret.

In the aftermath since my impeachment speech, gossip columns were written about me and commentators in the electronic media who knew nothing of what they spoke contributed to wild speculation. Let me put that speculation to rest. My sin was to stray from my marriage in violation of the Seventh Commandment. I've made peace with my wife and my God and nothing else matters. In addition, I have forgone the opportunity to serve my country as the Speaker of the House of Representatives, a job for which I was well prepared. That's a heavy price indeed, yet with God's help, life has gone on.

On the lighter side, I figured out that if one considers all the people of the world who never had a shot at being Speaker of the House and put them in one universe, it's a very large universe. Then take all the people who have served as Speaker of the U.S. House of Representatives and that's a very small universe. But, consider the universe of those who have fallen between the other two. That's a very exclusive universe since to my knowledge, I am the only Speaker-elect in U.S. History who did not actually go on to become Speaker of the House! Lucky me.

Once again, I'd chased a windmill; I'd reached for the brass ring and missed it. But as I left Congress, I fully expected to become more financially secure than I had ever been before. And that's what I did, but not without misgivings about what might have been. However, as I was to learn, making money ain't necessarily the same as keeping it.

January 6, 1999

Dennis Hastert of Illinois was elected and sworn in as Speaker of the House of Representatives for the 106th Congress of the United States.

The next day, the U.S. Senate began impeachment proceedings, the second in history, against President William Jefferson Clinton. Unfortunately, the Senate did not take the effort by the House as seriously as we had. The Majority Leader of the Senate and my old friend from Mississippi, Trent Lott, never fully bought into the idea of impeachment and as was noted in the recent Fox News production, "Scandalous," he and his colleagues gave short shrift to the arguments of Chairman Henry Hyde and his Impeachment team.

The country had only endured the impeachment process once before in history when, following the Civil War, President Andrew Johnson was impeached by the House of Representatives. Apparently, records of the actual trial in the Senate are sparse or non-existent, so there were no clear guidelines nor precedent for the Senate to follow.

I likened the process to my days as a criminal prosecutor and had assumed the role as head of the Grand Jury in the House of Representatives, while the Senate was to play the role of Petit Jury, thereby making it the "finder of fact" to weigh the charges brought by the House. If they followed through as I'd envisioned the Constitution required, that process would have compelled the Senate to call witnesses to testify to the charges so that Senators could determine for themselves whether the witnesses and the charges were credible.

Instead, the Senate seemed determined to do no more than was absolutely necessary in order to put the issue in the rear view mirror. Most of them assumed that Clinton would never be convicted, so Trent and his colleagues agreed to a process that virtually ensured that outcome. I was disappointed when I learned that instead of calling witnesses, the Senate's role in the proceedings was to be minimized by simply permitting Hyde's prosecution team to summarize the facts alleged by the witnesses.

The Constitution envisions a full trial, but this turned out to be nothing more than a presentation of appellate arguments. The statements of witnesses like Paula Jones, Kathleen Willey, and Juanita Broaddrick, the lady who claimed that she had been raped by Clinton, if acknowledged at all, were not presented by the witnesses themselves. None of the women alleged to have had consensual or non-consensual relationships with the President were heard. Most especially, Monica Lewinsky, the White House intern whose blue dress bore tell-tale Clinton DNA that proved his perjury under oath, never appeared in person before by the Senate. Her previously taped deposition was played for the Chamber, but no one was permitted to confront her or propound questions to her. As a result, the Senate was given a sterile recitation of charges and presentation of facts bordering on total boredom. When it was over, no one was surprised that the Senate returned a verdict of "Not Guilty."

The President was acquitted on all charges. Apart from this especially lurid chapter, he had enjoyed a relatively successful two terms in the White House. And nine years later when Trent Lott closed out his own successful tenure as Senate Majority Leader, the keynote speaker at his retirement ceremony was none other than former President William Jefferson Clinton.

*****

When Tom DeLay and I conferred about a possible replacement shortly before my resignation speech, I intended that Dennis Hastert might be a place holder until someone of greater stature could be selected by the Republican conference. He seemed like a nice guy but my first impressions of him beyond that turned out to be simply wrong. While he was a friendly and jovial back-slapping pol, his experience as a high school wrestling coach had ill prepared him for the role of Speaker of the House. He wasn't a man of vision, eloquence or conservative ideology. He had served in Congress for twelve years, but he hadn't chaired a committee; he hadn't sponsored legislation, and in fact, he hadn't done much of anything to earn the title of Speaker other than to have become Tom DeLay's Chief Deputy Whip. In short, he was a partisan vote-counter. Little did I think he would be permitted by the Conference to remain in place for eight years thereby becoming the longest serving Republican Speaker in history. That he did is a remarkable failing among those who refused to rock the boat by electing someone to the Speakership who might have been more competent. However, since I had played such an important role in clearing the deck for him in the first place, I can only accept most of the blame myself.

In fact, he was a disaster. He avoided public appearances like the plague. He couldn't give a sensible speech. He had no discernible philosophy. He depended solely on Tom DeLay for organization and direction. His staff was primarily parochial and limited. His political approach was to win at any cost and to hell with his adversaries. And in general, he had no sense of the role required of his responsibilities and position. Upon my departure, I had given him a foot-thick binder filled with notes on what would help him become a good Speaker, and if he read any part of the thing, I'd be surprised.

I viewed the Speakership as being partisan to a degree, but more as a leader who understood that he was Speaker for the entire House of Representatives, not just his own Party. I believed that despite their natural partisan leanings, Tip O'Neill and Tom Foley had been credits to the office. Newt Gingrich had certainly been a firebrand and a constant thorn in the side of the Democrats, but he was more than qualified for the office, and he was commonly accepted as being one of the brightest people in government, let alone the Congress. Because of our experience with Speaker Jim Wright, whom I believed had not lived up to the post, I felt that the Speaker should rise above the petty partisan wrangling of the day by letting the Majority Leader assume that role, subject to the Speaker's broad supervision.

As noted before, Tom DeLay was an extremely effective Whip. But Hastert rarely reigned in Tom's overreaching partisanship and disregard of the rules of fair play. Hastert's failure of leadership contributed to members indulging corrupt outsiders like Jack Abramoff, and he failed to limit the excesses of his own staff. Worse still, he abandoned the very philosophy that enabled the Republican majority to balance the budget, reduce government regulation, and scale back the size of government. Catastrophically, he disregarded warnings about legal and ethical transgression of members. Explicit inappropriate communications between Congressman Mark Foley (R-FL) and underage Congressional pages was the straw that broke the camel's back. In 2006 that straw cost Republicans the majority that all of us had worked so hard to attain.

I believe the Speaker's role to be one to protect the institutions of the entire House. The Parliamentarian, the Ethics Committee, the Intelligence Committee, and the House Administration Committee must be run efficiently and fairly so that, to the degree possible, they would serve all the members and not just a select and favorite few. I'd intended that the Appropriations Committee would continue to restrain but not eliminate the use of earmarks, reserving to the members of the committee and the full House the responsibility to see that well-meaning amendments to Appropriations bills were allowed in the interest of the country regardless of sponsorship. Parochial or partisan earmarks were to be rejected so as to not overload or undermine the system or the budget. I did not believe in allowing projects to be included simply because it might help a specific member politically in his District. As chairman, I had turned down many questionable earmarks proposed by members simply for political reasons. Of course, I was sometimes overruled by the Speaker or the leadership, but most of the time I prevailed.

As noted earlier, the hysteria against earmarks among current members of Congress and much of the Press is just foolish. The President plans his budget through OMB and submits it to Congress. It is replete with his priorities, another word for earmarks. The Constitution endows Congress with the "power of the purse," meaning that the cost of government must be considered and voted on by Congress as the legislative branch of government. "The President proposes and the Congress disposes," we always said. As detailed earlier, if the Congress gives up all authority for earmarks, then it essentially abdicates the rights of individual Congressmen to uphold their Constitutional budget responsibilities. All wisdom does not reside in the executive branch of government. Private citizens have the Constitutionally protected right to petition their elected Representatives. Many of them have wonderful ideas to advance the country, and those would never see the light of day but for a Congressional earmark. The trick is for members of Congress to exhibit judgment, responsibility, and restraint. Earmarks should be allowed sparingly and judiciously. And waste in government should be attacked in a far more thoughtful and strategic manner than just uttering platitudes or espousing bans on earmarks.

Finally, allowing well-considered, justifiable earmarks from backbencher majority or minority members simply was and always will be good politics and wise legislative policy, for it gives them a stake in the game. Members who would otherwise consistently oppose legislation might have reason to vote "yes," thereby ensuring passage of difficult bills. Earmarks are incentive for both minority and majority members (including "Freedom Caucus" members) to support Appropriations bills instead of opposing them in the name of party politics or knee-jerk ideology. Most importantly, bipartisan earmarks promote Congressional control over the Treasury in accordance with the Constitution instead of faceless, unelected executive-branch bureaucrats.

I believe I was a good chairman of the House Appropriations Committee. I'd served on the committee since 1981 when Trent Lott talked me onto it. I'd studied the habits and techniques of Chairmen Jamie Whitten, Bill Natcher, and David Obey. I learned how to preside over a committee meeting, granting equal time and opportunity to all members to participate in the process. The power of the majority was to prevail on the merits of legislation, rather than through under-handed political tactics.

The power of ideas was impressed upon me by the likes of my incredible friend, the late NFL quarterback and Congressman, Jack Kemp (R-NY). Good ideas, if given a fair and open hearing, will prevail of their own weight, and bad ideas will falter. And so as Appropriations chairman, I succeeded in advancing the Republican message, in curtailing wasteful spending, in eliminating unnecessary and redundant programs, and in creating an environment that led to a balanced budget for the first time in many years.

Likewise, in co-chairing the Ethics Rules Revision Committee with my former colleague and now Senator, Ben Cardin (D-MD), I strived to make rules to protect members from scurrilous, politically-motivated ethical charges, but still encourage the charging, and if warranted, conviction of those who had genuinely stepped beyond boundaries to benefit themselves.

I'd intended to restore the role of the Budget Committee to one of oversight, enforcement, and direction so as not to become a wholly separate Appropriations Committee desiring to duplicate and complicate the Appropriations process. I always said, "There are really only four numbers of relevance to the Budget Committee, which after all was only created by the Watergate Babies when they created the Budget Act of 1974. Those numbers are: 1.) How much did we raise last year? 2.) How much did we spend then? 3.) How much do we expect to raise this year? And 4.) How much of that would we like to spend?"

The Budget Committee could call witnesses from the Joint Economic Committee, the Congressional Budget Office, the Office of Management and Budget at the White House, and other relevant committees to arrive at those numbers. The whole process wouldn't take more than a few days at most. Once they arrived at a final number for the Discretionary Budget, they could give it to the Appropriators and instruct them through the Speaker to develop bills within that ceiling. If Appropriators subsequently spent a dollar over the number provided, Appropriations bills could be rejected in Conference or on the House floor or vetoed by President. Budget restraint would be enforceable, and the Budget Committee would bear the responsibility for setting the level of Federal spending for the year.

This was my view while I was Appropriations chairman, and it still is. But the then-chairman of the Budget Committee, John Kasich, wanted not only to determine the level of spending for the country, but to dive into individual Appropriations bills and determine the amount to be allocated to each line item. In short, he wanted to be an Appropriator. We were friends, but we fought about this repeatedly, and I generally won unless the Speaker overruled me. To give him his due, John was excellent at playing to the press, and he played a major role in convincing the American people that a balanced budget was both desirable and achievable. Continuing in that fashion after some years, John defeated an incumbent and was elected Governor of Ohio where he did a fine job under difficult conditions. Regrettably, his bid for the Presidency, in which he refused to accept his defeat in the primaries, reflected his Budget Committee ego.

That we collectively handed the new Speaker a virtually balanced budget was of no moment once Denny Hastert advanced to the Speakership. President George Bush (43) proffered his own spending priorities, and Hastert abandoned any pretense of oversight or enforcement on runaway spending. For the better part of his tenure, there was no enforcement, no relevance, no restraint, no discipline, and ultimately, no reason to maintain Republicans in office.

Because he did not enact my proposal for bringing members back to Congress for normal working days, most of them took to heart Newt's suggestion to leave their families at home. Once home, they needed to spend time campaigning, but their families understandably wanted still more of their time at home. It was only natural for them to want to lengthen their weekends and avoid coming back to Washington to as great a degree as possible. In the '70s and '80s, we used to come in on Monday mornings, begin debate on the floor with some possible votes on Monday afternoon, set committee meetings on Tuesday, Wednesday, Thursday, and sometimes Friday mornings. More recently, members want to arrive in DC Tuesday evenings, and if they can, they leave town on Thursday evenings. That was fine by Speaker Hastert, since he'd left his family in Illinois and preferred to be there rather than in DC anyway. (Unfortunately, the light scheduling of Congressional business persists today.)

That meant that all the committee, subcommittee, and political meetings had to be set at the only time possible, which was usually on Wednesday and Thursday mornings. It doesn't take a Mensa Society member to understand that members were rarely at their committee or subcommittee meetings. Even chairmen were often absent. Hence, if they weren't there, they either didn't hold meetings, or if they did, they had to delegate the business to the staff. When it came time to determine which amendments, riders, or earmarks were admitted to a bill, it was the staff that made the decisions. When members leaned on staff to admit extra earmarks, rather than argue with a member of Congress about the merit of his amendment, the staff person naturally caved in much of the time. Thus, Congress moved from a time when a small number of earmarks were considered, to one when thousands of them were included in the bills regardless of merit. Worse yet, President Bush (43) accepted much that his Republican Congress threw at him. In eight years he rarely vetoed an Appropriations bill. Is it any wonder that the American people lost faith in the Republican mantra of "fiscal responsibility?"

Aggravating their lack of fiscal discipline was their tendency to solve imagined problems while forgetting why their constituents sent them to Congress. The political desire to "do something" seemed to click into action every time the political environment got tight. In 2002, when Enron and WorldCom collapsed and corporate officials got caught with their hands in the cookie jar, even Republicans were not content to let the judicial system work. Instead, to show they were "doing something," they foolishly jumped into action and passed "Sarbanes–Oxley," thereby adding incredible complexity and added liability to management burdens of American corporate executives. As a result, more and more companies either moved offshore for corporate governance or took themselves off the public stock exchanges.

Moreover, the reporting system for political contributions has gotten increasingly complex since the first campaign finance laws were passed in 1974. Whereas the intent of the original law was to simply create transparency so that voters would know who was contributing to which candidates, Republicans and Democrats teamed up to pass "McCain–Feingold," which was so patently cumbersome that much of it has now been ruled unconstitutional by the U.S. Supreme Court.

And solely for short term political advantage, Republicans initiated an entirely new mandatory entitlement, "Medicare Prescription Drug, Improvement, and Modernization Act of 2003" calling for the federal government to provide prescription drug coverage for all Medicare recipients, regardless of their ability to pay. To guarantee passage, Tom DeLay kept the vote on the floor of the House open for forty five minutes, beating the previous record of fifteen minutes set by the Democrats in the '90s. Republicans were supposed to be the Party of smaller government that played by the Rules. None of these bills were consistent with Republican principles, but Republican President Bush (43) signed each one into law.

Tom DeLay is a good man. He wasn't an academic over-achiever, but he was a remarkably gifted organizer and a most vocal conservative. He was an exceptional Whip from the time we took the majority until 2003, when he was elected Majority Leader. He repeatedly delivered the votes for the Republican majority when they were most needed, so much so that the media dubbed him "The Hammer" for his ability to keep his troops in line.

But he lacked sympathy for oversight, and Denny wasn't up to providing it. As years passed, Tom controlled the agenda and grew arrogant in his role as Majority Leader. It didn't help that he surrounded himself with people who were more arrogant than he. "Earmarks" were allowed in bills without regard to their merit or benefit to the country. It appeared that Tom manipulated the process for political purposes for his favorite members . . . and lobbyists. Some of them lost the ability to distinguish between a valid political agenda and their own personal interests. Then Congressman Randy "Duke" Cunningham, the only Navy "Ace" in Vietnam, was charged and later convicted for having concocted a "price list" for bribes before he would introduce legislative adjustments. And the press was replete with allegations of Jack Abramoff's illicit relationship with various Congressmen for which he was later sent to prison.

Democratic District Attorney Ronnie Earle indicted DeLay in south Texas on what were clearly bogus charges, and it was hinted that Tom might also be charged federally in the Abramoff affair. When the state charges were formally launched against Tom, he might have rallied public support to his side because of the clear unfairness of partisan attacks against him. But Tom was never one to go down without a fight. He fought at every juncture and used every tool at his disposal. When for his own purposes, he was seen manipulating the very Ethics Rules that Ben Cardin and I had formulated and enacted in the late '90s, the Ethics Committee closed down and virtually ceased to function. DeLay politicized the committee, and Hastert did nothing to restrain him. That was too much. Tom resigned in September 2005, and Denny Hastert was lost. His philosophy, his organization, and even his brains were gone. In taking out Tom DeLay, the Democrats had chosen their target well.

America grew weary of Republicans and suspected that they had lost their way. Yet, Republicans still might have retained the majority in Congress, had it not been for the Mark Foley scandal in the latter days of October 2006.

Speaker Hastert should have put the brakes on Tom, but Denny was incapable of standing back from the fray to assess what was best for Congress. He implemented the "Hastert Rule" to prevent any legislation no matter how worthy from reaching the House floor without support from a majority of the Republican conference. This alone effectively eliminated any hope for bi-partisan legislative initiatives. He surrounded himself with sycophants and arrogant staffers who may have been loyal to him, but weren't up to the job of running the Speaker's Office. Their failures were numerous, but the worst one blew up just in time to cost them the Republican majority.

Congressman Mark Foley (R-FL) was a leading member on the Ways and Means Committee as well as chairman of the House Caucus on Missing and Exploited Children. One of Foley's additional assignments was to oversee the welfare of the Congressional Pages. No evidence ever surfaced of improper physical contact, but almost a year ahead of the election, rumors passed among members and staff that the quiet and conservative Foley been emailing unwanted sexual messages to one or more of the male Pages. His actions were brought quickly to the attention of the chairman of the NRCC, Congressman Tom Reynolds (R-NY) and the successor to House Majority Leader Tom DeLay, John Boehner (R-OH), the subsequent Minority Leader and later Speaker of the House. Both Reynolds and Boehner said publicly that they had told Speaker Hastert and his staff about the problem as soon as they heard about it. Hastert denied that anyone ever told him anything, but Boehner and Reynolds contended that he had told them he'd take care of it.

Democratic Congressman Dale Kildee (D-MI), a former Catholic Seminarian and a good man, shared responsibility over the Pages with Foley. Once advised of Foley's actions, the Speaker could have worked with Kildee to remove Foley. But Hastert apparently swept the issue under the rug for a year until it re-emerged just days before the election of 2006 when Foley's emails to one of the Pages erupted in the press. Foley was disgraced, the issue became the final blow in a bad year for Republicans, and the majority for which we had worked for forty years was lost. Democrats regained the majority, and Nancy Pelosi became the first female Speaker of the House.

His eight years as Speaker ended when Hastert resigned from Congress in 2007. A month or so later, Gregg Jarrett of Fox News aired a TV segment on Hastert, the lovable old "Coach" of the Republican majority, now the minority. Jarrett claimed that before he'd left office, Hastert had bought some land in subterfuge next to his own farm, placing it in an innocuous trust under a name not his own. He then allegedly induced a U.S. Government funded highway to be built across his own farm land, the land in trust, and land belonging to an eighty-two-year-old neighbor who did not want the highway in the first place. Once he left office, he flipped the trust land and sold it for a couple of million dollar profit.

Unfortunately, that wasn't the end of the Hastert saga. In May 2015, Dennis Hastert was indicted on a number of counts alleging banking violations and lying to an FBI agent. He was charged with withdrawing $3.5 million to pay off a male blackmailer whom he had allegedly abused sexually while he was a high school wrestling coach. Once made public, the charges were so sufficiently incendiary that they abruptly ended Hastert's political and professional career. He resigned from his law firm, his boards, and virtually any other vestige of Washington life. He subsequently plead guilty to some of the charges and was sentenced to fifteen months in prison. No one can condone what he had done, but I certainly empathize with the devastating turn of events in his life. Fortunately, my own humiliation is long past. His will last forever. But this story casts new light on why he didn't act to curtail Mark Foley before we lost control of the House of Representatives. I suspect Foley does not share my empathy.

The Hastert Speakership was found by the American people to have squandered the trust we handed him. He took a Party and a country that were in good fiscal condition, permitted earmarks and Congressional spending to go wild, ran up an intolerable deficit, and set the stage for the destruction of the Republican majority. So it was that in 2006, Republicans ceded control of the House of Representatives to Nancy Pelosi's Democrats. Incredibly, Speaker Pelosi apparently learned nothing from Hastert's mistakes for despite her pious assertions that she would preside over the "most ethical Congress ever," she compounded the politization of the job beyond anything anyone could have imagined.

If someone had told me when I was chairman of the Appropriations Committee years earlier that Nancy Pelosi, then a member of the committee, would become Speaker of the House, I would have responded with a belly laugh. I vividly recall seeing her hand rise in committee for recognition on almost every subject we debated over my four years as chairman. When given recognition, she would rise and take the most extreme "San Francisco Democrat" or "hard left" position on virtually every subject. I'd look at my watch, give her the allotted five minutes to discuss the issue at hand, and politely gavel her down when her time was up. She rarely won a vote, but we always remained cordial and friendly just the same.

Meeting her in person, one is struck by her gracious and friendly demeanor. She is an effective politician, but also an extraordinarily effective fundraiser for the Democrat Party and liberal causes. As Speaker, she was still the quintessential "San Francisco Democrat" that I knew so well back then, but I learned quickly that my earlier belly laughs were misplaced. For four long years, there was never any doubt that she was Speaker of the House. She was rarely non-partisan, bi-partisan, or fair. She is an ideologue who viewed her role as one entrusted with the responsibility of "saving the planet" (her words) with the hardest, most left-wing agenda imaginable.

Nancy is a most personable and nice lady when she is not wearing her political mantle. But in her official duties, she was the least likely person to compromise on any subject. She served with Ben Cardin and me as a member of our Ethics Rules Revision Task Force in the late 1990s. As Ben and I made our way through the arcane and tedious process of improving the rules, two members, one Republican and one Democrat, demonstrated little desire to ever compromise in debate. The Democrat was Nancy Pelosi. As Speaker, she was as tough and unforgiving a leader as we have had in modern times.

For example, she summarily removed the venerable "Chairman" John Dingell (D-MI), the longest serving and an extremely capable member in the House of Representatives, from the chairmanship of the Energy and Commerce Committee in favor of her bright but more compatible ally, Henry Waxman (D-CA). All activity in the House during her rein had to be processed through the Speaker's Office or approved by her good friend, George Miller (D-CA), who shared her leftist ideology. Regular order and the traditional committee process utilizing independent committee chairmen and subcommittee chairmen were usurped and became virtually non-existent.

Nancy Pelosi's domination of the House of Representatives pushed the very limits of the U.S. Constitution. Transparency, bipartisanship, and respect for minority rights were given ample lip service, but in practice they were virtually ignored in favor of high-handed and roughshod treatment of the minority, most especially with the 2010 passage of ObamaCare."We have to pass the bill so that you can find out what is in it," said Speaker Pelosi. And they did exactly that, yet we are still unraveling the disastrous consequences of that bill rammed through Congress, despite overwhelming public opposition. Nevertheless, ever-convinced of their ability to control the economy, with the wholehearted cooperation and assistance of Speaker Pelosi, Senate Majority Leader Harry Reid, Congressional leaders of the Democratic Party and the mainstream press, the Obama administration set about changing the American healthcare system. Without a single Republican vote, they succeeded in accomplishing what Hillary Clinton failed to do in the early '90s. They packaged, passed, and adversely impacted one-sixth of the American economy. The ObamaCare program was ill thought out from birth, and it has only become progressively worse with time. Without a complete overhaul or replacement, it will continue to devastate what is left of the amazingly productive healthcare delivery system of the United States. The 2016 election of Donald Trump and a Republican Congress has provided hope that we might rectify the damage, but the obstacles are monumental and Republicans so far have been unable to replace ObamaCare in Trump's first year in the White House.

In 2010, notwithstanding the worst Democratic defeat at the polls in fifty years, Pelosi continued her blitzkrieg advance of the leftist Obama agenda in a lame duck session of Congress by pushing through the Dodd-Frank Financial Regulation Bill to further Democratic domination of the U.S. financial industry. Senator Chris Dodd (D-CN) and Congressman Barney Frank (D-MA), the two men most responsible for protecting Fannie Mae and Freddie Mac, insisted on regulating the industry without eliminating the two major institutions that accelerated our financial collapse in the first place. They did very little to manage or control the "too big to fail" Godzillas of the banking industry, and they didn't touch, let alone terminate, the role of Fannie Mae and Freddie Mac in the mortgage industry. But they did manage to endanger community banks and other small businesses with ever burdensome regulation in "Dodd-Frank."

Speaker Pelosi was resoundingly chastised in the November 2010 elections when eighty-seven new Republicans and only nine new Democrats were elected to the House of Representatives, but that didn't stop her. Her tenure as Speaker was a disaster for America, yet still the Democrats remained loyal to her by repeatedly electing her as Minority Leader—notwithstanding their overwhelming defeat at the polls in 2010, 2012, 2014, and finally in the Trump sweep of 2016. Largely because of her leadership, Republicans captured control of more State House seats, Legislatures, and the Congress since the 1920s. And yet to this very day, she clings to power as she recently announced her intent to run once again for Speaker if the Democrats retake the majority in 2018.

Yet I still blame former Speaker Hastert for allowing her to come to power by not exerting intelligent discipline over the Republican Congress. He was far happier on his farm in Illinois than he was as Speaker, and he should have recognized that and gone home after his first two years on the job. He finally did leave in 2007 as the longest serving Republican Speaker in history, whereupon the Fox News expose' provided a fitting epitaph for his tenure.

*****

Barack Obama served as President from 2009 to 2017. As an unrepentant socialist, he did all in his power to provide the "change" he promised the American people. Despite his devotion to Keynesian spending and domination of American industry through ever expanding government intervention, none of it worked. His tenure provided the longest period of recession or near recession of any in American history since the Great Depression of the '30s. Unemployment declined officially, but when people who gave up looking for work were added to the statistics, the actual unemployment level never really dropped below 9 percent or 10 percent in most of his presidency. In the inner city, young people whom Obama professed to champion experienced levels of unemployment well over 50 percent or higher. Crime in his old neighborhoods of South Chicago reached epidemic proportions. He virtually doubled the aggregate debt of the nation from $10 to $20 trillion, and that was after George W. Bush himself had doubled the debt to $10 trillion.

When Obama first ran for President, I listened to his speeches and was convinced that he wanted to turn our Constitutional laissez faire free market democracy into a managed socialistic system. I was so convinced of it that I had a box of bumper stickers printed in May, 2008: "SOCIALISM: Change for the worst!" They remained on my cars and those of my kids until the 2016 election season began.

Keynesian economists cling to the belief that increased government spending keeps the economy afloat. If that were true, the Soviet Union would have been the strongest economy in the world. Thankfully, it collapsed in 1989. Life in America cannot be improved by simply raising taxes. Draining the private sector of seed corn capital can only impede growth and retard our economy. It hasn't worked anywhere it's been tried whether in the Soviet Union, the U.S. during the "Great Depression," or anywhere else in the world. And it failed miserably during the Obama administration, which escalated unofficial unemployment—including people who have given up looking for work. These were the very people Obama and "progressives" professed to champion! Clearly, their philosophy has utterly failed. Cuba, Venezuela, and North Korea offer the worst examples of "progressive" failure, but almost any large city in America is testament to the irresponsibility of the leftist agenda. Economic redistribution simply doesn't work! It hasn't worked in the past, and it is highly unlikely to in the future. But it does stifle innovation and competition, and without them, growth is stifled and a stagnant economic pie is consumed from within.

My favorite snippet, "That government is best which governs least," is as true today as ever. If we are to solve the problems of low productivity, high unemployment, and inadequate investment, we must rely on government no more than is absolutely necessary. Certainly there must always be some degree of government regulation to keep men from destroying one another. But government produces virtually no wealth; it bleeds the private sector and redistributes wealth to lesser productive channels. The private sector is the true generator of wealth, but it can only remain so if encouraged to flourish in a free and lightly regulated capitalistic society. When a nation tries to replace the private sector by government spending and dictate, it strangles the goose that lays the golden egg and the nation will cease to be wealthy.

The financial collapse of 2008 occurred because of just such government overreach. When it became increasingly clear that the next

President was to be Barack Obama and the Bush tax cuts of 2003 would be allowed to expire, Congressional intervention in the market place also began to take its toll. Sarbanes-Oxley, the highly intrusive law passed by Congress in the wake of the Enron scandal, discouraged public companies from decisions that might benefit both stockholders and the U.S. economy. Worse still, Congressional demands upon the banking sector to lend money to people who had no way to repay what they had borrowed contributed heavily to the collapse of the housing industry and the bursting of the banking bubble.

The Community Reinvestment Act of 1977 was based on the best of intentions to encourage investment by aspiring homeowners. Banks were pressured by regulators to lend to people who did not meet minimum risk standards and who years earlier would have been denied loans. These new loans were packaged, then insured by FHA and sold to quasi-government agencies, Fannie Mae and Freddie Mac. Real estate values were pumped up by unwarranted speculation, with banks making money on every transaction while exercising little if any due diligence over the quality of their loans. The bubble popped, and America and the world were thrown into the deepest recession since the Great Depression.

It took several years of deflation to finally be replaced with a gradual return to normalcy. Had Donald Trump not been elected President in 2016, we might never have emerged from the depths of slow growth. He's been in office for over a year, and his significant reduction of government regulation together with enactment of the largest tax reduction package in 30 years has accelerated growth in this country beyond anything critics like Paul Krugman might have imagined.

*****

As much as I blame Speaker Hastert for punting away the Republican majority in 2006, I blame myself even more for creating the conditions enabling Denny to become Speaker. I had a chance to change the country for the better. I have no doubt whatsoever that I could have worked with and ridden herd on Tom DeLay, run the Congress in competent and amicable fashion, tempered the hard edge of partisanship, and provided competent guidance for the House. I might have done so, but my own failings stopped me in my tracks! It was indeed my own fault, and I am heartily sorry for what I wrought through my self-centered narcissism—I apologize to my wife and children, to my constituents and the people of Louisiana and to my fellow Americans. I would have been a good Speaker, and I have no one to blame but myself for not making that happen. It's now up to our younger generations to overcome the harm that I and those who followed me have inflicted on this wonderful country of ours.

May God continue to bless America.

Postscript

By and large, life has been good to me. I've had a number of careers, all of them relatively successful. While I never cared for the private practice of law, I loved serving as a criminal prosecutor in the Federal, State and Local levels.

Congress was wonderful while I served in the minority and even more so in the majority. I thrived in the process, and while I never had a spare dollar to spend, I was able to raise my family in suburban Virginia and send all four children off to college by refinancing my home seven times in nine years.

Since leaving Congress, I've established a first class lobby firm, The Livingston Group, and together with my partners and associates, we have enjoyed a great deal of success. My co-founding partners, Allen Martin and Paul Cambon and I have worked together for over forty years and my assistant, Jane Graham, has been with us for some thirty nine years. We've built our organization together, and I've been fortunate to have had such a great team of people to work with.

For those who view the word "lobby" as a four-letter word, I'll simply say everyone has the Constitutional right to petition his or her elected representatives. But not everyone has the time or the understanding of the legislative process to do it properly. No one fears the hiring of an attorney to get them through the judicial process in the courts. Likewise, if one finds need to petition a legislator for or against an issue of importance to him, he wouldn't go to a person who has no earthly idea of how the process works. Instead, he would seek out people who have years of experience in the process.

I have worked in the legislative process for over forty-one years, and the people in my firm have brought their talents and experience to the table to represent clients and help them find their way through the legislative jigsaw puzzle. We are proud of what we do. We do it with honor and dignity, and we reject the gratuitous attacks on our profession by those who demagogically appeal to ignorance for their own purposes. Likewise, we condemn those who bend the rules to their own ends, just as we applaud effective and reasonable rules of enforcement to clean out those who take undue advantage of the system.

Our client base has enabled us to work with domestic corporate, educational, and non-profit clients, and we have enjoyed a strong international practice aimed at improving relations between the United States and multiple foreign partners.

Fortunately, my success has extended beyond my business. All of my kids have made me extremely proud. Rob ("Shep" to us) received his BA and subsequent MBA. He tried accounting for a couple of years and woke up one morning and yelled, "I hate this stuff." He now lives in Georgia with his wife, Sissy, and three wonderful children, Caroline, Robert, and William. He has been quite successful as a federal law enforcement agent and he loves going to work every single day.

My youngest son, David, graduated from LSU on the extended plan and tried his hand in the securities brokerage business for a few years. He did reasonably well until the "dot.com" crash of the early 2000s slowed him down, but he bounced back and now represents a major investment firm. He, his wife Nance, son Barklie and daughter Alexandra live in New Orleans.

My daughter, Susie, adopted at age six from Taiwan, is a beautiful five-foot ten-inch Eurasian combination of Chinese and German. She is married to an outstanding ophthalmologist, Kevin Kirchner, and they also live in New Orleans with their curly red-headed children, Kevin Jr. ("Little Shep") and Katie and Richard.

In the spring of 2006, I recall pinching myself because things had been going so well for me. Although we had many friends whose properties were devastated, none of our family lost property in the wreck of Hurricane Katrina. My firm was flourishing in DC, and I was making more money than I ever could have anticipated.

*****

But I think I may have had a foreboding that it couldn't last. It didn't. Our second son, Richard, was the only one of my children who (at age thirty-seven) had never married. But he was engaged to a beautiful young lawyer, and they were to have married in May of 2007.

Rich, a big, handsome, laid-back young man, was our only "Type B" child and was most like his mother in temperament. He wasn't a great student and was often frustrated by his inability to absorb information as quickly as his classmates, but he had a perseverance that often astounded me. He was frequently on award winning soccer and football teams, and he always had lots of friends. A left handed, right-brained, slow moving youngster, Rich became a fine athlete, an artist and a musician, and he was possessed of an incredible sense of humor. He stood six-foot three-inches tall, was great looking and was just a really nice guy without a mean bone in his body.

After graduating from high school, he took off for the next six months to visit a friend whose family was attached to the U.S. Embassy in Paris. He enrolled in the American School there, and he must have really enjoyed Paris for his final academic record was so bad that he couldn't use it as a credit for future college enrollment. On his return to the U.S., he flunked out of Ole Miss after the first semester.

Three years in the Army did a lot for Richard. He enlisted and served with distinction at NSA, Fort Meade, Maryland, and in Korea in an intelligence billet. He emerged from the Army well organized and full of realization that he didn't want to do that for the rest of his life.

So Richard enrolled in Savannah College of Art and Design (SCAD) where he developed his skills as an artist, musician, and computer guru. He graduated in three years and went to work for Oracle for a couple of years. When he found himself spending too much time in what he called Oklahoma "Shitty," he quit and tried his hand selling for a digital signals firm until they collapsed in the "DotCom" era. So he went back to school.

To our great delight, Richard followed the example set by his older brother and earned an MBA from the University of New Orleans in two years. Rich tried his hand at setting up a musical promotion company to take U.S. talent to Central America, and he was getting his life together. He became engaged to a bright and attractive young lady lawyer firm Charleston, SC. To earn some money in the meantime, he started a hurricane-cleanup company with a cousin and some day-workers. He taught himself how to climb, trim, and remove dead trees from property damaged in Hurricane Katrina.

The company was doing fairly well. He'd bought, rented, and begun paying for lots of heavy equipment including a truck, trailer, stump grinders, cherry pickers, climbing equipment, saws, and the like. As he developed his business, Rich found that keeping workers trained and on the job proved difficult at times. Much of the time, he just did the jobs himself as he was in extraordinarily great shape.

He owned his own house that he'd bought on the GI Plan two or three years earlier, and he was attempting to put away some money for his pending marriage when he took on a job for a friend of his on July 25, 2006. It was a damp gloomy day, overcast but not rainy, and the tree he was to trim was well within the size that Rich could handle. When his crew was working, they'd removed trees in excess of one hundred feet high. This time, his crew didn't show up.

Rich told his friend and client, "Brad, if you will simply watch the ladder and send me stuff up when I ask you to, I'll take care of this tree, and you'll see what a great business this is. I bet you'll quit your job, join me, and never work for anyone else again."

Rich climbed to the top of the wet tree, fixed his safety lines in place, and came back down about a third of the distance to the ground where he would begin cutting the first set of branches. Always safety conscious, he was bedecked in a harness with all his ropes intact.

But the safety harness and lines had a metal core that Richard hadn't noticed. High voltage power lines stretched across the property roughly three feet above where Rich had settled in the tree. As Brad looked up from the ground, he didn't see Rich touch the lines. But he did see a spark, and Rich jumped. "I can't move!" he said to Brad, as he seemed to twist in his rigging. Then he slumped over a tree limb and died. The power had arced and taken our beautiful son.

Our tall, handsome, nice, witty and generous son Richard was gone from our world. His death almost killed Bonnie, and God forbid she ever has to go through anything like that again. Richard was a wonderful son to both of us and was much loved by his brothers and sister.

2006 was not a good year for the Livingstons.

Awakening

In the aftermath of Richard's tragic death, I've had the opportunity to evaluate things in my life that have been important and those that I'd have best avoided altogether. First and foremost, I've been fortunate for the past fifty-two years to have Bonnie at my side as a steadfast and loving partner and wife. I find our union has grown more happy and rewarding with every passing day. We've been blessed with four great kids, nine grandchildren, and now one beautiful great-grandchild. I have made many mistakes. I was probably not ready for marriage at the age of twenty-two and I failed in my responsibility.

By the grace of God, my family stuck with me and I with them.

Until late in life, I was never significantly religious. My father was Catholic, my mother, Episcopalian. I was baptized in my father's church and sent to Catholic schools in my early years. When he was no longer in my life, my mother made me go to Mass on my own, but I soon learned that I could instead sneak away and spend the time reading comic books across the street at Weinberg's Drugstore.

Switching schools in fifth grade to St. Martin's Episcopal School weened me from Catholicism, and I was confirmed as an Episcopalian where I remained until long after my marriage. But Bonnie is an ardent Catholic and she took the kids to Mass every Sunday. One of my great regrets was that I didn't join them except at Christmas and Easter.

My progression through law, politics, and business was left fairly well without spiritual guidance of any meaningful sort. In fact, I felt I didn't need it, and I was wrong. Had I realized it in time, I may not have made the mistakes I made, and I might have been a great Speaker of the House. Circumstances may have been different, and we might not have lost our dear Richard.

I think it was his death that compelled me to dig deeper into the true reasons for my, for our, existence. I've read a lot of history, and I just couldn't ever justify the origins of the Church of England and its derivative, the Episcopalian Church. So I gradually returned to the Catholic Church. I began to attend weekly Mass regularly with Bonnie and to appreciate that so many of my goals I'd set for myself really didn't matter in the larger scheme of things. Women, fame, or money, none of that will mean anything when we are called to our Maker. I had risked my marriage. I had achieved a maximum role in politics and within a few days was to become the third highest ranking official in the United States. Then quite suddenly, all that I had worked for over more than twenty years was wiped out in short order.

I left Congress and made a lot of money only to narrowly avoid bankruptcy in the last couple of years. And yet, I've survived. I have my life, my wife, my kids, my grandchildren, a great-grandchild, my business, and reasonable health for a seventy-five-year-old man. I may have chased too many windmills, but I've actually caught a few. And Hillary Clinton is not President!!! What more can a man ask for?

When our Founders completed their work on the Constitution, Ben Franklin said we had "A Republic . . . if you can keep it."

Well, in 1994, Americans gave Republicans the majority. In the elections of November 2006, Republicans crashed and burned and lost control of both the House and the Senate. All our success in 1994 was overcome. Franklin might have said, "They couldn't hold on to it."

But then, neither could the Democrats in 2010. In Navy terms, Republicans now "have the Con." Under Speaker of the House John Boehner and Speaker Paul Ryan, Republicans have gained the Presidency, the House, and the Senate and have made major advances among state governors and legislatures. But have they learned to govern? Can they keep it? That remains to be seen.

Appendix

Farewell Speech on House Floor:
H11970 CONGRESSIONAL RECORD — HOUSE
December 19, 1998

Mr. LIVINGSTON. Mr. Speaker, I rise with the fondest hopes that the bitterness engendered in this debate will at its conclusion be put aside, and that all members will return to their families for the holidays mindful of what has been done here by we as agents of principle. We have fulfilled our duty to our magnificent Constitution.

Yes, our young men and women in the uniformed Armed Services have in these last few days set about the task of ridding the earth of the threat of weapons of mass destruction in the hands of an enemy of civilization, Saddam Hussein, and they have performed their tasks with valor and fortitude, that we may freely engage in this most unpleasant aspect of self-government as was envisioned by our forefathers.

I very much regret the enmity and hostility that has been bred in the Halls of Congress for the last months and years. I want so very much to pacify and cool our raging tempers and return to an era when differences were confined to the debate and not of personal attack or assassination of character.

I am proud to serve in this institution, and I respect every member of this body. Each of us stands here because a majority of roughly 600,000 people had the confidence to vest us with this authority to act as their agents in a representative democracy.

When given the chance, we often find that aside from political and partisan differences we have much in common with one another. But we never discover what that common ground may be with the gulf between the sides of this narrow aisle.

The debate has done nothing to bring us together, and I greatly regret that it has become quite literally the opening gambit of the intended Livingston speakership. I most certainly would have written a different scenario, had I had the chance.

But we are all pawns on the chessboard, and we are playing our parts in a drama that is neither fiction nor unimportant. Indeed, it is of utmost significance in the course of American history, and my desire to create an environment for healing must take lesser precedence than must the search for responsibility, duty and justice within the format provided by the U.S. Constitution.

I believe we are in active pursuit of these goals, and I give great credit to the gentleman from Illinois (Mr. HYDE) and the gentleman from Michigan (Mr. CONYERS), and Mr. Tom Mooney and all the members and staff, majority and minority, of the committee on the Judiciary for their deliberate and conscientious effort on this most difficult task.

We are nearing completion, and however the vote turns out, no one may say that we did not own up to our constitutional responsibility as members of Congress in a careful, respectful and insightful debate. Much credit is due our presiding officer, the gentleman from Illinois (Mr. LAHOOD), who has done an outstanding job.

Mr. Speaker, we differ on process. The minority believes that we acted too hastily in view of the troops in the field, and that we omitted an alternative from the options available for consideration. We in the majority believe we have properly begun the debate after setting aside a whole day to honor and praise our troops and the effort that they are extending on our behalf. General Schwarzkopf, the commander of the troops in Iraq several years ago, agreed with us on the *Brian Williams Show* on MSNBC just two nights ago. We believe, we believe that the Constitution envisioned that censure not be a part of the debate on whether or not to impeach the President, and we are supported there by comments by then majority leader Tip O'Neill during the Nixon impeachment proceedings.

So there are differences in process; what about substance? The minority has maintained that the President has not perjured himself and that even if he did, such perjury was not intended within the term "high crimes and misdemeanors" delineated in Article 2, Section 4 of our Constitution.

Surely no President has been impeached for perjury, but at least three Federal judges have been impeached and convicted under the perjury statutes, and so perjury, a felony punishable by up to five years in the penitentiary, is a crime for which the President may be held accountable, no matter the circumstances.

Perjury is a felony, as I have said, and fully 116 people are serving time in Federal prison as we speak for perjury today, and, yes, there have been several instances of people going to prison following convictions for perjury involving lies under oath under sexual circumstances.

The average citizen knows that he or she must not lie under oath. Ms. Christine Simms of Rockville, Maryland, wrote to the Committee on the Judiciary just two weeks ago and said, and I quote:

> I too was called upon to give answers under oath in interrogatories during a civil proceeding. Truthful answers to those questions would be embarrassing to me, and what I knew exposed me to criticism and had a potential to ruin my life, particularly as it related to my children whom I love very much. In short, I was scared to tell the truth. However, I did just that. I could not lie when I was sworn to tell the truth, no matter what the risks nor the degree of temptation to take the easy way out. Parts of my life have been difficult since that time because elements of that testimony have been used to scorn me. But I as a common citizen was compelled by my conscience to tell the truth.

Yes, our Nation is founded on law, not on the whim of man. We are not ruled by kings or emperors, and there is no divine right of Presidents. A President is an ordinary citizen, vested with the power to govern and sworn to preserve, protect and defend the Constitution of the United States. Inherent in that oath is the responsibility to live within its laws with no higher or lower expectations than the average citizen, just like Ms. Simms.

When the President appeared at the deposition of Ms. Jones and secondly before the Federal grand jury, he was sworn to a second oath, to tell the truth, the whole truth and nothing but the truth, so help you God. This, according to witnesses to the Committee on the Judiciary and before the Special Counsel, he did not do. For this I will vote to impeach the President of the United States and ask that his case be considered by the United States Senate, that other body of this great Congress, uphold their responsibility to render justice on these most serious charges.

But to the President I would say: Sir, you have done great damage to this Nation over this past year, and while your defenders are contending that further impeachment proceedings would only protract and exacerbate the damage to this country, I say that you have the power to terminate that damage and heal the wounds that you have created. You, sir, may resign your post.

And I can only challenge you in such fashion if I am willing to heed my own words.

To my colleagues, my friends and most especially my wife and family: I have hurt you all deeply, and I beg your forgiveness.

I was prepared to lead our narrow majority as Speaker, and I believe I had it in me to do a fine job. But I cannot do that job or be the kind of leader that I would like to be under current circumstances, so I must set the example that I hope President Clinton will follow.

Mr. Speaker, I will not stand for Speaker of the House on January 6, but rather I shall remain as a back bencher in this Congress that I so dearly love for approximately six months into the 106th Congress, whereupon I shall vacate my seat and ask my Governor to call a special election to take my place.

I thank my constituents for the opportunity to serve them; I hope they will not think badly of me for leaving. I thank Allen Martin, my chief of staff, and all of my staff for their tireless work on my behalf, and I thank my wife most especially for standing by me. I love her very much.

God bless America.
Robert L. "Bob" Livingston (R-LA)

Acknowledgments

It's taken me almost twenty years to write this book, but it's still a short summary of a lifetime of experience. Bonnie has shared over two thirds of that life and as she often says, I've made the living and she's made the living worthwhile. She has given me four great kids, nine grandchildren and by last count, one beautiful great-grandchild. It's been a wonderful ride.

As I wrote bits and pieces of *The Windmill Chaser* as well as material for a possible second book, I never really intended to bring it to closure until last year. I was planning on simply leaving it for my grandchildren to peruse once I'd departed the earth. But about a year ago, Robin Cleveland, a former colleague on Capitol Hill who retired from her positions as foreign policy advisor to Senator Mitch McConnell (R, KY) and to Paul Wolfowitz, Director of the World Bank, and began work on a dissertation for her Ph.D. She asked to interview me about my success as a southern Republican in attracting African American votes.

In the course of the interview in my office, she casually suggested that because of my stories and history, I should consider writing a book. I told her that in fact I had accumulated substance for a book, but that I hadn't really intended to do much with it. Well, she encouraged me to pull it together, so here it is. With much gratitude, I wish to thank the now Dr. Cleveland but for whom I would never have finished this work.

Thanks also to Bob Tucker of the Jones Walker Law Firm in Baton Rouge, Louisiana, who provided valuable and free advice on copyright which led to discussion about potential publishers. Because of Bob, I found James D. Wilson Jr. of the University of Louisiana at Lafayette Press who quickly expressed interest in my work and but for whom I would definitely be saving material for my grandchildren. James has been enormously helpful to the finished product. And I must thank my friend and former press assistant, Quin Hillyer, with whom I consulted about this work when it was in its infancy and who eagerly pitched in to provide a list of media contacts by which to launch the final product.

But most of all, I want to thank all my family and many friends, supporters, and voters for their steadfast support even when I let them down. My mother, Dorothy Billet, got me through difficult early years and beyond. My sister, Carolyn Teaford, was an ongoing quiet supporter throughout my life. Bonnie and my children, Shep, Richard, Dave, and Susie have been the rocks on which I stand and have provided me reason for living. They together with their wonderful spouses and our perfect grandchildren are all that really matter.

To all the wonderful people who have stood by me as friends, working in my campaigns or simply voting for me, I can't thank you enough. I enjoyed virtually all my time in Congress, so I thank all my Republican and Democrat friends who made my life in Congress so enjoyable.

And last but not least by a long shot, I want to thank all the fantastic people who worked with me in Congress and later in The Livingston Group located only two blocks from Capitol Hill. I came to Washington thinking I'd be here for two or four years and now, forty-one years later, we are still here. Allen Martin and Paul Cambon and I have worked together the entire time. Allen was my first winning campaign manager and my chief of staff on the Hill and he's doing great things as our firm's managing partner, despite a threat of cancer that he has contained for well over twenty years. Paul was my driver in 1977 and he became one of the foremost appropriations experts on and off Capitol Hill. The three of us were joined by Jane Graham who has been a wonderful assistant in Congress and since for almost forty years.

Since leaving the Hill, The Livingston Group (TLG) has been blessed with our partners including Rick Legendre, who served as my district representative and then helped form TLG until he retired in 2006. Martin Cancienne, Bernie Robinson, and Lauri Fitz-Pedado also became partners, and Lorraine Kuchmy joined us from the George W. Bush White House to become our Chief Administrative Officer. They are all a great team and we have been on a roll ever since we left Congress.

Finally, I cannot close without thanking the great team at the Jones Walker Law Firm and most especially, Chris Johnsen, the managing partner of their Washington office. Chris saw the commercial potential awaiting Paul, Allen, Rick and me for a successful lobbying venture, and only with his support and guidance was The Livingston Group created and enabled to prosper.

Thank you one and all!

Index

Robert L. Livingston Jr. was elected to the United States House of Representatives in a special election in 1977—the first Republican to represent Louisiana's First Congressional District in over one hundred years. He was re-elected to eleven successive terms. He served as a Member of the House Appropriations Committee through most of his time in Congress, and for the maximum period of six years on the House Select Committee on Intelligence. From 1995 through 1998, he served as the Chairman of the House Appropriations Committee. He was chosen by his peers to serve as Speaker-designate for the 106th Congress. Following his departure from Congress in February 1999, Mr. Livingston established a successful lobbying firm known as The Livingston Group.

Before his almost twenty-two years in Congress, Livingston practiced law in both public and private fields for nine years. As an Assistant United States Attorney from 1970-1973, he served as Deputy Chief of the Criminal Division of the U.S. Attorney's Office. Livingston also served as Chief Special Prosecutor and Chief of the Armed Robbery Division of the New Orleans Parish District Attorney's Office (1974-1975) and as Chief Prosecutor for the Organized Crime Unit of the Louisiana Attorney General's Office (1975-1976).

Livingston earned Bachelor of Arts and Juris Doctorate degrees from Tulane University, and is a graduate of the Loyola University Institute of Politics. In 1981, he received an Honorary Doctorate from Our Lady of Holy Cross College in New Orleans, LA, and in 1990, an Honorary Order of the Coif from the Tulane Law School. Livingston served in the United States Navy from 1961 to 1963 and received an honorable discharge from the U.S. Navy Reserve in 1967.

Livingston lives with his wife, Bonnie, in Alexandria, Virginia, and New Orleans, Louisiana. They have three sons and a daughter, nine grandchildren, and one great-grandchild.